STEINBRENNER!

DICK SCHAAP

G.P. PUTNAM'S SONS
NEW YORK

The author gratefully acknowledges permission from Michael
and Anne Yeats, Macmillan Publishing Co., Inc., and A. P.
Watt Ltd. to reproduce lines from *Collected Poems* by William
Butler Yeats. Copyright 1919 by Macmillan Publishing Co.,
Inc., renewed in 1947 by Bertha Georgie Yeats.

Library of Congress Cataloging in Publication Data

Schaap, Dick, date.
    Steinbrenner, George Michael, 1930-   . 2. Baseball—
United States—Team owners—Biography. 3. New York
Yankees (Baseball team) I. Title.
GV865.S79S3   338.4′7796′0924 [B]   82-581
ISBN 0-399-12703-8   AACR2

PRINTED IN THE UNITED STATES OF AMERICA

From this arises the question whether it is better to be loved rather than feared, or feared rather than loved. It might perhaps be answered that we should wish to be both: but since love and fear can hardly exist together, if we must choose between them, it is far safer to be feared than loved.

—Niccolo Machiavelli
The Prince

Show me a good and gracious loser and I'll show you a failure.

—Knute Rockne

For the memory of Joan McLeod,
for the presence of Trish McLeod,
and for the future of Karen Joan.

STEINBRENNER!

Author's Note

From the beginning, the subject flatly opposed the writing of this biography, which was too bad, because I feared I would not have the opportunity to sit with George Steinbrenner and discuss the controversies he has created, the character he has become, the books he liked to read when he was an English literature major at Williams College, the songs he liked to sing when he stood in the back row of the Williams Glee Club. I wanted to offer George Steinbrenner a chance to rebut some of the charges that have been leveled at him, a chance to explain some of his actions that have struck reasonably objective observers as calculating, callous and even cruel. I wanted to tell him that, since I do not pretend to comprehend the mysteries of building a ship or amassing a fortune, arts Steinbrenner clearly has mastered, I admire above all else the fact that he treats so many athletes not like prima donnas, but precisely the way he treats other human beings—even if I do not necessarily approve of the way he treats those other

human beings—sometimes generously, sometimes shabbily, sometimes brutally, sometimes gently. He has a
wonderful belief that healthy young men who are being
paid from one hundred thousand to one million dollars a
year, give or take a few incentive clauses, should earn their
salaries, should work as hard as less richly rewarded
people, and he believes that, since he is the man who pays
those salaries, he has a right to be angry, and to display
that anger, when he feels he is not getting his money's
worth. I like that, and I like, too, Steinbrenner's love for
New York City, and his love for winning.

Our relationship, before I set to work on this book, was a
good one, not intimate, but certainly cordial, friendly. The
last time I interviewed him, before the book, was in the
spring of 1981, in Florida, when I was doing a story for
ABC's *World News Tonight* about the possibilities of
peaceful coexistence, that is, whether or not the outfield at
Yankee Stadium was large enough to contain both Reggie
Jackson and Dave Winfield, two of the nation's most
muscular and, in different ways, self-confident million-
aires. The interview was conducted in West Palm Beach,
where the Yankees were playing an exhibition game
against the Atlanta Braves. George was sitting behind the
Yankee dugout, and in order to ask him a few questions
during the game, without ruining the view of other
spectators, I had to slide into his row and kneel at his feet.
"While I'm here," I said, cramped, yet trying to be cheerful,
"should I kiss your ring?"

"Cut that out," Steinbrenner said, annoyed.

"If I can't kid *you*," I said, "who can I kid?"

Steinbrenner laughed, seemed to relax, then said he had
no worries about Jackson and Winfield sharing both the
outfield and his affections. "I think the Winfield-Jackson
combination is going to be great," he said. "It's going to be
like Mantle and Maris, like Ruth and Gehrig." I don't
think Steinbrenner *accidentally* put Winfield's name ahead

of Jackson's, making Winfield the "one" of the one-two combination, elevating him to the level of Mickey Mantle and Babe Ruth. Steinbrenner may simply have been referring to their positions in the Yankee batting order, Winfield directly in front of Jackson, or, more likely, he may have been unable to resist an opportunity to needle Jackson. Steinbrenner almost never does anything by accident.

I have been reporting on Steinbrenner and his Yankees since the day the team became Steinbrenner's Yankees. At the beginning of January 1973 I attended the news conference at Yankee Stadium announcing the sale of the Yankees to a group of twelve businessmen, a group assembled by George Steinbrenner. I had never before heard his name. I may have said hello to him that day, but I certainly didn't bother to interview him. I assumed that Steinbrenner, like most owners, probably had nothing terribly exciting to say. The next time I attended a major Yankee news conference, I again did not interview George Steinbrenner, mostly because he was not present. On the final day of 1974, I was one of several journalists called away from New Year's Eve parties and summoned to an office across the street from Shea Stadium, the Yankees' temporary home while the City of New York refurbished Yankee Stadium, to celebrate the signing of Catfish Hunter, a righthanded pitcher, to a five-year contract that made him baseball's first instant millionaire. It was an historic and expensive moment that Steinbrenner did not witness because, as a result of violating federal election laws, he had been temporarily suspended from active management of the Yankees. Six years later, both Steinbrenner and I were able to attend a similar news conference, commemorating his greatest athletic expenditure, the awarding to Dave Winfield of the richest contract in baseball history, a contract guaranteeing Winfield, over the next decade, considerably more money than Steinbren-

ner and his associates had paid for the whole Yankee organization in 1973. The Winfield party was held at Jimmy Weston's, a Manhattan restaurant which had become one of Steinbrenner's favorites. The proprietor, Jimmy Weston, was a former St. John's University basketball player and a former New York City detective, and coincidentally, during the mid 1970s, when I was editor of *Sport* magazine and my office was only half a block from Jimmy Weston's, I used to eat many of my lunches there. Occasionally, I even got to sit at the secluded corner table Steinbrenner later favored.

I witnessed, too, one of the most historic Yankee moments *on* the field, the game in which Reggie Jackson hit three home runs to end the 1977 World Series and lift the Yankees to the first world championship of Steinbrenner's reign, the first for any Yankee team in fifteen years. After the game, in the chaos of the locker room, both Jackson and Steinbrenner agreed to appear with me early the next morning on NBC's *Today* program, for which I was then the resident sports correspondent. I picked up Jackson at six A.M. at his Fifth Avenue apartment—he had come in only an hour earlier, the doorman warned—and then together we called for Steinbrenner at his hotel residence, the Carlyle, on Madison Avenue, only four blocks from Jackson's apartment. Steinbrenner had managed a little sleep, perhaps three or four hours, and I thanked him for getting up so early. "I wouldn't have done it for anyone else," Steinbrenner said, which made me feel very special, very flattered. I have since discovered that Steinbrenner takes great delight in making people feel special, feel singular, but that when he says, "I'm doing this just for you," or, "I'm saying this just to you," he may well have done the same thing, or said the same thing, for a number of people. Still, he did not get up at six A.M. for everyone, and for that appearance on *Today,* which impressed my employers as much as it impressed me, I am still grateful.

I'm also grateful that, during his ownership of the Yankees, George Steinbrenner has always invited me to his Opening Day and World Series celebrations at Yankee Stadium, pregame gatherings in the Great Moments Room, which is decorated by pictures of significant events in the life of the stadium, from championship fights to football games. And I appreciate that he has always helped me purchase tickets for postseason games, for playoffs and the World Series, reserving for me excellent seats that have brightened my image both with my employers and with my friends. Even in the fall of 1981, when I was well at work on this book, defying Steinbrenner's expressed wishes, he still endorsed my request to buy World Series tickets, and he again invited me to his pregame parties, to share the bar and the buffet with Cary Grant, Kirk Douglas, Danny Kaye, Shelly Hack, former New York Mayor John Lindsay, current New York Mayor Ed Koch, New York Governor Hugh Carey, tennis player Arthur Ashe, author Gay Talese, attorney Roy Cohn, the Los Angeles Dodgers' owner Peter O'Malley and Jack Kent Cooke, television host David Susskind, *The New York Times'* executive editor, A. M. Rosenthal, and a few hundred more of his closest friends. So far as I could detect, Steinbrenner himself never came into the Great Moments Room for the pregame festivities—he had a more private private room for himself, Jimmy Cagney, Joe DiMaggio and other immortals—and so I did not have a chance to thank him personally, or a chance to attempt to overcome his resistance to this biography.

Of course he knew about the project. I wrote to him at the start of the 1981 season, telling him that I was going to work on this book, and telling him that I hoped he would cooperate, would share with me some of his experiences and some of his impressions. He did not reply, not directly. I did get a phone call from Larry Wahl, then the publicity director of the Yankees, advising me that George was not pleased by my plan, that he would like me to abandon it. I

declined. A few weeks later, Wahl resigned, which was purely a coincidence, even though he did take a job with ABC, my base, too. Then, in August, immediately after the end of baseball's first massive mid-season strike, I wrote to Steinbrenner again:

> Now that that other thing is out of the way, can I buy you a meal, a drink or a cup of coffee at the Pewter Mug [in Steinbrenner's home town of Cleveland], Weston's or even the Court Deli near the Grand Concourse [in the shadow of Yankee Stadium and the Bronx County Courthouse]?
>
> I'd like to talk to you—even if I have to do all the talking—about the book I'm working on. It's easy for me to find critics, knockers, enemies—they're always available—but I really want to be able to talk to your friends. And from my contacts with them so far, they really want to talk about you—affectionately. But for some strange reason, many of them seem to have lost their memories (as well as my phone number).
>
> We've always had a good relationship, which I appreciate, and I'd like to keep it that way. You got up at six in the morning for me once; I'll meet you at any hour you say any place.

Steinbrenner responded within ten days, remarkably quickly for a man with his schedule, and with his feelings toward the project. His letter made it clear that he opposed my book chiefly because he intended to write his own story of his life. "It has been my thought and desire for a long time that someday I would write a book, not just about baseball, but about everything I have been involved with," he said. "I think I would write a book that would be so enlightening in so many areas that it could be a great seller. I had planned to . . . donate the proceeds to charity; in fact, I already have the charity picked out."

14

Steinbrenner said he considered me a good friend, someone he had always trusted, but he feared that I was using our relationship for my own profit, trying, as he phrased it, "to make a killing off of my life and career." He insisted that only he could tell the true story of his experiences. "What I have been through in my lifetime I would like to think that many needy people, particularly the young kids who it is my plan to benefit, would benefit," he wrote.

Still, he said, he was willing to sit down with me and explain precisely why he did not want me to write a biography of George Steinbrenner. He said he expected to be in New York the weekend of September 4 and suggested we might get together then.

I attempted to contact Steinbrenner the weekend of September 4, but he was understandably preoccupied, busy firing one manager and hiring a new one, an experience that even he does not yet find commonplace. I settled for writing to him once again:

> When you wrote and said you'd be in New York this past weekend, you couldn't possibly have anticipated how newsworthy the weekend would be. I did try to reach your office a few times, but with no luck . . .
>
> I still would like to get together at your convenience to discuss the points you bring up in your letter.
>
> I do want to mention a few things here. First, I am positive that the book I have in mind and the book you have in mind—to write yourself— could coexist easily, without overlapping; there are so many things that can be said in the third person that cannot be said in the first—and vice-versa. Second, as far as using the relationship that has developed between us, I plead guilty; I'm afraid that's the nature of being a journalist—making the best possible use of

your relationships with people; I don't think that's necessarily evil. And third, in reference to your fear that I might "make a killing" off your life and career, I hope you're right. After all, I do write *professionally*.

I look forward to seeing you.

That was the end of our correspondence—literarily, we presented no threat to the letters of George Bernard Shaw—until I submitted a request to purchase postseason tickets, which ended: "On the *other* front, I'd still like to get together and chat—whenever you have an opening." The response was a call from Gerry Murphy, Steinbrenner's administrative assistant, telling me where and when to pick up my tickets. I paid for the ones to the American League championship series, and to the World Series; the ones to the intradivisional playoffs, against Milwaukee, were, I was informed, a gift from Mr. Steinbrenner. The day after the Yankees eliminated Milwaukee, two days after Steinbrenner delivered a famous, or infamous, speech, or tirade, which had everything, or nothing, to do with the Yankees winning the decisive game—the alternatives depending on your point of view—I sent a gift to Steinbrenner at the Hotel Carlyle, a bottle of Dom Perignon to thank him and to toast his latest victory.

At the same time I was seeking to confront Steinbrenner, I was contacting his friends, his enemies and his acquaintances, from childhood up to the present, trying to piece together as complete a portrait as possible of the man who owned the Yankees. Steinbrenner had gotten to many of them before I did, particularly to his closer friends, and had asked them, or had told them, depending on the extent of his influence, not to talk to me. Only a few obeyed him to the letter—and refused to talk, or even to accept my phone calls—but I was stunned by the number of otherwise powerful and courageous men, including corporation presidents and working newsmen, who would talk about

Steinbrenner only if their identities were protected. "If George decides he's going to get you," one wary source insisted, "he'll get you." Some people sought to turn aside questions with humor. "I'm not going to say anything," said Jeff Torborg, a bright and articulate Yankee coach who had already announced he was resigning to become baseball coach at Princeton University. "He could buy the school and fire me." Torborg laughed easily, but a few weeks later, although Steinbrenner did not buy Princeton, he did the next best thing. He made an offer so attractive that Torborg elected to pass up Princeton and, instead, remain with the Yankees, first as a coach, eventually as an executive.

Surely the most tongue-twisting, and logic-twisting, response came from a small group of Steinbrenner's friends who, after some verbal sparring and a few rounds of drinks, offered me a deal: "If you promise not to tell George that we told you that he told us not to talk to you, we'll talk to you." They did, and what they had to say was overwhelmingly favorable to George.

A different, but fairly typical experience occurred with Eddie Sapir, who is both a judge and a practicing attorney in New Orleans, a man accustomed to resisting pressure. Sapir's clients include Billy Martin, the former Yankee manager, who is one of the two dominant characters (Reggie Jackson is the other), aside from the protagonist himself, in George Steinbrenner's life in the past decade. Eddie Sapir and I have several mutual friends, including Joe Namath and Namath's attorney, Jimmy Walsh, and when I phoned Sapir one night, while I was in New Orleans to do a television report, and told him that I wanted to speak with him the next day about George Steinbrenner, Sapir seemed absolutely delighted. "I couldn't think of a better friend, or a tougher enemy," Sapir said. "He's brilliant. He's a genius." Sapir's client, Martin, had said some terrible things about Steinbrenner in his ghost-written autobiography, *Number 1*, but Sapir

insisted, "I don't have a bad word to say about George Steinbrenner."

The next day, in his chambers, Judge Sapir didn't have a word to say about George Steinbrenner, good or bad. Sapir wore a red checkered shirt, open at the neck, a loosened black knit tie and blue jeans, which gave him a very casual and youthful appearance for a judge. He measured his words carefully; he was apologetic, and embarrassed. He had assumed, he said, that I had George's blessing to write a biography—which might explain the tone of his initial comments—but in checking with George shortly before our scheduled conversation, he had discovered that George was withholding his blessing. Since his client, Billy Martin, was still being paid by the Yankees, fulfilling a contract that was in force when Steinbrenner fired him in 1979, Sapir felt he had no choice but to accept Steinbrenner's suggestion and not speak to me—even though he had nothing but nice things to say about the man. I not only understood Sapir's delicate position; I loved it. The whole episode revealed more about George Steinbrenner than Sapir could have revealed in a month of interviews.

Not long after the necessarily brief encounter with Sapir, I took my son, a Yankee addict, up to the stadium to see a game. During batting practice, I bumped into the man who probably spends more time with Steinbrenner in New York than anyone else, William Denis Fugazy, who is in the limousine business and who, in the days before Muhammad Ali and multimillion-dollar purses, promoted a few heavyweight championship fights. When Bill Fugazy decided to get out of the boxing business, he wrote an article about his experiences for the *Saturday Evening Post,* an article that—another coincidence—I ghosted. Fugazy greeted me at Yankee Stadium half warmly and half warily. He mentioned that he would like to get me and Steinbrenner together, so that we could avoid any misun-

derstandings. I confessed I wouldn't mind at all getting together with George. Then Fugazy invited me, and my son, to watch the game from Box 332, Steinbrenner's private box, which overlooks home plate and the rest of his domain. I accepted. Steinbrenner, unfortunately, from my point of view, was not in New York, but his box did not go to waste. Several of Fugazy's relatives were there; so was Mike Forrest, a furrier who is a regular member of Steinbrenner's New York crowd. Three or four innings into the game, Roy Cohn arrived, the attorney, the former aide to Senator Joseph McCarthy. Cohn was an old acquaintance; we had been on opposite sides of a divorce action. When Cohn, knowing how Steinbrenner felt about my work-in-progress, spotted me with Bill Fugazy and Mike Forrest, a look of horror crossed his face, as if the shade of Robert F. Kennedy, his old enemy, had returned to haunt him. If it is any consolation to Cohn, neither Fugazy nor Forrest revealed any details, intimate or otherwise, about their friend, George Steinbrenner. Both have assured me, at other times, that George is a magnificent human being, a great American and a credit to his race.

Fugazy and I did talk a few times after our encounter at Yankee Stadium. He called to let me know that George wanted to see me, was willing to talk to me. I was to call George's secretary, tell her that George had told Bill to tell me to call her, and then she would make an appointment for me. I called George's secretary and repeated the whole complicated message. She never did make an appointment for me. Irv Kaze, the latest Yankee publicity director, did call to say that George would see me before Thanksgiving. After Thanksgiving, Kaze called to say that George would see me before Christmas. After Christmas, Kaze called to apologize.

Fugazy called again, after I had interviewed Barbara Walters, with whom I work at ABC News. She knows Steinbrenner better than any other journalist, and her

comments about their relationship were lively, witty and intelligent. She, obviously, was not intimidated by Steinbrenner. "Don't bully me," she told me she once said to him, only half kidding. "I don't work for you."

"The only reason Barbara talked to you," Fugazy said, "was that Roone wanted her to. Roone's afraid you might do a hatchet job on George, and Roone really likes George." I'm not certain whether the repeated references to Roone— Roone Arledge, my boss, the president of ABC News and ABC Sports—were supposed to intimidate me, but they did amuse me. I wouldn't have insulted Barbara Walters by asking her if she spoke to me only because Roone Arledge wanted her to, and I was positive that Arledge had more important things to worry about than whether I wrote a book vilifying George Steinbrenner or one beatifying him.

Barbara Walters was very helpful. So were several other people who were not afraid to have their names used. Bill Sharman, who coached the Cleveland Pipers when George Steinbrenner owned that now-defunct basketball team, finds it painful to converse, after laser surgery on his vocal cords, but he took the time and effort to write a note about his experiences with Steinbrenner. Jim Polk of NBC News, who, in his days with the Washington *Star-News,* did the investigative reporting that exposed Steinbrenner's involvement with Watergate and led to his indictment for violating federal laws, not only provided me with his original articles, but also sent me a letter several thousand words long, detailing his encounters with Steinbrenner. Roy Meyers, the coauthor of a series in the Cleveland *Press* in 1975 on Steinbrenner and his legal problems, and now the press secretary to Senator Howard Metzenbaum of Ohio, was more than generous with his recollections.

I could not possibly list all the people who shared their memories and their feelings, and many of them, of course, would be very nervous if they were listed. Most of the others are mentioned in the text, or in the acknowledg-

ments at the end of the book. It is no exaggeration to say that nearly every person I have spoken to, professionally or socially, since I started working on this book has offered either a fact or an opinion about George Steinbrenner. Dennis Smith, the literary fireman who wrote *Report from Engine Company 82,* mentioned to me over dinner one evening that Steinbrenner had just agreed to give all the receipts from one Yankee game in 1982 to the families of New York City firemen and policemen killed in the line of duty. One of my daughters went to a play at a small theater in New Jersey and reported a plaque outside the playhouse identifying George Steinbrenner as a benefactor. Unsolicited, casual acquaintances told me that they loved George Steinbrenner, or hated him.

Steinbrenner and I had our first conversation after I began working on this book the night the 1981 World Series ended, the night the Los Angeles Dodgers destroyed the New York Yankees, the night the Yankees embarrassed George Steinbrenner so badly he felt compelled to apologize to the people of New York. When the game ended, and with it Steinbrenner's hopes for a third world championship in his nine Yankee seasons, an ABC News camera crew and I hurried to the basement of Yankee Stadium and positioned ourselves opposite the elevator that descends from Steinbrenner's office to the locker-room level. We wanted to catch Steinbrenner coming off the elevator for two reasons, first because it might provide the best opportunity for a quick one-on-one interview, second because the setting seemed so appropriate. Three nights earlier, in Los Angeles, after the fifth game of the Series, Steinbrenner had—he said—encountered a pair of abusive Dodger fans in an elevator at his hotel and, as a result, he had a swollen lip and a damaged hand, but you should have seen the other guys. Actually, no one had seen the other guys; they had vanished immediately after the incident.

Bobby Freeman, the cameraman, and Jim FitzGerald, the soundman, and I waited outside the elevator. We waited perhaps fifteen minutes. Then the elevator came down, the door opened, and Steinbrenner emerged, flanked by newspaper reporters and security men. He was wearing his executive uniform, blue shirt, blue suit, blue-and-maroon-striped tie, blue eyes understandably cold, gray hair freshly cut and impeccably combed. He came straight from defeat, straight from drafting his public apology. His team had played horribly, driving thousands of fans out of the ball park and millions away from television screens long before the final out. His pride was hurt; so was his pocketbook. When he stepped off the elevator, I was the first person he saw, microphone in my hand, camera at my side. He could have been forgiven if he had sworn, or screamed, or swept past me. But, instead, George Steinbrenner reached out his hand, shook mine and said, "Hi, pal."

Three months later, he invited me to visit him in Tampa. I did, and, finally, we talked about almost all the subjects I had wanted to discuss, about Williams and Watergate, about Martin and Jackson, about shipping on the Great Lakes and baseball in the big leagues. His words are scattered throughout the book, and concentrated in the final chapter, which deals with my trip to Tampa.

He couldn't have been a more gracious host.

—Dick Schaap
New York City
February 1, 1982

1

George M. Steinbrenner III had every reason to be happy. At fifty-one, even though he carried perhaps ten or fifteen pounds more than he would have preferred, he enjoyed robust health. His wealth stopped just slightly short of infinity. His power, especially his power to hire and fire, was awesome, and his fame, his celebrity, for a man who did not sing or dance or act for a living, who did not throw or hit or catch a ball professionally and who was legally enjoined from holding national office, was unparalleled. Only a few months earlier, the television program *Sixty Minutes,* which can be a harsh judge of humans and their motives, had profiled him most favorably, the story ending with Steinbrenner, baton in hand, absolutely beaming, conducting a university orchestra playing "The Stars and Stripes Forever." Equally stirring, *Playgirl* magazine had just named him one of "The Ten Sexiest Men in America," thrusting him into the company of such distinguished men

as Mikhail Baryshnikov, Dan Rather and Gene Kelly. Yet with all these riches, George Steinbrenner clearly was not happy.

Steinbrenner was unhappy because the New York Yankees, the baseball team he owned and operated, were at this point, a few weeks into the second half of the 1981 season, losing more often than they were winning, a situation he could neither comprehend nor tolerate. The Yankees were to Steinbrenner, to his image and to his self-esteem, approximately what San Simeon was to William Randolph Hearst, and each Yankee defeat shook him like the seismographic tremors that periodically threatened every castle on the Pacific Coast.

That the Yankees were already guaranteed a spot in the postseason intradivisional playoffs, the bizarre system created after the baseball strike of 1981, did not pacify Steinbrenner. He had publicly given his word to the fans, to the little people, as he liked to call them, that the Yankees would not be complacent, that they would not let down in the poststrike half of the 1981 season, that they would maintain the effort and the enthusiasm that had enabled them to finish the prestrike part of the season with the best record in the Eastern Division of the American League. But now the season was slipping away, and the Yankees were not winning even half their poststrike games. George Steinbrenner bristled. *They* were not keeping *his* word.

During the next two weeks, the last week of August and the first of September, Steinbrenner would be very busy, even by his own standards, which border on the obsessive. He would labor mostly over the telephone, maneuvering, manipulating, persuading, informing, demeaning, soothing, threatening, explaining, demonstrating most of his strengths and most of his flaws, inspiring abuse and, usually grudgingly, admiration and, most important, headlines, always headlines.

Steinbrenner's fortnight of almost Machiavellian activity would focus primarily on two men who had, in different ways, displeased him: the man who had for almost five seasons been the star of his baseball team, Reggie Jackson, and the man who had for almost five months been the manager of his baseball team, Gene Michael. The two men were, to a considerable degree, Steinbrenner's creations, which made his discomfort even more acute.

True, Jackson had been an athlete of vast demonstrated talent and matching ego when he came to the Yankees late in 1976, lured by the then-outrageous offer of almost three million dollars for five seasons, but Steinbrenner had given Jackson, besides the money, an arena and a city in which both his talent and his ego could flower to their fullest. Michael, in his prime a far lesser ballplayer than Jackson, but a far greater diplomat, was Steinbrenner's protégé, a lean and hungry lieutenant risen through the ranks, from big-league coach to assistant to the owner to minor-league manager to big-league general manager to, finally, hand-picked Yankee manager.

But Jackson, late in August of 1981, was experiencing the most severe batting slump of his career, a slump that had persisted all season, and Michael was guilty of a more grievous sin—displaying resistance to Steinbrenner's suggestions, Steinbrenner's guidance, Steinbrenner's ideas on how to lift the Yankees out of their poststrike doldrums. Specifically, when Steinbrenner had insisted that the slumping Yankees hold a practice session on their first day off during the poststrike half of the season, Michael, arguing that the workout was unnecessary, had said, "If you're ordering me to do it, then I'll do it, but I'm going to tell the players it's your practice."

"Tell them anything you want," Steinbrenner had responded. "I think it has to be done, and I'm signing the paychecks."

Jackson, in the final year of his five-year contract, knew that at the age of thirty-five he had to produce a strong season if he wanted to earn a new and even more spectacular contract from the Yankees or, as a free agent, from any other team, and Michael, after several years of standing and sitting at Steinbrenner's side, knew that the boss could tolerate neither defeat nor—as much as he said he didn't want "yes" men—contradiction. Jackson, the athlete Steinbrenner himself would have loved to have been, and Michael, the surrogate son, had much more reason than their employer to be disheartened. They were not too happy with each other, either.

On August 25, 1981, at Yankee Stadium, Steinbrenner's castle in the Bronx, manager Michael sent someone named Aurelio Rodriguez up to pinch-hit for Jackson, an obvious insult. Rodriguez, if he was known for anything, was known for his fielding. It was as if a director had asked a chorus boy to show Olivier how to act. The next night, Michael kept Jackson out of the lineup, even though the Yankees were facing a righthanded pitcher, the kind of pitcher Jackson, a lefthanded hitter, habitually destroyed. "Maybe he can't do it here, I don't know if he can do it next year," Michael told a group of reporters, the implication being that Jackson was on the brink of being finished, his talent faded, his value eroded.

"It makes me sick to see someone like that sitting and judging my ability," Jackson countered the following morning. But Jackson was not convinced the judgment was purely Michael's. "His name," Jackson said, "should be Gene Michael Steinbrenner."

At that moment, as he sat over breakfast with a gifted young columnist for the New York *Daily News*, Mike Lupica, Jackson was more angry with George Michael Steinbrenner than with Gene Michael. Steinbrenner, through his hired hands in the Yankees' front office, had ordered that Jackson undergo immediately a thorough

physical examination, from eyes to toes, to determine whether his muscular body was betraying him. Michael's deprecating words seemed, to Jackson, to issue from Steinbrenner's mouth, words aimed, like the physical examination, at reducing Jackson's market value.

"There is no doubt in my mind that they are trying to plant seeds of doubt about my physical well-being," Jackson told Lupica. "They want any team that might sign me next year to wonder about my condition. That's their game. I just don't want to play it any more. They're trying to humiliate me, and I just don't care. Four, five years ago, I wouldn't have let them humiliate me this way. I would have told them to stuff the physical, and let them suspend me. Now I just give in. I hate giving in, but I give in."

Jackson, psychologically, was in a position that was new to him. Not just *giving in;* that was only part of it. Much more significant was *why* he was giving in. He was afraid. He feared George Steinbrenner. Once, fresh from the courtship that persuaded him to become a Yankee, Jackson thought that he and Steinbrenner might be friends, social equals, partners in a certain sense, twin Colossuses bestriding the baseball world. Later, Jackson discovered firsthand what a perceptive writer named Tony Kornheiser eventually surmised, that "as soon as he hires you, George Steinbrenner loses all respect for you"—a phenomenon of pursuit-conquest-scorn not uncommon in male-female relationships. Even then, when he realized that he had miscalculated their closeness, Jackson for a while still enjoyed playing games with the owner, matching wills and wits. But in time Jackson came to realize that he could not win, that Steinbrenner did not lose such wars, that Steinbrenner, who did not mind at all being likened to Patton, could inflict permanent psychological damage, especially upon a psyche so fragile as Jackson's. Like so many professional athletes, Jackson had been pampered and stroked since childhood, told over and over how gifted he was, how

wonderful, none of which prepared him well for criticism or, for that matter, for reality. It was no surprise that Jackson exhibited symptoms of classic paranoia—delusions of persecution and delusions of grandeur—mixed, of course, and sometimes confused with moments when he was truly persecuted, moments when he was truly grand. "When they start messing with your mind, trying to foul it up," Jackson said, "the best thing is not to get into it, not with a guy like Steinbrenner. He's a tough act, man."

Jackson's tone fluctuated between defiant and fearful, and fearful won. Even though he insisted that his troubles were mental, Jackson took the physical Steinbrenner demanded—a general examination, a neurological examination and an ophthalmological examination—and passed each test. Then he was expected to fly to Tampa, Florida, to meet Steinbrenner for dinner and conversation, presumably the psychological part of the examination. Jackson was expected on a specific flight by Steinbrenner, who maintained a base in Tampa for business and personal reasons. Tampa was the heart of his vast shipbuilding holdings, the site of the race track and the resort hotel he owned, and was not too far south of the Ocala horse farm where he bred and raised thoroughbreds, one of whom, he hoped, would one day win the Kentucky Derby. Steinbrenner also headquartered his family, his wife and children, in Tampa, out of the glare of New York publicity. As hard as Steinbrenner seemed to work sometimes to thrust himself and his baseball team into headlines, he worked just as hard to keep his family out of the spotlight. He told more than one interviewer that personal questions were off limits, that he wanted to preserve his children's privacy because he feared publicity might tempt kidnapers. He did not offer any equally logical reason for shielding his wife.

Steinbrenner had arranged for his older son, the oldest of his four children, to go to Tampa Airport to pick up Jackson. But Jackson had no intention of flying to Tampa.

The previous day, when Cedric Tallis, the executive vice-president of the Yankees, and Lou Saban, the president, had informed Jackson that he was to take a physical and then go to Tampa, Jackson had reluctantly agreed to the physical—contractually, the team had a right to demand he undergo a physical at any time—but had said that he would not go to Tampa to eat a meal with Steinbrenner. Tallis had insisted upon making a plane reservation for Jackson anyway, either because he suspected Jackson might change his mind or, more likely, because he was afraid to tell Steinbrenner that Jackson did not intend to fly to Tampa. Tallis, an unobtrusive man, had spent most of his adult life working in baseball, and people who knew him well said that he had a very fine baseball mind. People who knew him well also said that he endured an incredible amount of abuse from Steinbrenner. "You know what?" Tallis told an acquaintance around the time of the Jackson physical. "The other day, on a conference call, in front of a bunch of people, George called me an asshole!" Tallis shook his head. "I can't take much more of this," he said.

Clearly, Steinbrenner intimidated Tallis; he did not have quite the same effect on Saban, who had spent most of his adult life working in football. At one point during his football career, Saban had coached at Northwestern University, and one of his assistants in the 1950s was a young man named George Steinbrenner. More than twenty years later, after Saban had won and surrendered coaching jobs at West Point, at the University of Miami and with the Buffalo Bills, Steinbrenner hired him and gave him his first baseball job, a job with a prestigious title, president of the New York Yankees. The president answered directly, of course, to the man listed in the team's official directory simply as "Principal Owner."

No one told the principal owner that Jackson was not flying to Tampa until an hour or two before the scheduled dinner meeting. Then Jackson himself placed a call to

Steinbrenner, and the two men talked for an hour and a half, a real conversation, their best in a long time, each man making points, each man listening. Steinbrenner said he was delighted that the tests had shown that Reggie's problems were not physical. The problems were "upstairs," Steinbrenner said, meaning in the head. Jackson said he had known that all along. Both men made plans to be in Chicago the following day, Jackson to rejoin the team for a series against the White Sox, Steinbrenner to observe.

At the end of the conversation with Jackson, Steinbrenner called the reporter who was covering the Yankees on a daily basis for the New York *Daily News,* Phil Pepe. Even though Pepe and Lupica worked for the same paper, they were, Steinbrenner knew, more rivals than compatriots. Steinbrenner knew, too, how to play on that rivalry, how to use it for his own advantage. Steinbrenner had become expert on feeding stories to favored reporters, stories that would present his point of view, and at this time, Pepe, even though he was clearly no sycophant, ranked among his favorites.

Ironically, Lupica had once been one of Steinbrenner's favorites. They had even traded needling correspondence in print, correspondence initiated by Lupica, who, writing from London after covering the tennis at Wimbledon, mentioned proudly that he was sitting in Samuel Johnson's favorite chair at Ye Olde Cheshire Cheese off Fleet Street, prompting Steinbrenner, who had majored in English literature at Williams College, to respond, "You know how I am about the American flag, John Philip Sousa and the Fourth of July. Well, if you really knew your English literature, you'd know that this Johnson is the same cat who wrote, and I quote from memory, 'I am willing to love all mankind, except an American.'"Steinbrenner did not bother to mention that Johnson also said, "Patriotism is the last refuge of the scoundrel."

But then Lupica's columns grew increasingly antagonis-

tic toward Steinbrenner, even vicious. Lupica once referred to Steinbrenner as "an owner who brings whole new dimensions to the term 'manic-depressive,'" and in calmer moments, Lupica called him "a liar . . . a tyrant . . . a graceless lout . . . a statesman in the Alexander Haig mold." Understandably, the owner turned against the columnist. This put Elaine Kaufman, the proprietor of Elaine's, New York's fashionable East Side saloon, in a delicate position. Steinbrenner and Lupica—as well as, for instance, Woody Allen, Norman Mailer and Jacqueline Onassis—were regulars at Elaine's, and Elaine valued both the World Series championship ring George had given her, which she wore around her neck, and the more sensibly priced Wimbledon T-shirt Mike had given her. She had to be very careful to give both Steinbrenner and Lupica choice tables—lesser areas of the restaurant were good enough only for gawkers and unknowns—without putting them too close to each other. One night, in the men's room at Elaine's, Steinbrenner encountered Dan Jenkins, the journalist and author of *Semi-Tough,* who was dining with Lupica. "How can you sit with that little shit?" reporter Jenkins reported Steinbrenner inquiring.

Soon Lupica began to hear that Steinbrenner was spreading unkind rumors about him, calling him not a lout or a liar, but names even less flattering. Lupica never had more than hearsay evidence that Steinbrenner was the source of the vicious stories—and Steinbrenner himself later vehemently denied it—but, in his anger, Lupica called Edwin T. Broderick, vice-president and general counsel for the Yankees, and told Broderick that Steinbrenner should stop spreading such slander if he valued his reputation as a good husband and father. Whether the threat had anything to do with it or not, the stories apparently stopped circulating. Lupica continued to attack Steinbrenner in print, and Steinbrenner continued to feed baseball stories to Phil Pepe.

31

Steinbrenner called Pepe the night of the physical to insist that he had not tried to embarrass Jackson. "If I wanted to humiliate him, if I wanted to make him look bad, so no other club would sign him," Steinbrenner told Pepe, and Pepe repeated, "I would have done nothing. I would have just let him do what he's doing. I would have let him die." Steinbrenner said he wanted Jackson to take the physical for his own benefit. "If there's something wrong," the owner said, "I want to help him. When a guy's going good, when he's hitting .300, and he's cocky and he makes mistakes—which Reggie can do—that's when I'll whack his ass, physically, mentally, any way. But when things are going bad and he's trying hard, I'm not going to come down on him, I'm not knocking him, I won't be on his ass. Now, when he needs me, I'm there for him."

The same day that Steinbrenner's comments popped up in Pepe's story, the New York *Post*, a newspaper with a lust for overstatement, headlined its report of Jackson's physical: "George's Ugliest Hour . . . Boss Twisted Knife as Reggie Crumbled."

What the *Post*, in its fervor to sell papers, called his "ugliest hour," Steinbrenner seemed to feel was nothing more than a merciful moment—and the enormous gap between those two viewpoints dramatized what Tony Kornheiser, in a profile of Steinbrenner in *The New York Times Magazine*, once called "The Blue Spotlight Theory."

"George Steinbrenner does not photograph well in black and white," Kornheiser wrote. "Blue is his favorite color, his best color. It is said that under a soft blue light a Phyllis Diller can look like a Phyllis George.

"Steinbrenner carries a metaphorical soft blue spotlight around with him, and plugs it in and shines it on himself when the questions get hotter than he cares for . . . Steinbrenner speaks fluent blue."

The trouble with Steinbrenner's "blue spotlight" explanation for the Jackson physical—he simply wanted to help

a valued and once-productive employee achieve peace of mind—was that, if Steinbrenner's motives were so pure, the physical would have been arranged quietly and tactfully, and certainly not scheduled for a day when the rest of the team was starting a road trip, when Jackson's absence was conspicuous, when frustration and headlines were inevitable. But quiet tact was never Steinbrenner's strong suit. Quiet tact never sold tickets.

The day after his conversation with Jackson, Steinbrenner turned metaphorically red, red with rage, and, uncharacteristically, had almost nothing to say, even to favored reporters. The cause of Steinbrenner's fury, and his reticence, was his disciple, his hand-picked manager, Gene Michael.

Early in the evening of August 28, perhaps an hour before the Yankees were to play the Chicago White Sox, Michael sat in the bare room allotted to visiting managers in Chicago and spoke to a small circle of reporters, who thought they were going to hear about a meeting Michael had just had with Reggie Jackson. But Michael did not have Jackson on his mind. He read from notes, and chose his words carefully. The night before, the Yankees had lost for the tenth time in seventeen games since the midseason strike, and, predictably, the defeat had inspired George Steinbrenner to call Michael. "He said, 'Gene, I think I'm going to have to let you go,'" Michael told the impromptu news conference. "I said, 'George, do it right now, don't wait. I can't manage with that hanging over my head.'"

Michael went on to say that he didn't know how serious Steinbrenner's threat was, or how imminent the firing might be, but he said he was speaking out "to save face" and because "I want people to know how tough it is to manage the way it is right now." Michael said Steinbrenner had come very close to firing him in May and, more recently, Steinbrenner had threatened him with dismissal after almost every defeat. "After we lose a ball game,"

Michael said, "it's my fault. I made the wrong move. I did this. I did that. It's really tough to manage that way. He's threatened me in front of the coaches."

The manager said that Steinbrenner was coming to the game in Chicago that night, which meant that he might be fired before the night was over, and, incidentally, he and Steinbrenner had agreed on one thing: Reggie Jackson was going to be returned to the regular lineup. Michael conceded that he knew what he was getting into when he took the managing job. He knew Steinbrenner would call him and prod him and advise him, just as Steinbrenner had called and prodded and advised Michael's immediate predecessor, the 1980 manager of the Yankees, Dick Howser. "With Howser," Michael said, "George used to come to me and tell me to tell Dick that he was going to fire him. But Dick never heard about it because I never told him. I didn't think he needed that."

Then Michael went out to the dugout to guide his team against the White Sox, and the reporters, who in covering the Yankees had become masters of turmoil, experts at confrontation, charges and countercharges, went to search for Steinbrenner, to provoke his reaction to the latest revolution in his ranks. Steinbrenner showed up shortly after the game began and sat in a box seat behind the Chicago dugout, which gave him an excellent view of the game and a better view of the Yankee dugout. The reporters found him and summarized Michael's news conference for him, citing the manager's remarks that Steinbrenner had been harassing him and threatening to fire him. "I have no comment," Steinbrenner said. Then he commented, "Any discussions I have with my managers are not public. They're supposed to be between my manager and me. If he knows that [he's going to be fired], he knows more than I do. If he thinks that [speaking out] will help, that's his problem. Maybe he thinks that will serve some useful purpose, to cement him in, I don't know. I don't

want to talk about it any more. He's said enough for everybody already."

Steinbrenner and Michael both watched the Yankees beat the Chicago White Sox decisively, with Reggie Jackson, physically fit and batting fifth, contributing two hits. After the game, Steinbrenner did not fire Michael, nor threaten him, nor praise him. Even though both men were camped in Chicago for the weekend—Steinbrenner, besides inspecting his Yankees, was checking out some of his equine athletes at Chicago's Arlington Park—the manager and the owner did not speak. Neither tried to call the other. They communicated only through the reports of their words in the newspapers.

The next day, Saturday, August 29, the press corps surrounding the Yankees grew, with columnists from the *Daily News* and the *Times,* plus a network television crew, descending upon Chicago, drawn by the scent of blood. Some of the newsmen also smelled a plot. No matter what any of them thought of George Steinbrenner personally, no one could deny that the man had a genius for publicity, for stirring up controversy, for keeping his team and himself in the sort of headlines that sold seats. It was no accident that the attendance at Yankee games had risen every single year after a syndicate headed by Steinbrenner purchased the team from CBS for ten million dollars, a bargain price, on January 3, 1973. The attendance was 966,328 in 1972, and it was almost three times as high, 2,627,417, in 1980. It was also no accident that the Yankees' number of victories had climbed almost as dramatically, from 79 in 1972 to 103 in 1980; Steinbrenner claimed, and no one knowledgeable contradicted him, that he had turned the Yankees into a profitable enterprise, but that all of the profits went back into the business, many millions into signing free agents and developing young talent.

The more cynical among the newsmen, especially those

who reached Chicago on Saturday, wondered if the Jackson physical and the Michael eruption hadn't been carefully orchestrated by Steinbrenner, twin events calculated to produce more victories and, at the same time, greater attendance. Steinbrenner's gift for orchestration was so well known the cynics even suspected that the owner might have ordered the manager to rebel, to scream out publicly, first to keep the Yankees in headlines, where Steinbrenner knew they belonged, and second to unite the team behind Michael, to get the players to work harder to defend their "harassed' manager from their "heartless" owner. (It was not an unknown tactic in football, the sport in which Steinbrenner himself was schooled, for a coach to lift his team to greater performances by uniting the team against him; the Green Bay Packers of the 1960s, then the dominant team in professional football, used to say that their coach, the late Vince Lombardi, drove them so hard, pushed them so far—"he treats us all the same—like dogs," one of his players said—that they took out their rage toward him on opponents. Lombardi, not coincidentally, was frequently compared to Patton, Steinbrenner's military hero.)

When the question was put to Jackson—Is George Steinbrenner Machiavellian enough to do this, to promote a war between himself and Michael simply to bring you and Michael together?—Jackson smiled. "He might be, he just might be," Jackson said. Then, as he walked past the office in which the manager had delivered his modest emancipation proclamation the previous night, Jackson leaned through the doorway and called to Michael, "Thanks, thanks for taking the heat off me."

Michael smiled back, but wanly. The reporters who had witnessed his performance the night before swore that either Michael was sincere, that he was honestly unable to tolerate Steinbrenner's threats any longer, or that he was a

finer actor than had ever appeared in any of the Broadway productions Steinbrenner helped to finance.

"Has George ordered a complete psychiatric exam for you?" one of the newspapermen asked Michael.

Michael seemed relatively relaxed, much more at ease than he had been twenty-four hours earlier. His nickname was "Stick," for his long, lean frame, but he was made of sturdy stuff. He said that he did not regret at all what he had said, that he felt it had to be said, and had to be said then, before he got fired, before his credibility could be tarnished. He said he had not heard from the owner all day.

Then, for the second night in a row, Michael and Steinbrenner shared a pleasant experience, watching the Yankees beat Chicago, this time with Jackson hitting a home run, his first home run in thirty-four games, the longest drought of his professional career. Michael watched the game from the dugout, of course, and Steinbrenner from somewhere in the stands, neither discovered nor disturbed by reporters. His wife also viewed the game, from a box seat behind the Yankee dugout. Bill Kane, the team's traveling secretary, sat with Joan Steinbrenner and later reported that George had sat in less expensive seats, among the fans, among the little people, signing autographs, cheering for the Yankees, permitting the fans to buy him a beer or two. "He had a great time," Kane dutifully noted.

Kane was among the veterans of the Yankee organization, a survivor of twenty seasons, the first dozen as a statistician, hired originally by Mel Allen, the voice of the Yankees throughout the 1950s, their most glorious decade. After Steinbrenner bought the team, Kane became traveling secretary, responsible for shepherding managers, players and coaches from city to city, hotel to hotel, ball park to ball park, and, at the same time, catering to the owner's

slightest whim. Kane, according to a variety of sources, some of them reliable, held the Yankee record for being fired by Steinbrenner, or for being threatened with being fired—most recently on August 21, the day after the Yankees held the workout that Steinbrenner had demanded, and Michael resisted. Kane left his office half an hour early the day of the workout, and Steinbrenner, already upset by his team's play and his manager's attitude, was furious. The next day, Steinbrenner summoned Kane, who had a limp from childhood polio, to his office and informed him that, for leaving early, he would be docked a day's pay. Kane protested, arguing that he needed the day's pay very badly. Steinbrenner reportedly replied, "If you think you can get as good a job anywhere else, in your condition, go ahead and take it."

The story might be distorted, or even false, but that Kane was a frequent target of Steinbrenner's ire was irrefutable fact, supported by Steinbrenner's friends. Even his old friends in Cleveland, where Steinbrenner grew up and where he first flourished as a businessman, knew the owner's feudal attitude toward Kane. They remembered Steinbrenner the evening of a Yankee game in Cleveland, sitting at table fourteen in the Pewter Mug, his old hangout, glancing around the table and asking, "Who wants tickets for tonight?" He counted the requests, then called the ball park and asked for Bill Kane. No one could find Kane. "If he doesn't call me back in five minutes," Steinbrenner thundered, in front of his Cleveland friends, "he's fired."

Still, threatening to fire a man and telling him, "If you think you can get as good a job anywhere else, *in your condition*," were certainly not the same thing. One remark rang ultra-tough, the other downright cruel. Steinbrenner never did measure his words too carefully; diplomacy was not his game. Whether he actually made the remark to Kane or not, he was—even the people who liked him

38

agreed—capable of being cruel. Occasional cruelty was one of what he liked to call, almost casually, "the dents in my armor." "I'm no angel, don't get me wrong," Steinbrenner once said to Ira Berkow of *The New York Times*, "but the man with no dents in his armor, let him step forward. I try to do the best I can. And sometimes—as much as I don't want to—I have to inflict pain. But I also inflict some joy." A neat, and curious, phrase: I *inflict* joy.

Perhaps, from a practical standpoint, the bottom line was that Steinbrenner did not fire Kane, not in August of 1981 or any other time, and Kane did not quit. Kane even admitted to friends that he was accustomed to being fired; when he first joined the Yankees, Mel Allen would fire him, or threaten to fire him, every time he made a statistical error. Steinbrenner not only did not fire Kane; quite conceivably, after one or more of his threats, he may have given Kane a raise. Even the people who found Steinbrenner distasteful would not have been surprised if he had given Kane a raise; it would have been in character. "George buys off pain," said Tony Kornheiser, who did *not* dislike Steinbrenner. Kornheiser, fully cognizant of Steinbrenner's dents, conceded that on balance he liked the man, for his accessibility, for his bluntness and for his charm.

After the second straight victory over Chicago, Reggie Jackson poked his head into the manager's office once more and shouted, "One more day, you still got the job, one more day." Then Reggie went back to his locker, pumped up by his home run and by the war he and Michael were waging against Steinbrenner. For a fleeting moment, Jackson might even have thought that he and Michael were winning the war. "I'm writing my book," Jackson said, "and when George reads it, he'll think *The Towering Inferno* was a wienie roast."

That night, Michael unwound in the bar in the hotel in which the Yankees were staying. He talked about a man

who had kept calling him in his hotel room the previous afternoon, urging him to let his star pitcher, Ron Guidry, pitch a full nine innings against Chicago. The man told Michael he would be crazy if he used a relief pitcher. "About the third time the guy called," Michael said, "I picked up the phone and he just started right in, 'Listen, asshole . . .'" Michael sipped his drink. "And I thought it was George," he said.

The Yankees won their next three games, stretching their winning streak to five games, and in two of those three victories, Jackson drove in the winning run, and in the other he hit a three-run home run. Jackson was hitting. The Yankees were winning. The owner had good reason, once again, to be happy.

But not Steinbrenner. He was, he later said, agonizing, torn between his genuine feelings for Gene Michael and his deeper feelings for discipline and loyalty. He liked Michael; he loved discipline and loyalty. He ordered Cedric Tallis and Bill Bergesch, the Yankees' vice-president for baseball operations, not to contact Michael, not to talk to him, to transmit any messages through Bill Kane. While Michael was getting the silent treatment, George himself remained silent, not responding to calls even from favored reporters, not drumming up a single fresh headline. His agony must have been almost unbearable.

When the five-game winning streak ended, followed by two defeats in a row, Steinbrenner broke his silence, called Phil Pepe of the *Daily News* from his American Ship Building Company office in Tampa and responded to Michael's statements of a week earlier. "I consider it the maximum double-cross," Steinbrenner said. "I'm so disappointed in him. So disappointed. You can't say those things about your boss and expect to get away with them." Then Steinbrenner asked Pepe, "How long do you think you would be working if you said those things about your editor?"

Steinbrenner added that he was disturbed because

Michael had not been "a good soldier," and that his initial reaction when he learned of Michael's remarks, a blend of anger and disappointment, had not subsided. "Usually, when something like this happens," Steinbrenner said, "I feel differently the next morning. In this case, the more I think of it, the more I feel the same way I felt when he first said those things. Nobody ever pressured him. Nobody ever interfered with him. The only thing I ever ordered him to do was to have a practice, and that's because he forced me to do it. I told him I thought the way we were playing the guys needed to have a practice. He didn't want to have a practice, but I insisted."

Steinbrenner then turned his blue light on the silent treatment Michael had encountered. The lack of communication was not to ostracize Michael, the owner said, but to soothe him. "I told my people, 'Stick doesn't want your interference, so we won't interfere with him,'" Steinbrenner said. "'Don't call him any more. Don't interfere with him. Stay away from him.'"

The owner stopped just short of announcing Michael's dismissal. The same day, at the ball park in Kansas City, the Yankees' latest stop, NBC Sports was preparing for a rare Friday night network baseball game, the Yankees against the Royals, with Tony Kubek and Joe Garagiola broadcasting. Both men were familiar with Michael's situation; both men were familiar with Steinbrenner, and one of them was even on good terms with him. Kubek, himself once the Yankee shortstop, in the Mantle years, the years before Michael, and before Steinbrenner, came up with the idea of calling Steinbrenner, to get his thoughts on Michael for the network telecast. Kubek presented the idea to Mike Weisman, the producer for NBC Sports, and suggested that Garagiola place the call. Kubek knew that Steinbrenner would not talk to him.

Kubek and Steinbrenner stopped talking in the spring of 1978 when Kubek, covering the Yankees at their Florida

training camp, granted an interview to a writer from the Fort Lauderdale *News* and spoke openly about his feelings toward Steinbrenner. The story appeared under the headline: "Blame for Baseball Trauma Rests With Owners—Kubek." Within the article, Kubek was quoted, accurately, saying of Steinbrenner, "He has one of the most expnsive toys in the world, and what he does is manipulate people. He's not the only one, either. The same is true of most of the owners in baseball. Steinbrenner won't let anybody relax. It's what I call his 'corporate mentality.' He throws a fear into everybody . . . He makes the players fear for their jobs. That's his theory, and it works. But it's not a pleasant way to have to play."

Steinbrenner found the comments so fascinating he had the article photocopied and a copy sent to each major-league owner, with a postscript: "How's this for the mouth that bites the hand that feeds it?" Steinbrenner spoke to executives at NBC Sports, to the president of the American League and to the commissioner of baseball, implying strongly that Kubek should be fired. The commissioner, Bowie Kuhn, who was then having one of his periodic feuds with Steinbrenner, called Kubek and said, "Now you know how I feel when I have to deal with people like him."

When the 1978 season began, and Kubek still had his job, Steinbrenner plotted to get even. NBC's first "Game of the Week" featured the Yankees against Texas, and Steinbrenner knew that Kubek would attempt to conduct pregame interviews with the Yankees. Steinbrenner told Mickey Morabito, then the publicity director of the Yankees—a job with no more security than managing the team—that if any of the players spoke to Kubek, he, Morabito, would be fired. Morabito, properly fearful, spread the word. Steinbrenner later insisted that he never told any player not to talk to Kubek, and technically, of course, Steinbrenner was telling the truth. Ironically, or perhaps predictably, a few of the Yankees did talk to

Kubek, deliberately antagonizing their boss, and Morabito did not get fired, reinforcing a suspicion that Steinbrenner relished, much more than firing people, toying with their emotions. "George is the neighborhood bully," Kubek said.

Garagiola, on the other hand, always had a friendly relationship with the Yankee owner, for a variety of reasons. For one, Garagiola was a national celebrity, a regular on the *Today* program, when Steinbrenner was still in Cleveland, dreaming of getting to know celebrities, barely dreaming of someday being one himself. For another, Garagiola was a much more extroverted person than Kubek, much more concerned with being liked, by nature and by choice a cheerleader more than a critic. For a third, Joe Garagiola, Jr., fresh out of law school, had been hired by Steinbrenner, first as assistant to the president of the Yankees, then, after he passed the bar exam, as in-house counsel. Young Garagiola had never been fired, but had, in 1977, decided to quit, along with Marty Appel, who was then the team's publicity director, so that the two of them could form a company to represent athletes. "Joe and I went in together to say we were leaving," Appel recalled. "We had been rehearsing over and over what we were going to tell him: 'We've decided to take a cue from your own life. At one point, you decided to go out on your own, and we've come to that point in our lives.' He briefly tried to talk us out of it, but he said he wouldn't stand in our way. He was very gracious, but it was the most frightening experience I ever had." Joe Garagiola, Jr., later became Tony Kubek's agent.

Garagiola placed the call to Steinbrenner from Kansas City and explained that he wanted to do a brief interview. Steinbrenner, who had already spoken to Pepe, agreed. Garagiola suggested that Steinbrenner think about what he wanted to say, then said that he would call back in an hour. An hour later, Garagiola called again and recorded an interview that lasted less than two minutes. There was

one key sentence. "Joe," Steinbrenner said, "if you stood up in front of your boss at NBC and said those things I heard, I don't know if you or Tony would be broadcasting this game tonight."

The implication was clear: Michael's position was, at best, precarious. After the interview was recorded, NBC played it back for, among a few other people, Joe Donnelly, a reporter for the newspaper *Newsday*. Half an hour later, still well before NBC was going on the air, Steinbrenner called back and told Garagiola he had reconsidered, he did not want the interview to be broadcast. Garagiola passed the word to Weisman. "He wants us to kill the tape," Garagiola said.

Weisman got on the phone with Steinbrenner and explained that he could not kill the tape, that, among other reasons, Joe Donnelly had already heard the tape and had made notes. "Steinbrenner went crazy," Weisman recalled. "He said, 'You double-crossed me,' and then he hung up. A few minutes later, he called again. 'How could you do this?' he said. 'You better not play that tape on the air. Let me tell you, I'm on the [major-league baseball] television committee, and NBC will get shit all over.'"

Understandably nervous, Weisman called his boss, Art Watson, the president of NBC Sports. "Was he aware we were taping him?" Watson asked.

"Sure," Weisman said.

"Was it edited at all?" Watson asked.

"No," Weisman said.

"Then go ahead and play it."

NBC played the tape on the air, but not before playing it for Michael, who was offered the opportunity to respond. Michael declined, discreetly, then placed his own call to Steinbrenner. The two men talked for almost an hour, but at the time, neither reported what was said. Steinbrenner later reported, however, what was not said: Michael did not

apologize for his remarks a week earlier, and this lack of an apology was going to be fatal.

Then, armed with the knowledge that their manager once again was on the brink of being fired, the Yankees responded with a 4–0 victory, a victory in which Ron Davis pitched brilliantly in relief, and Reggie Jackson hit safely for the eighth straight game. "Gene Michael has been the best manager I've ever had," Davis said afterward, "and in the back of my mind, I thought, 'If I blow this, I may see another guy here tomorrow.'"

Once again, Jackson fired a postgame comment into the manager's office. "Call him 'The Cat,'" Jackson suggested to the writers interrogating Michael. "The man has nine lives."

But, even though the Yankees won again on Saturday, giving Michael seven victories in nine games since his outburst, he had run out of lives. Friday night, after the conversation with Michael that included no apology, George Steinbrenner called Bob Lemon at Lemon's home in Long Beach, California, and asked Lemon to fly to Tampa. Lemon, fresh from the barbershop, where he had listened to the boss' comments on NBC while his hair was being clipped, sensed the situation. A member of the Baseball Hall of Fame for his pitching skills, Lemon knew how Steinbrenner operated from personal experience. In 1978, he had become the fourth Yankee manager of the Steinbrenner era, hired in midseason when Billy Martin was dismissed for the first time. The following year, in a reversal of roles, Lemon became the fourth Yankee manager to be scuttled by Steinbrenner, and he was succeeded by, of all people, his predecessor, Martin. Martin gave way to Dick Howser in 1980, and Howser to Michael in 1981, and now, logically, by his own brand of logic, Steinbrenner wanted Lemon to replace Michael.

Steinbrenner knew he would not have to offer Lemon a

contract. Lemon already had one: The contract he was working under in 1979, when Steinbrenner dropped him as manager, was still in effect, until the end of 1981. Steinbrenner had an expensive habit of paying his managers after he discarded them, and in Lemon's case, the owner felt a special obligation. Lemon's son, Jerry, died at the age of twenty-six in an automobile accident in the fall of 1978, a tragedy that drained from Lemon all the satisfaction of winning the World Series that year. The following season, understandably, Lemon was not the same man he had been before his son's death; his mind wandered from baseball; winning was *not* the only thing. In June, Steinbrenner removed Lemon from the manager's office, but kept him on the Yankee staff, briefly as general manager, a meaningless title, then as a scout.

Lemon flew to Tampa on Saturday, and was greeted by the offer he had anticipated. "Do you want to manage the Yankees again?" Steinbrenner asked.

"Yep," Lemon replied.

That settled, Lemon was dispatched to Kansas City, and Bill Kane was given the assignment of getting Michael out of Kansas City without encountering the press. Dave Szen, the second Yankee publicity director of the season, who was about to be replaced by the third, was given the job of releasing the official announcement about Michael and Lemon, and Steinbrenner himself notified Michael, then set about explaining through the newspapers to the public why the change in managers had to take place. Steinbrenner's blue light glowed brilliantly.

His early-morning phone calls woke up Phil Pepe of the *Daily News* and Jane Gross of *The New York Times*. Typically, Steinbrenner started right in explaining himself without identifying himself. "It took me three or four sentences to wake up and realize who was calling," Jane Gross said. Then Steinbrenner, in another typical ploy,

said that everything he was going to say was "off the record." Gross waited till Steinbrenner finished, then negotiated for the right to attribute some of his comments, some of his rationale for firing Michael.

"I feel like a father scorned," Steinbrenner told Gross, in injured tones. "I feel like I have a son who has done something wrong and isn't mature enough to admit it."

"I nurtured him, he was like my own son," Steinbrenner told Pepe, with equal feeling.

No one from the New York *Post* received a wake-up call from Steinbrenner, but before the day was over, the *Post*'s Henry Hecht reached the owner. "This is the most agonizing decision I've made since I've owned the Yankees," Steinbrenner said, in what the *Post* blissfully labeled "an exclusive interview."

Between the exclusive interview, and the negotiated quotes, using varying words and varying details, but a consistent tone, Steinbrenner carefully disseminated his side of the story, his account of the decisive Friday-night conversation with Michael.

"I was just on my way out when Stick called," Steinbrenner recalled, "and I said, 'Hot dog, he's come to his senses.' I told him, 'Stick, if you feel I threatened you, I didn't mean to. I'm not an easy guy to work for.'"

(Parenthetically, Steinbrenner added, "That's me. That's my dent. It's one of the dents in my armor, and I can't remove it.")

"'I'm sorry if you feel I threatened you,'" Steinbrenner quoted Steinbrenner saying to Michael, "'but I own this team, and when you take on your boss publicly, you can't just get away with it.'

"I begged him to say, 'I'm sorry,' but he wouldn't say it. I wasn't going to put him up in front of a microphone. I just wanted him to say he made a mistake, that he was sorry for what he said."

("I never heard him 'begging' me to apologize," Michael said later, without disputing the gist of Steinbrenner's version.)

"'I've got no reason to apologize,'" Steinbrenner quoted Michael saying to Steinbrenner, "'because I didn't do anything wrong.'

"I couldn't spank him," Steinbrenner continued, "but I had to let him know somehow that he was wrong. And I can't teach him by having him just ignore me. It's not the way I operate. A boss can be totally wrong, you know, but he's the boss, and he worked to get there.

"Discipline is the most necessary condition for success, corporate and sports. No leader, whether in the army or in a school or in a company or on a team, can let one of his employees say to him, 'Get off my ass or fire me.'"

On Sunday morning, when Steinbrenner did fire Michael, the deposed manager forgot to ask who was succeeding him. He got the word later from a reporter. Then he got a phone call from Lemon. "I told him," Lemon said, "'You never know. I'll keep the seat warm for you.'" Then Lemon went out to the ball park and was greeted by Graig Nettles, the Yankees' third baseman, an athlete with a reputation for brilliant fielding and stinging comments. "Condolences, Meat," Nettles said, using the nickname, "Meat," that Lemon habitually used for almost everyone else.

"I never got any credit for being bright," Lemon replied cheerfully. "Nobody ever accused me of that."

Lemon was in a good mood, obviously happy to be back on the field, the impact of his son's death softened by time. Lemon was sixty, seventeen years older than Michael, and considerably less impetuous. He explained why he again accepted the hazardous job of managing the Yankees. "George has been awfully good to me," Lemon said. "I'm still a company man. If he wanted me back as manager,

48

that made me feel good. When he replaced me before, it may have been more for my own good. With the problems I had, some of the incentive was lost. It took me a while to realize that what he did was right."

Lemon said he could see at their meeting Saturday that Steinbrenner was honestly upset about firing Michael, genuinely disturbed by what he considered a betrayal by a trusted aide. The owner, accustomed to attacks from other quarters, pulled up short of saying to Michael, "*Et tu.*"

Then Lemon began his second tour as Yankee manager, matching strategies with another former Steinbrenner manager, Dick Howser, who had only a few weeks earlier taken command of Kansas City. "I don't want to say Gene's better off," Howser said, "but when the guillotine is over your head, it's better to have it happen. Sometimes it's a relief. In my case it was." Howser was fired after winning 103 games in his season as manager; only five teams in Yankee history had won more games.

Lemon's new reign started with a victory over Howser's Royals, and while the Yankees were in the clubhouse, saying mostly nice things about their departed manager, mostly nice things about their new manager and mostly diplomatic things about their owner's maneuvering ("It was just a matter of time," Reggie Jackson said; "It was out of our hands," Graig Nettles said), Michael was boarding a TWA flight to New York. When he reached LaGuardia Airport, he tried to avoid waiting newsmen by slipping out the back door of the plane and going straight to the baggage area, but the reporters cornered him there. Michael's eyes were bleary. He needed a shave. He didn't need another drink. He was friendly, and grateful for words of support, but he said that at the moment he had no comment to make about the firing. When a TWA employee told him he had a call coming in on the airline courtesy phone, he picked up the receiver and said, "Hello? Hello?

Hello?" No one responded. Michael hung up the phone and smiled wryly. "I wish the telephone in our dugout hadn't worked," he said.

At that moment, as he carried his suitcase out of LaGuardia, Michael was the only man who had managed the Yankees during the Steinbrenner era who was not still managing a major-league team. Ralph Houk, the incumbent when Steinbrenner took title to the Yankees, managed the Boston Red Sox in 1981; Bill Virdon, Houk's successor, managed the Houston Astros; Billy Martin, next in line, managed the Oakland A's; Bob Lemon was back managing the Yankees and Dick Howser managed Kansas City. Remarkably, each of the four who'd been hired by Steinbrenner—excluding Houk, whom Steinbrenner inherited from CBS—guided their teams into the postseason playoffs in 1981, strong circumstantial evidence that when Steinbrenner picked managers, he picked winners. The reverse side of that circumstantial evidence was that when Steinbrenner fired managers, he fired winners.

When Steinbrenner fired Michael, most of the owner's cherished little people, the cab drivers, the cops, the waiters, the elevator operators, the doormen, the receptionists, the army of New Yorkers who were constantly in touch with strangers, the mass of New Yorkers who felt compelled to share their observations on everything from the Ayatollah to the AWACS, sided with the deposed manager. Generally, they felt sorry for an admirable, dedicated man pushed beyond his endurance by a harsh, belligerent boss. The little people had a lot of trouble identifying with a jowly millionaire. But one newspaper columnist, Dick Young of the *Daily News*, who had been covering major-league baseball in New York for more than thirty years, had no sympathy for Michael. "In the real world, you don't dare the boss to fire you," Young wrote. "You don't dare the boss to do anything. If you take his money, you do as he wishes. When you reach the point

where you believe it is not worth it, it is, perhaps, humiliating, then you find another boss. Gene Michael can sit back and collect $125,000 a season for the next two years. That's one thing about working for George. The money takes the sting out of the humiliation."

But Young, who often sided with baseball management against the players, was a lonely voice. In most of the public print, Steinbrenner was vilified. In Young's own paper, Thom Greer called the owner "a tyrant, heartless and cold," and said that a "flogging in Times Square would be too good for George." In *The Sporting News,* the self-anointed Bible of Baseball, Ray Fitzgerald wrote, "I can think of only one man who might, just might, fit the high standards necessary to manage the New York Yankees. First, we'd have to fit him for the Yankee uniform. A 42 around the waist would be just about right, with a 15 ½ red neck and padded shoulders . . . shoes small enough to fit into his mouth . . . and . . . the biggest hat size available. His name would be emblazoned on the pinstripes . . . S*T*E*I*N*B*R*E*N*N*E*R . . . the only one who could possibly do the job. I see George Steinbrenner, unregistered egomaniac and all-time second guesser, firing his team and playing all nine positions himself." And in *The New York Times,* the dean of American sportswriters, Red Smith, winner of the Pulitzer Prize, a craftsman revered for his gentle wit, savaged Steinbrenner: "George M. Steinbrenner III has been fuhrer of the Yankees since 1973 . . ." Smith's judgment was, perhaps, the unkindest cut of all. Steinbrenner, one of his former employees later pointed out, was sensitive to all criticism, but especially sensitive to any criticism that highlighted his German heritage and hinted of Fascism. "George is the original some-of-my-best-friends-are-Jewish," the ex-Yankee official said, "and, to be fair, many of his are."

Yet Steinbrenner did not explode when he saw the latest in a series of *Daily News* cartoons drawn by Bill Gallo,

cartoons depicting Steinbrenner as a puffed-up Prussian soldier, General Von Steingrabber, wearing an Iron Cross with the Yankee symbol carved into it. Gallo believed that his cartoons, none of which depended on subtlety for their impact, amused Steinbrenner. "Whenever his friend Bill Fugazy sees me," Gallo said, "he just shakes his head and smiles and says, 'That Steingrabber, that Steingrabber.'"

Right after Michael's dismissal, Gallo drew General Von Steingrabber talking to his mistress, a Wagnerian woman labeled "Mata Money." Steingrabber said, to Mata, "Hello, Liebchen, I'm home—und I had a maff-a-lous day. I fired der manager again. That always makes me feel so goodt . . ."

"Ach, mine cute little strudel-puss," the mistress responded, "you are so brave, so excitingly impulsive . . . such a grabber mit der headlines . . . keep it up . . . sweetie . . . und always der house will be full up to der rafters!"

The New York Times, on its editorial pages, expressed basically the same sentiments, with considerably more dignity. "Do all the firings indicate that the Yankee owner is a tyrant, a perfectionist, a meddling amateur?" the *Times* wondered. "Maybe. What is clearer is that as a producer of theatrics, he is an adept professional. Even at the risk of painting himself a capricious villain, each firing implies action and incites interest . . . Look who's on the front page."

The front page . . . or der headlines . . . George Steinbrenner dominated both. The end of the first week of September 1981 was, in a certain sense, in George Steinbrenner's special world, like the end of a Shakespearean tragedy, *Hamlet,* say, or *Macbeth,* bodies scattered about the stage, but with one very important difference: In *Hamlet,* and in *Macbeth,* the protagonist was among the corpses.

In real life, in George Steinbrenner's life, the protagonist was very much alive. In fact, George Steinbrenner was

almost happy. The Yankees were winning. He had a manager who would not contradict him. And Reggie Jackson was hitting—even if his will to remain a Yankee was broken.

"George Steinbrenner can afford to lose Reggie Jackson now," said a former Yankee executive, "because George Steinbrenner now is bigger than Reggie Jackson."

Bigger than a superstar.

Bigger than any other owner in sports.

Bigger than life.

And not even a decade had passed since George Steinbrenner came out of Cleveland, practically unknown, and said, when he bought into the New York Yankees, "I'm going to spend more time with my family. I won't get involved with the team."

2

In the middle of the nineteenth century, a German immigrant named Philip J. Minch settled in Vermilion, Ohio, just west of Lorain on the shores of Lake Erie, and founded the Minch Transit Company, a shipping fleet operating on the Great Lakes. His daughter, Sophia Minch, clearly an unusual woman, went to college at Oberlin, assembled a priceless collection of Civil War music, married a man named Henry Steinbrenner and, when her father died, became president of the shipping company. Soon after the start of the twentieth century, the company, by then known as the Kinsman Marine Transit Company, became the first tenant in the John D. Rockefeller Building in downtown Cleveland, and over the next half century, with Kinsman operating out of the same headquarters, the presidency passed to Sophia's son, George M. Steinbrenner, and then to his son, Henry G. Steinbrenner. Hank Steinbrenner was not only superbly bred for the shipping business; he was superbly educated for it. He was a naval

architect, a marine engineering graduate of the Massachusetts Institute of Technology, one of the most distinguished schools of engineering in the United States, and he had been one of the school's most distinguished athletes. In 1927, Hank Steinbrenner had become the first, and last, man to win a national outdoor track and field championship for MIT, the 220-yard low hurdles, an event later discontinued, dropped from collegiate track meets. The event vanished, but the Steinbrenner imprint on MIT athletics survived. In 1977, when the school got a new three-hundred-thousand-dollar track, the facility was named Henry Steinbrenner Stadium, primarily because the money for the track was a gift celebrating Hank Steinbrenner's fiftieth college reunion, a gift from his two daughters and his son, George M. Steinbrenner III, principal owner of the New York Yankees, a man who, for most of his life, had been trying to do things that would please and impress his father, not, however, with noticeably great success.

George M. Steinbrenner III, great-grandson of Sophia Minch Steinbrenner, was born on the Fourth of July, 1930, a celebration of patriotism during the dawn of the Depression. No record indicates that young Steinbrenner suffered during the Depression, but considerable evidence exists that he learned quickly to think of himself as a patriot, a flagwaver and even, in the words of an earlier George M., who was also born on the Fourth of July, a Yankee Doodle Dandy. But if the accident of his birthdate influenced George Steinbrenner, the personality of his father unquestionably influenced him more. "Always work as hard as, or harder than, anyone who works for you," Henry Steinbrenner counseled, and the only son listened.

Athlete, engineer and businessman, Henry Steinbrenner was tall and austere, proper and stern, brusque and outspoken, a man of his word and a man of great wealth, a protector of the traditional values. When George

Steinbrenner's two younger sisters, Susan and Judy, began to entertain what were then known as "gentleman callers," their father, wearing a black suit and tie, would sit in a corner of the living room, quiet but hardly inconspicuous. "It's a wonder either of them ever got married," George Steinbrenner once told a friend.

George was born in Rocky River, Ohio, only a few miles west of downtown Cleveland, and he grew up only slightly farther west, in a century-old colonial house on a twenty-acre farm in Bay Village, a lakeside suburb that looked as if it had been lifted out of New England, tree-lined streets dotted with colonial and Cape Cod houses, a peaceful village free of industry. A man named Jeff Kurz, who lived in Bay Village in the early 1950s, took away one vivid impression of Henry Steinbrenner. The elder Steinbrenner had come to Kurz's stepfather's truck garden to buy vegetables. As Steinbrenner was leaving, walking toward his car, Kurz's stepfather looked at him and said, "He could buy and sell all of us." Kurz never forgot those words, and the power they implied, and Kurz's wife, Jean, always remembered that Henry Steinbrenner, and his shipping friends and rivals on the Great Lakes, were known as men who were honorable, who trusted each other, who did not need contracts formalized, but could rely on handshakes, a closed circle of staid, solid men who attached considerable importance to their families, not big spenders, but good providers.

George's mother, Rita Haley Steinbrenner, an attractive but reserved woman, a devout Christian Scientist, was of Irish descent, and from her, George later suggested, he acquired a sense of compassion, a feeling for the underdog. George was very close to his mother—even when he was grown, and married, and had children of his own, he phoned his mother every day—but the father, and the father's values, dominated. "My dad demanded things that I didn't always like or understand," George once said, "but

looking back there's nothing I would change about the way I was brought up. I got some gentleness from my mother, but I got toughness from Dad." Another time, speaking of his father, George said, "He was a typical German father— very strict, a great teacher, very difficult at times. He was extremely competitive, and he taught me to be. I had some great teachers in life, but it all comes back to Dad. Whatever good there is in me is him. Whatever's bad is me."

In 1981, when the good Steinbrenner and the bad Steinbrenner were inspiring daily headlines, Maury Allen of the New York *Post,* writing a series of articles about the Yankees' owner, asked a friend of his, a psychiatrist, for an instant analysis of Steinbrenner. "It seems a classic case of a filial relationship with a strong father," said the psychiatrist, who knew Steinbrenner only through reading about him and seeing him on television. "His aggressiveness, his toughness, his meanness to employees all come from his inability ever to please his father. No matter how much success he achieves, he can never achieve the perfection his father demands. The complexity of the man is that he wants desperately to be loved by his father while knowing it cannot happen. Some human beings are congenitally incapable of expressing affection. George Steinbrenner would give a World Series ring if his father would hug him to his breast and say, 'I love you.'"

As a youngster, by his father's decree, George always wore a tie and a jacket to grade school, which subjected him to both verbal and physical abuse from less elegant and more violent schoolmates, who did not suspect that some-day George Steinbrenner would grow up to be named, by *Penthouse* magazine, the best-dressed businessman in America, a tribute to shirts designed by Bill Blass and to suits frequently selected at Barney's, the giant New York men's clothing store. Steinbrenner, incidentally, once attended a party given by Bob Guccione, the founder and

publisher of *Penthouse,* but at the party, Steinbrenner refused to pose with a group of attractive young women, in revealing outfits, called Penthouse Pets. Steinbrenner refused to pose not for fear of offending his father's morals, or his mother's, or his own, but because, he said, kiddingly, he didn't want to make his players jealous. A few months later, Steinbrenner resisted being the subject of *Playboy's* monthly interview because, he said, he feared that the magazine was not consistent with the Yankee image. He did not soften when he was reminded that the images of President Carter, Walter Cronkite, Buckminster Fuller, William F. Buckley, Jr., and Princess Grace of Monaco had all managed to survive the *Playboy* interview.

By the age of nine, again by his father's decree, George had his own business—a thriving poultry trade that kept him in, among other things, baseball cards and James Fenimore Cooper novels. "Dad didn't give me an allowance," George explained. "He gave me chickens. I'd get my money through them. I'd get up early, clean the roosts and then sell the eggs door to door. It was called The George Company. When I went away to school, I sold the company to my sisters, Susan and Judy. It became The S & J Company." Steinbrenner sold the franchise for fifty dollars.

At the age of fourteen, George was sent off to Culver Military Academy in northern Indiana, not far from Chicago, a school founded late in the nineteenth century and designed to prod the sons of the wealthy into shape for college. The accent was military, but the school's more famous graduates succeeded in the arts—from Josh Logan, the director, to Ernest K. Gann, the novelist, to Hal Holbrook, the actor. Steinbrenner entered Culver two years after Holbrook graduated, in 1944, right at the end of World War II, when the line between patriotism and militarism was still blurred by recent combat, when the achievements of MacArthur, Patton and Eisenhower were

not so much history as current events. Steinbrenner was certainly not an outstanding student at Culver, but he did manage an A+ in military science and, for a while, considered a military career. Later, in his business prime, Steinbrenner was called, even by friends, and sometimes to his face, "General" or "The U-Boat Commander," and Neil Walsh, a New York insurance man and city official, once said, "We always tell George that it was a good thing his great-great-grandfather came to America. If he hadn't, we would have lost the war."

At Culver, Steinbrenner was a versatile athlete, an end on the football team, a basketball player and, in the family tradition, a hurdler. His father had taught him hurdling when he was twelve, and George became so proficient in that delicate and demanding art that, when he was older, he was swift enough to compete against a fellow Clevelander, Harrison Dillard, the 1952 Olympic hurdling champion. He was not swift enough to defeat Dillard; hardly anyone was. Still, George was good enough to beat most lesser hurdlers, though never good enough to please his father completely. Once, when he had won two races and finished second in a third, George recalled his father saying, "What the hell happened? How'd you let that guy beat you?"

The one major sport Steinbrenner conspicuously did not play at Culver was baseball. "I never was a good baseball player," he admitted. "I never played it. Track was my sport in the spring." Yet George was, he confirmed many times, a dedicated baseball fan, if a slightly schizophrenic one, split between cheering for his hometown team, the Cleveland Indians, and being awed by the visiting titans, the New York Yankees. "When the Yankees came to town," Steinbrenner said, the day he purchased the team, "it was like Barnum and Bailey coming to town. I don't mean that they were like a circus, but it was the excitement. They had these gray uniforms, but there was a blue

hue to them. I'll never forget watching them. Watching them warm up was as exciting as watching the game. Being in Cleveland, you couldn't root for them, but you would boo them in awe." Steinbrenner used to go to the headquarters for visiting teams, the Hotel Cleveland, which was perched above the railroad station, and sit in the lobby and stare at the Yankees, at Joe DiMaggio and his teammates. DiMaggio was a hero; so was Lou Gehrig or, equally, Gary Cooper, the actor who portrayed Lou Gehrig. "I hate to think how many times I've watched *Pride of the Yankees* on television," Steinbrenner said. "I watch it every time it's on."

When Steinbrenner was in his teens, his hometown team often provided a sturdy challenge to the Yankees. In 1948, the year Steinbrenner graduated from Culver, the Indians not only won the American League pennant, but, with Bill Veeck, a master showman, operating the team, set an American League attendance record that would survive for thirty-two years, until it was broken in 1980 by George Steinbrenner's Yankees. (By then, Veeck and Steinbrenner were unfriendly rivals. Veeck was running the Chicago White Sox, a marginal team artistically and financially, and he made no secret of his dislike for Steinbrenner.) The Indians also won the pennant in 1954, with a remarkable pitching quartet of Bob Feller, Mike Garcia, Early Wynn and Bob Lemon, the future Yankee manager, plus, at third base, the Most Valuable Player in the American League in 1953, Al Rosen, who would become, a quarter of a century later, under Steinbrenner, president of the New York Yankees.

In his final year at Culver, Steinbrenner brought his grades up from the lower quarter of the class to the upper quarter, an achievement that helped him win an award for all-around excellence when he graduated in 1948. But he hardly made an indelible impression on his classmates. Another member of Culver's Class of 1948, Senator Lowell

Weicker, the Connecticut Republican, said in 1981 that he could not remember anything at all about George. But the school remembered Steinbrenner. In 1971, almost a quarter of a century after his graduation, he was named Culver's Man of the Year, in recognition of his postgraduate accomplishments and of his generosity, gifts to Culver ranging from film equipment to scholarship funds to an all-weather track, the George M. Steinbrenner track. With the opening of Culver Girls Academy in 1971, the school became coeducational, and as soon as each of Steinbrenner's children reached high-school age, he shipped them off to Indiana.

Helped by a strong recommendation from the Culver dean, Steinbrenner gained admittance to Williams College, one of New England's Little Three (with Amherst and Wesleyan), the so-called Potted Ivy League, a prestigious school nestled among the Berkshire Mountains in a corner of Massachusetts near the New York and Vermont borders, a school known equally for high academic standards and a lively social schedule. Fraternity parties at Williams were legendary, but Steinbrenner, even though he joined Delta Kappa Epsilon, a house dominated by athletes, was hardly a wild undergraduate. "George wasn't exactly your 'Animal House' type," a classmate and fraternity brother, George McAleenan, recalled. "George had a good regimented upbringing. He was not spontaneous. He was always in control. He had a certain amount of reserve, and always retained a bearing of dignity. He was very polite and very organized." Steinbrenner did not smoke and did not drink and did not complain about Williams' compulsory chapel attendance. On Sunday mornings, he would take his yellow Plymouth convertible and chauffeur elderly women to the Christian Science Church in Williamstown.

McAleenan, who became president of the Peninsular Oil and Gas Company, knew Steinbrenner's father. "I don't

think George ever measured up to his father's standards," McAleenan suggested. "His father was a world-class hurdler. George was good, but he wasn't an Olympian. George is a competitive person, and he wanted to achieve the degree of success his father enjoyed. That might be the key to George's desire to succeed. He is driven to exceed his father's successes."

At Williams, Steinbrenner continued to run the hurdles, competing at Madison Square Garden, setting a variety of Williams records, becoming captain of the track and field team in his senior year. But he gave up all other sports until, in his senior year, he went out for football. He played halfback. In 1954, a story appeared in the Columbus *Citizen* headlined, "The Amazing MISTER Steinbrenner," and said that after graduating from Williams, Steinbrenner "signed as a free agent with the New York Giants and played defensive halfback," a facet of his life Steinbrenner, not famous for his humility, never mentioned after he purchased the Yankees and became a part-time New Yorker. The New York Giants had no record of anyone named Steinbrenner ever playing for them, and their 1952 guide listed no one named Steinbrenner on their roster for training camp. If he did play for the 1952 Giants, he would have to have used an assumed name. Among the names he could have assumed were Frank Gifford, Kyle Rote, Charlie Conerly, Tex Coulter, Emlen Tunnell or Arnie Weinmeister, all of whom did play for the Giants in 1952. None of them ever recollected a wealthy young teammate from Williams. The same Columbus *Citizen* story that awarded Steinbrenner a professional football career also said, "His athletic performances in track and football earned him the honor of being selected as one of the twenty-five outstanding athletes in the country for 1952 in a poll conducted by a board of New York sportswriters." A survey of veteran New York sportswriters failed to turn up a single man who could recall voting for George Steinbren-

ner as an outstanding athlete. The Columbus *Citizen,* later merged into the *Citizen-Journal,* may have been the New York *Post* of its day and area.

The source of the fictitious achievements probably was not Steinbrenner himself. He had a sense of his own shortcomings in football. At least, as cosports editor of the Williams *Record,* the student newspaper, he wrote of his skills disparagingly. "Right From The Record," the young wordsmith called his column, and late in October 1951 he wrote, "Just about five weeks ago, yours truly was displaying some very meager talents as a football aspirant on Coach Len Watters' edition of the 1951 Purple 'gridiron horde.' I spare no haste in setting you readers straight— my abilities as a football player were as obscure as my gridiron feats which numbered a big 'Nothing.' However, during those weeks, I really got to know the 42 ballplayers and the three great coaches who have given Williams a ballclub to be proud of. True, enough praise cannot be heaped upon the ballplayers and a 'never say die' spirit which makes the New York Giants look like strictly bush league stuff. But being connected with the team, one can see some other very vital instruments in these three 'Frank Merriwell' victories."

As a writer, Steinbrenner apparently believed that the use of quotation marks excused the use of clichés. He was, remarkably enough, very tolerant of defeat in certain circumstances; when Williams lost its opening football game one season to Princeton, 66–0, Steinbrenner not only praised the "powerful Princeton aggregation," but also consoled "a game bunch of ballplayers from the Berkshires who though they knew they were way out of their class, took a pretty severe shellacking like good sports men." Steinbrenner was less tolerant of another group of men— professional sportswriters. When the Associated Press, in 1951, after its annual poll of sportswriters, named Dick Kazmaier of Princeton "Outstanding Male Athlete of the

Year," Steinbrenner enthusiastically attacked the selection. "I cannot understand how these men who are supposedly competent sportswriters could come to such a unanimous vote on such a 'poor' decision," he wrote. Then, in a sentence heavy with negatives and with hyperbole, Steinbrenner added, "I do not wish to argue the fact that Kazmaier is not a great football player—no one can deny this—but to call him the 'Athlete of the Year' is like comparing 'hyperion to a satyr.'" The failure to capitalize "Hyperion" was probably the fault of a printer unfamiliar with *Hamlet*. Steinbrenner went on to accuse "these so-called experts" of "a decision of mediocrity," and concluded, "These gentlemen are way wrong—their choice is as much out of place as 'Dolly Madison at a Sunday milk punch party.'" Steinbrenner himself would have voted for Bob Richards, the pole vaulter, or Ben Hogan, the golfer, or Stan Musial or Bob Feller, the baseball players, over Kazmaier—and the funny thing is that, in retrospect, he probably was right.

Steinbrenner the columnist was not always right. He loved to make predictions, to pick the winners of football games and other sporting events, and more than a quarter of a century later *Newsweek*'s Pete Axthelm wrote that George "still cherishes the memory of the time he picked the Kentucky Derby winner for his readers." Steinbrenner's memory was playing tricks on him. In the Williams *Record,* Steinbrenner predicted the outcome of three Kentucky Derbies: He chose Hill Prince to win the 1950 Derby, Battlefield to win the 1951 Derby and Tom Fool to win the 1952 Derby. When Battlefield was scratched in 1951, student Steinbrenner, who had gone to New York to watch the running of the Wood Memorial, a tuneup for the Derby, switched his selection to Big Stretch. Middleground won the Derby in 1950 (with Hill Prince second); Count Turf in 1951 and Hill Gail in 1952. Steinbrenner didn't have much luck in baseball, either. His hometown prejudice showing,

he chose the Cleveland Indians to win the American League pennant in 1952, chose the Indians' Luke Easter to dominate the American League batters and chose the Indians' Sam "Toothpick" Jones to be Rookie of the Year. He also wrote, "Veeck's St. Louis club starts long climb that will find them near top by 1955." Cleveland came in second, which wasn't bad, and Easter, although his average slipped to .263, did hit thirty-one home runs. But to call Sam Jones "Rookie of the Year" was like comparing Hyperion to a satyr. Jones won only two games in 1952. And Bill Veeck's St. Louis Browns, after finishing next-to-last in 1952, were no longer in St. Louis by 1955; they were in Baltimore, and they were still in next-to-last place. In pro football, Steinbrenner picked the New York Giants to win the National Football League championship in 1952, presumably with or without his help in the defensive backfield; he should have picked his hometown team, the Cleveland Browns, who won the title against Detroit. To be fair, Steinbrenner did have an excellent record of picking the winners in college football games; by his own count, he got eighty-two percent right one year, which, as he pointed out in his column, put him far ahead of Pigskin Pete of *The Sporting News*. Even as a college sportswriter, Steinbrenner realized that not everyone loved him. In his farewell column, trying to pick his words carefully, he wrote, "I know there are some among you who would just as soon I said nothing. To this group I can only say that even though you have criticized my writing in the past—I still consider you among my more rabid readers—for at least I have the satisfaction of knowing that you read the column."

Steinbrenner, no matter what the Columbus *Citizen* said, was not Superman at Williams, but he was an incredibly active and diversified student. President of Purple Key, the athletic honorary society, and a member of Gargoyle, the senior honorary society dedicated to "the advancement of Williams in every branch of college life,"

Steinbrenner was also deeply involved in things musical. He played in the college band one year, entertained at the piano at fraternity parties and spent four years in the glee club, the final year as president. Steve Sondheim, the Broadway lyricist (*West Side Story,* for example) and composer (*A Little Night Music*) was at Williams at the same time, and Steinbrenner told writer Marie Brenner that he stood behind Sondheim in the glee club. "I could sing better than he could," Steinbrenner reported, a contention Sondheim, years later, did not dispute. Sondheim did point out, however, that he did not stand in front of Steinbrenner in the glee club, primarily because he, Sondheim, never belonged to the glee club. Steinbrenner's memory was playing tricks on him again. Even after he bought the Yankees, Steinbrenner continued to spend some nights at the opera and some at the ballet, which prompted him to brag to writer Tony Kornheiser that "he knows the difference between arabesque and *changement de pieds*, and how many people in baseball, he wants to know, know that?"

He was not a distinguished student at Williams—"I wouldn't even be able to get in today," he says—but not from any lack of commitment. He studied. He did his work. "I like the expression that a Yale president once used in a speech," Steinbrenner once said. "He told alumni, 'Pay attention to your A and B students, because they will return to teach physics and chemistry at your school. But remember your C students, too, because they may return to give you a new physics or chemistry building.'" Steinbrenner, remembered as a C student, did select an ambitious subject for his senior thesis. He wrote about the heroines of Thomas Hardy's novels, about Bathsheba in *Far From the Madding Crowd,* about *Tess of the d'Urbervilles,* about Sue Bridehead in *Jude the Obscure,* about passions unsanctioned by the church and about marriages that failed, that turned empty, as Hardy's own first marriage did. Hardy

wrote of "the fundamental error of their matrimonial union; that of having based a permanent contract on a temporary feeling." No copies of Steinbrenner's thesis survive—unless he has one hidden away. His observations would be interesting, considering that Steinbrenner's one and only marriage, while it has endured, has been severely strained, and considering that many of his acquaintances sense that for Steinbrenner, unlike many powerful men, the sexual drive is not only not a primary one, but not even a major one. If Hardy's words from *The Hand of Ethelberta* ring true—"a lover without indiscretion is no lover at all"—then Steinbrenner is no lover at all. He has been a model of discretion; the only woman his name has been linked with in his celebrity years has been Barbara Walters, the television news star, and both Steinbrenner and she insist that they are simply good friends, which is not only possible, but probable.

On a note more frivolous than Hardy, Steinbrenner, according to the Williams yearbook, received fairly prominent mention in the class elections. He tied for ninth in the balloting for "Most Versatile" and tied for fifth in "Done Most for Williams." He came in tenth in "Best Build," and while he did not get any votes for "Handsomest," he placed a strong second among "Thinks He Is." It probably was only good-natured kidding, but Steinbrenner also tied for second in two categories, "Shovels It Fastest" and "Class Griper." Surprisingly, he was not mentioned among "Most Likely to Succeed" or "Hardest Worker."

Steinbrenner graduated in June of 1952, as the Korean War was winding down, joined the Air Force, was commissioned a second lieutenant and was assigned to Lockbourne Air Force Base in Columbus, Ohio, by good fortune only a couple of hours' drive from Cleveland. He was named, by continued good fortune, aide to the commanding general, and soon found himself heading the sports program for the base. Before Steinbrenner arrived at Lockbourne, the

sports program had been sagging, and the number of AWOLs rising. He elevated the sports program and, apparently as a direct result, reduced the number of AWOLs. His basketball team engaged in such competitions as the Columbus Basketball League and the Central Ohio AAU, and in two seasons won eight of the ten tournaments it entered. The team's most notable achievement, according to the Columbus *Citizen,* its credibility diminished somewhat by its New York Giants story, was an 84–77 victory over Rio Grande, a college not from Texas, but from Ohio, its name pronounced Rye-oh, rhyming with bayou. The Columbus *Citizen* did not invent Rio Grande; the college actually was well known in basketball circles in 1954, mostly because of a center named Clarence "Bevo" Francis, who was the first college player to score one hundred points in a game.

George also coached the Lockbourne baseball team. "I won a championship with my team," Steinbrenner told Harry Reasoner on *Sixty Minutes,* "and I didn't know anything about baseball. But I bought a good book and I just stayed one page ahead of the team, and that's the way I coached." When Steinbrenner was coaching Lockbourne, a young man named Bob Sudyk was playing baseball for Ohio State, first base on the junior varsity. One day the Ohio State junior varsity went to play at Lockbourne, and as the team got off its bus, Sudyk recalled, "I heard someone yelling, yipping and yowling, and I thought, 'Who the hell is that guy?' It was George. He wanted to play the varsity, not the junior varsity. We won the game, the jayvees, and that got him even more upset." Sudyk went on to become a sportswriter in Cleveland and, in fact, was with Steinbrenner, whom he admired greatly, the night in 1972 George thought he had purchased the Cleveland Indians. The deal fell through, which turned out to be a break for Steinbrenner. "George would have brought a winner to Cleveland," Sudyk said during the 1981 World

Series in New York, "but this stage is made for him."

In the Air Force, as always, George Steinbrenner was not content to be occupied merely with sports. Even though he did find time to set an Air Force record for the 440-yard low hurdles, he had to have something else going. He started a business. "For George, the word has never been day-dreaming, it's day-scheming," one of his oldest friends, Pete Smythe, a Cleveland realtor, once said. "At Lockbourne, George got to sitting around trying to come up with some way to make money, and what he came up with was sort of an early-day coffee cart. He got a franchise because—well, you know how government workers are about coffee breaks—it saved time and made the whole operation on the base more efficient." The military version of The George Company used six pick-up trucks and served some sixteen thousand military and civilian personnel, leaving Steinbrenner with enough income and enough free time to enjoy a busy social life in Columbus. "He used to come to Ciro's Supper Club," Alex Clausen, then a baseball coach at Ohio State University, remembered. "The girls went ga-ga over him. He used to drink 7-Up, with a cherry in it." Eventually, Steinbrenner went into the restaurant business with Clausen, partners in a Columbus branch of The Pewter Mug. "He never bothered me at all," Clausen recalled. "Thank God he lived in Cleveland." But if Steinbrenner had offered any suggestions, Clausen said, "I would have listened to him. George is good at anything he does. He's intense at everything. He's a winner. I think he's a genius."

In 1954, discharged from the Air Force, Steinbrenner elected to stay in Columbus, to study for his master's degree in physical education at Ohio State, which had one of Woody Hayes' most awesome teams, undefeated Rose Bowl and national champions, led by Howard "Hopalong" Cassady, a halfback who, in 1955, won the Heisman Trophy, awarded annually to the outstanding college foot-

ball player in the country. Steinbrenner, of course, attended Ohio State football games—a photo in the Columbus *Citizen* showed the crew-cut young bachelor leaving the stadium after one game, arm in arm with an attractive cheerleader named Connie Sutton—and while less confident football fans might have dreamed of *meeting* Hopalong Cassady someday, Steinbrenner, conceivably, dreamed of *hiring* him someday. By 1981, Cassady was working for George Steinbrenner in three official capacities, as a scout in the Tampa area, as a coach for the Columbus Clippers, the Yankees' Triple-A farm team in the International League, and, during spring training, as a conditioning instructor for the Yankees themselves. Not a bad parlay: Cassady, the best college football player in the country in 1955, and Al Rosen, the Most Valuable Player in the American League in 1953, both playing in Ohio, both stars of championship teams in 1954, both wound up a quarter of a century later employed by a man who was, in 1954, a student of coaching at Ohio State.

The Columbus *Citizen* story on MISTER Steinbrenner in the fall of 1954 carried the sub-headline, "Former Lieutenant-Coach at Lockbourne, Millionaire's Son, Pro Grid Star, Enrolled at OSU; Plans Coaching Career," and the story raised three questions: Should George go into his father's million-dollar steamship business? Should he return to the professional football wars? Or would he fare best by testing his coaching abilities on the college level? The *Citizen* seemed to favor the third choice: "The future looks bright for the 23-year-old coaching phenom . . . Remember the name George Steinbrenner because in the years to come, the coaching greats may have to move over and make room for him." The last sentence was certainly prophetic.

During his year at Ohio State, George Steinbrenner met a teenaged coed named Elizabeth Joan Zieg, the tall, slender, blonde daughter of Jessie and Harold Zieg, who lived on Onondaga Drive in Columbus. Harold Zieg was a

real-estate developer, and his daughter, who used her middle name and pronounced it "Jo-Ann," was planning to major in dental hygiene and education. Steinbrenner attended his phys ed classes, dated Joan Zieg and served as an assistant coach, in football and basketball, at St. Thomas Aquinas High School in Columbus.

After one year of studying at the top of the Big Ten, at Ohio State, Steinbrenner took a job at the bottom, at Northwestern University, where despite Lou Saban as head coach and Steinbrenner as end coach, the 1955 football team lost all nine of its games. The next year, Saban and Steinbrenner were gone, Ara Parseghian moved in, and Northwestern began winning. Steinbrenner moved on, in 1956, to Purdue University, to coach the backfield under Jack Mollenkopf. By then, Steinbrenner had married Joan Zieg, on May 12, 1956, when George was twenty-five and Joan twenty. At Purdue, the star of the football team was the quarterback, Len Dawson, who, a quarter of a century later, remembered vividly what coach Steinbrenner had done for him. "It was my senior year," Dawson said. "He probably doesn't remember it. I had coffee with him one day late in the season. I had a sore shoulder, I'd missed a game, and he said something about playing when you're hurt. He said not him, but some of the other coaches were saying that I might be more concerned about the pro football draft than I was about finishing the college season. I guess he was trying to work some psychology on me, and what it did was it pissed me off. I played the final game, against Indiana, and I played pretty well. I passed through the pain. And I learned something about playing hurt. I lasted nineteen seasons in professional football, and for the first eleven of those seasons, I suited up for every game." How good a coach was Steinbrenner? Did he know football? "Hey," Dawson said, "I was twenty-one. Everyone knew more than I did."

Steinbrenner was tempted to continue in coaching, but

by 1957, his father wanted him back in Cleveland, to work with Kinsman Marine, which, in competition with the big steel companies' own fleets, was beginning to experience difficult times. Steinbrenner, who had spent part of his college summers working in the shipyards, learning the insides of the boats (called "ships" elsewhere, but "boats" on the Great Lakes), was about to become a father and needed more money than the modest wages of an assistant college football coach. That, plus the continuing desire to please his father, deprived college football coaching of George Steinbrenner. He became treasurer of Kinsman Marine, which then had five boats carrying iron ore, coal and, to a lesser degree, grain, and with his father set to work revitalizing the company. "We really worked like hell," Steinbrenner said. "We got out and pounded the bushes and we created some business by going to the steel companies and by really hounding them for business. The real turning point for the company came when Jones & Laughlin Steel Corporation made a decision to help the independents and signed a contract guaranteeing us tonnage. That was in 1960."

By then, even though he had really worked hard to help Kinsman flourish, Steinbrenner still had not earned his father's approval, his father's trust. In 1960, the year he turned thirty, George decided to go into a sports business for the first time. Against his father's advice and wishes, he sold his shares of Kinsman stock and put together a group of investors who for $125,000, purchased a basketball team called the Cleveland Pipers. The Pipers played AAU basketball, which was amateur basketball, at least in theory, and they played in an industrial league against such teams as the Denver Truckers and, probably the best known of the industrial teams, the Phillips 66 Oilers, who were sponsored by the Phillips Petroleum Company, which found openings for seven-foot-tall executives. The Pipers were coached in 1960 by John McClendon, who, in the late

1950s, led Tennessee A & I to three straight small-college national championships, and they had a number of gifted players, including, during the Steinbrenner years, Dick Barnett, who later played for the New York Knicks when they won the National Basketball Association championship, and Bevo Francis, the high scorer from Rio Grande. The Pipers were good enough to be selected, as AAU champions, to tour Russia, and good enough to win eight straight games in the Soviet Union.

Phillips Petroleum and Goodyear Rubber may have considered industrial basketball a worthwhile investment, but Henry M. Steinbrenner certainly did not. He ordered his son not to do basketball business on Kinsman time and Kinsman property. Once, one of George's friends told *Cleveland* magazine, Henry Steinbrenner walked into his son's office while George was on the phone discussing the Pipers. The father clicked the receiver down and reminded the son that he was working for a shipping company.

The son, however, was not lacking in ingenuity. He arranged to have a phone with a private line installed in his office, on a day, of course, when his father was out. The private phone fit neatly into a desk drawer, which was kept locked, except when George needed to conduct Piper business. A few of the Kinsman people knew about George's secret phone, but Henry Steinbrenner did not. Sometimes, when the son was absent from the office, the father used to complain to his secretary that he thought he could hear a telephone faintly ringing.

Many people went into sports businesses for fun as much as profit, but George took the Pipers very seriously. When the team won an exhibition game against the 1960 United States Olympic team, which had such celebrated stars as Oscar Robertson, Jerry West and Jerry Lucas, and the Cleveland newspapers gave the Pipers' victory only scant mention, Steinbrenner screamed at the editors. Whenever a referee made a call against the Pipers, Steinbrenner

screamed at the official. Whenever the team lost, Steinbrenner screamed at the players and at coach McClendon. Sometimes, in the middle of a game, George bolted from the stands to the court to make his points to players and officials. The games were played usually in Cleveland Arena, which was hardly Yankee Stadium; crowds were modest, and security was so lax that one night a game had to be halted because fans had stolen all the basketballs. Steinbrenner was so visible and so volatile the Cleveland *Press* called him "congenitally unsuited" to run the team. Steinbrenner felt no more warmly toward the *Press.* Once, when the Pipers held a news conference to announce the signing of a new player, and the *Press* barely noted the signing, Steinbrenner gathered his players, coaches and partners and told them that he wanted each of them to cancel his own subscription to the *Press,* and he also wanted each of them to call fifteen friends and tell them, too, to cancel their subscriptions. Several years later, Steinbrenner conceded that he may not have been the model sports executive, that even then he had dents in his armor. "I was too vociferous in exhorting my coaches and players from the stands," he recalled. "I'd get on their backs when I didn't think they were trying hard enough. I guess over-exuberance, enthusiasm and youth made me the kind of owner that, perhaps, I shouldn't have been."

John McClendon was the object of many of Steinbrenner's vociferous exhortations. "If he's the way I read in the newspapers," said McClendon, in 1981, "and I know he is, then he's just exactly the way he was then. If anything, he might have been a little . . . I was going to say 'worse' . . . but, well, a little less mature. He came on strong. All you had to do was win everything, and he'd be satisfied. He told me he never knew anybody like me. He couldn't upset me. I was very close to the players."

In 1961, with industrial basketball slipping, and a new professional league emerging, the American Basketball

League, founded and led by Abe Saperstein, the owner of the Harlem Globetrotters, the Cleveland Pipers switched from the AAU to the ABL. McClendon became the first black coach in professional basketball and, in the first half of a split season, led the Pipers to a first-place finish. But the club and, even more so, the league were having financial problems. Saperstein was using the Globetrotters as often as he could in the opening games of doubleheaders, trying to spark attendance, but the league, competing with the established National Basketball Association, couldn't catch on. Early in the second half of the season, after the Pipers had lost seven of nine games, which drove Steinbrenner to new heights of fury, the management of the Pipers held up the players' paychecks. The official reason was a temporary dearth of funds, but McClendon suspected that if the team had been winning, Steinbrenner would have found the money. McClendon resigned in protest, and after the players got paid, at least in part, the Pipers hired a new coach, Bill Sharman, a former star with the Boston Celtics in the NBA. "George decided to make a coaching change and bring me in from California," Sharman wrote in a letter in 1981, when he was general manager of the NBA's Los Angeles Lakers. "I was coaching the Los Angeles Jets the first half of the 1961–62 season, until our team folded because of financial reasons.

"Fortunately for me, the Pipers had some good players in Dick Barnett, John Barnhill, Connie Dierking, John Cox etc. and we wound up winning our division, the playoffs and the ABL championship!" The underlining was Sharman's. "I have to say that during my three months in Cleveland, George treated me extremely well. He gave me a furnished apartment, and tried to make things as comfortable as possible. However, I was always aware that he was a fierce competitor and definitely wanted a winner! He was very active in the front office, always asking what he (or we) could do to improve our club and record. So, I

knew he wouldn't be satisfied with anything except a championship. He would often come down to the dressing room after the games. If we won, he was very happy and in a great mood. If we lost, he would be upset and want to know all the reasons why. When the team was on the road and we won a game, often he would call and have me take the whole club out to dinner. George was always great and very generous as long as we were winning. But, <u>very impatient</u> if we didn't.

"When the season and playoffs were over, he didn't have enough money to pay us all our total amount due. However, a few years later George sent me a check to cover every cent he owed for the season and the playoff money.

"From my experience, George Steinbrenner is a very smart, intelligent person, and I like and respect him very much. <u>He's a winner!</u>

"If all his players had his intensity and worked as hard, they wouldn't lose many games."

When the 1961–62 season ended, with the Pipers champions of the ABL, Steinbrenner the basketball owner acted very much the way Steinbrenner the baseball owner someday would. He sought to strengthen his team, and to strengthen his competitive position. He negotiated, unsuccessfully, to get a franchise in the NBA, and, fully aware even then of the value of a superstar, negotiated, successfully, to sign the best college basketball player in the country, a young man who had been a hero in Ohio almost from junior high school, Ohio State's Jerry Lucas. The Cincinnati Royals of the NBA offered Lucas thirty thousand dollars a season, fantastic in those days; Steinbrenner offered forty thousand, plus a dazzling package of stocks and stock options. Lucas, an A student, made what he thought was the only intelligent decision; he went with Steinbrenner. But Lucas never received a penny from Steinbrenner, or from the Pipers, and he never played a game for George's team. The American Basketball League

folded in December 1962, and Jerry Lucas, after sitting out the 1962–63 season, joined the Cincinnati Royals the following season, for thirty thousand dollars a year, a bargain price for one of the most talented players in the history of basketball.

A story circulated that the only thing Lucas did receive from Steinbrenner was a bonus, a car, on which no payments were made. Supposedly, as Lucas and his wife were eating breakfast one morning, they saw the car disappear out of their driveway, repossessed. The story was wonderful, but, said Lucas in 1981, "I don't remember that happening." If Jerry Lucas doesn't remember it, it didn't happen. Lucas is a professional rememberer. By 1981, the former basketball player was a minister, specializing in teaching people how to memorize the Bible; the phone in his office was answered, brightly, with the message, "It's a great day to remember!" Lucas was perfectly qualified to teach memory. He himself had a photographic memory, which he used in small ways and large. He could remember the exact number of steps leading from the locker room up to the basketball court in every arena he had ever played in, and when he played for the New York Knicks, he memorized the first several hundred pages of the New York telephone directory. Anyone could call out a page number, and a line, and Lucas would respond with the name and listed telephone number. Lucas also did magic tricks and a variety of mental tricks. His favorite was to spell words with their letters arranged instantly in alphabetical order. For instance, if someone called out, "Alphabetical," Lucas would immediately respond, "A-A-A-B-C-E-H-I-L-L-P-T," which is "alphabetical" spelled in alphabetical order. Naturally, even twenty years later, Lucas remembered George B-E-E-E-I-N-N-N-R-R-S-T well. "I think he was very much like he is today," Lucas said. "Effervescent, eager, active, confident. A salesman."

When the ABL went down, leaving behind worthless

contracts, countless bills and its one enduring legacy, the three-point play, a bonus for long shots eventually adopted by the NBA, the Pipers sank, too, into bankruptcy, one hundred twenty-five thousand dollars in debt. George Steinbrenner personally had lost a quarter of a million dollars in two years, and his partners, as many as sixteen of them at one point, had also lost considerably. Steinbrenner did try one final desperate maneuver to cut his losses. After the ABL collapsed, he phoned a Cleveland advertising executive named Howard Marks, who had signed Lucas to a personal services contract, hoping to use Lucas as a wedge into the NBA, and offered to sell the Pipers, what remained of them, to Marks for seven hundred fifty thousand dollars.

"George, that's awfully nice of you," Marks later quoted himself as saying, "and I appreciate it, but I just can't afford that kind of money. I'll have to say no."

Steinbrenner called back the next morning, Marks recalled, and offered to sell the Pipers for five thousand dollars. Again, Marks declined. Steinbrenner was left in a position he hated; he was a loser. "When you're down," he said, "you don't want to see your friends, you don't want to go to places and restaurants. Human nature is funny. When you're down, a lot of people walk the other way. You find out who your two friends are."

Strangely, the bankruptcy of the Pipers served, in time, to strengthen Steinbrenner's image and his influence. Against the advice of his attorneys, he called his partners in the Pipers and he called the creditors, telling them that he would eventually pay them all back. First, dipping into his Kinsman salary, he paid off the creditors. "My father had a sporting goods business," Al Newman said several years later, "and George paid him every cent the Pipers owed." To pay off his partners, Steinbrenner bought an ore boat, formed a special company and divided the boat's earnings among the Piper partners until, in three years,

they were all paid off. "Now," Walter Knapp, a shipping executive who worked for Steinbrenner, said fifteen years later, "George's word is so good that if he said he needed ten million dollars to make a deal tomorrow, he'd have ten guys with a million each lined up tonight."

But in the middle of 1962, in trouble with the Pipers and at war, over the basketball business, with his father, his energy and resources spread precariously thin, Steinbrenner, not surprisingly, encountered marital difficulties. On July 7, 1962, Joan Steinbrenner filed a suit for divorce in Cuyahoga County Domestic Relations Court. She retained, as her attorney, Robert Krubansky, one of Cleveland's most prominent lawyers, a man of great influence, a dangerous opponent in a domestic battle, not unlike George's later-day friend in New York, Roy Cohn. Krubansky eventually became a federal judge, named to the bench by Richard M. Nixon.

At the time of her suit, Joan Steinbrenner lived on Bruce Road in Bay Village in a house whose value she placed at $38,500. She said her husband's income was similarly modest, $22,000 a year, and she listed his chief additional asset as a twenty-five percent interest in movie and television rights to a book called *The Sheppard Murder Case*. Sam Sheppard was, in the 1950s and 1960s, certainly the most notorious resident of Bay Village. An osteopath and a surgeon, Sheppard was convicted of murdering his wife and then, after a decade in prison, won a retrial and, defended by F. Lee Bailey, had his conviction reversed. Both trials drew national coverage. Sheppard was probably the most well-known person ever to come out of Bay Village, until George Steinbrenner.

Mrs. Steinbrenner, in her divorce suit, sought alimony and custody of the couple's two children, Henry and Jennifer. Two months later, Mrs. Steinbrenner dropped the suit, and her attorney explained that the couple had reconciled.

His marriage stabilized and his most disastrous business experience behind him, Steinbrenner began the series of moves that would lift him from twenty-two-thousand-dollar-a-year salary to a net worth so high in the millions even close friends hesitate to estimate his total fortune. In 1963, Henry M. Steinbrenner, by then in his late fifties, was ready to retire, convinced that the best days for the independent Great Lakes shipping fleets were behind them.

George Steinbrenner disagreed. He decided that if his father wanted to retire, he would take over Kinsman Marine and make it a bigger and more successful company. He would outdo his father. But first he had to purchase the company, or a controlling interest, from his father and from other stockholders, many of them relatives. He couldn't borrow sufficient capital in Cleveland, so he went to New York, looked up a schoolmate from Culver who had gone into the banking business, and negotiated a loan sizable enough—twenty-five thousand dollars, according to one report—to begin buying Kinsman stock. Back in Cleveland, buoyed by the initial loan, Steinbrenner was able to borrow more money and buy a controlling interest. Other small independent fleets were going out of business, and Steinbrenner bought their boats, then bought four larger ore carriers from U.S. Steel. As he expanded the Kinsman fleet, and upgraded the boats, and as he shifted the emphasis from carrying ore, a shrinking business, to carrying grain, Kinsman flourished, confirming Steinbrenner's faith in the future of lake shipping. Even after he moved on to much larger operations than Kinsman, Steinbrenner maintained a personal interest in the company that had been in his family for more than a century. In 1981, Kevin Patrick Smith, a graduate of the United States Merchant Marine Academy, a man who sold supplies to Great Lakes shipping fleets, recalled seeing Steinbrenner storming through the yard, demanding that

a door that was scraping noisily against its jamb be filed down immediately, or else. But Steinbrenner could no longer supervise everything personally, and, Smith said, "If you put me blindfolded in the engine room of three Great Lakes boats, I'd know which one is a Kinsman boat." How? "They're filthy," Smith said. "They're not kept up."

In 1967, Steinbrenner joined a group of investors, assembled by Thomas H. Roulston, the president of Roulston & Co., a brokerage firm in Cleveland, that bought 470,000 of the 1,197,250 outstanding shares of stock in the American Ship Building Company, a firm based in Lorain, Ohio, right next to Vermilion, where George's great-great-grandfather, Philip J. Minch, had settled in the 1840s. To avoid a proxy fight between the new stockholders of American Ship and the old, both sides agreed to elect George Steinbrenner president of the company. He didn't rename the firm The George Company, but he certainly reshaped it.

When Steinbrenner took command, the company had one small drydock and a few ships. That year, the company's revenues amounted to $46,953,770, its assets to $27,029,000 and its net worth to $14,747,448. He merged Kinsman Marine into American Ship, saw the size of the parent fleet swell to twenty ore carriers, plus stevedoring operations in five cities, plus the heart of the operation, the shipyard in Lorain that built boats to sail the Great Lakes. Under Steinbrenner, American Ship grew in size and in scope. The company soon became the dominant grain carrier on the Great Lakes, acquired the largest tugboat company in the area, moved into shipyards in Chicago and Toledo, began building and renovating one-thousand-foot tankers for U.S. Steel, branched into Tennessee to build river barges, towboats and marine deck hardware and, most ambitiously, purchased a shipyard from Tampa Ship Repair & Drydock Company in Florida, a shipyard specializing in the building of offshore oil drilling rigs and the repair of tankers, and expanded and improved that facility

so much that, within a decade, American Ship had a twenty-three-million-dollar drydock in Tampa capable of handling eighty-five percent of the world's bulk cargo fleet. The American public, of course, never noticed what Steinbrenner was achieving, and could not have comprehended it, but the stockholders of American Ship knew and understood. Within ten years, Steinbrenner and his shipping team tripled the company's revenues, quadrupled its assets and more than tripled its net worth. Steinbrenner performed similar mathematical magic on his personal resources, to the point that, in the 1970s, he bought Kinsman back from American Ship, restored it to the family and lured his father temporarily out of retirement to run the company once more. Finally, he had his father working for him.

Steinbrenner, stepping up from president to chairman of the board, put his stamp on American Ship, the same stamp he later put on the Yankees, the image of an owner in perpetual motion, making fierce and sometimes unreasonable demands of his employees, driving less energetic executives either into quitting or into despair, changing presidents almost as quickly as he changed Yankee managers, always adhering to his father's dictum, "Work as hard as, or harder than, anyone who works for you." Or, perhaps equally important, make it seem as if you do.

A football player from Purdue, a massive young man named Jim Bonk, went to work at American Ship and became executive assistant to the former coach, whose pace dazzled him. "Sometimes Mr. Steinbrenner would show up at 9:30 in the morning," Bonk told Everett Groseclose of the *Wall Street Journal*, "and say, 'Get an Executive Jet [a charter service] in here right away. I want to leave at 11:30 and be in New York for a meeting at 12:30. We'll catch lunch and be in Pittsburgh for a meeting at 3:00, and be back in Cleveland by 5:00.' That's just the way he operates—pure impulse." Bonk told the *Wall Street Journal* he

would often accompany Steinbrenner on his sudden trips, even though he couldn't quite figure out what his function was supposed to be. "I sometimes had the feeling," Bonk said, "he just wanted to have somebody there to jump, somebody to take a note or make a phone call. He just wanted somebody there to react." Bonk finally reacted the way many of Steinbrenner's subordinates did. He quit. Battered by the boss' peripatetic pace, he opted for a more peaceful life as a corporate accountant.

Steinbrenner never pretended he was easy to work for. "Some guys can lead through real, genuine respect," he once said. "There are some guys who people would walk through a wall for. OK, but I'm not that kind of a leader. I wish I were. An Eisenhower, when he was in the army, was that type leader. Unfortunately, I'm probably more of a George Patton. He was a gruff son of a bitch and he led through fear. I hope I don't lead through fear, and I would hope it was more love and respect, but maybe it isn't."

Later, near the end of the 1970s, he expressed similar thoughts. "My employees know I'm rough on them," Steinbrenner said, "and I am. I demand more of them than they think they're capable of. I don't know of any other way to lead. I can't be responsible for how my people feel. I never demand more of an employee than I demand of myself."

And, in the 1980s, he struck the same theme. "I'm not a tentative leader," he said. "I make a decision and then I've got to go hell bent for leather. People in this country don't want tentative leaders. That's why they voted Carter out of office—overwhelmingly. There are too many under-achievers in this country. I want my guys to perform up to their abilities, and beyond. And God knows they're getting enough money to do it. I can't be a nice guy about it. Church choirs are filled with nice guys. This country was built on people with guts who wanted more than they had—like the people in those little covered wagons who

went West and fought the weather and the Indians."

The people around Steinbrenner couldn't help but recognize his style, and some of them accepted it. "George is an overbearing, arrogant, arbitrary, authoritarian son of a bitch," Pete Smythe, his old friend, once said. "There's no denying that. But I just love him. We all do. You ask yourself why he can't be more like everybody else. Well, if he was, he wouldn't be George Steinbrenner."

"George is the essence of the Jekyll and Hyde mentality," said Campbell W. Elliott, after he had been president of American Ship Building Company, under Steinbrenner. To social acquaintances, to people he wants to like him, Elliott said, "George is the most charming guy in the world, a real Mr. Nice." But to his employees, to people he expects to produce for him, "George's attitude is that they're damn lucky to have a job—and if they don't like the way he treats them, they can just get the hell out." (That assessment—coming from a man who, at the time, considered himself a friend of Steinbrenner's, no longer an employee—made the story about George threatening and demeaning Bill Kane, the Yankees' traveling secretary, more credible.)

"Sure, he is tough to work for," said a third Cleveland friend, one who requested anonymity. "He's more than that. He can be a real son of a bitch. But when all is said and done, he's helped more people than any single guy in this town. But me work for George Steinbrenner? You wouldn't catch me dead doing that. Anything else I'll do for the man. But not that."

The emerging picture—of a man who is a pleasure to socialize with, and abominable to work for—was once analyzed for the *Wall Street Journal* by Harry Levinson, a psychologist who studied management personalities. "Executives who are harsh with their people often are expressing their own feelings of inadequacy and self-disappointment," Levinson theorized. But Levinson sug-

gested that the same men might be perfectly gracious in social situations, especially in social situations with people whose fame or wealth or position impressed them. "These are usually men with a very intense need to be loved by people in power," Levinson said. "They fawn after attention, affection and applause. [But] if people don't have power, their affection doesn't count."

The psychologist's analysis, neat and logical, almost captured Steinbrenner, but not entirely. Perhaps if Levinson's "people in power" were interpreted as father figures, the analysis would have hit closer to the mark.

A much simpler evaluation came from a man who worked for Steinbrenner in New York, and quit. "George Steinbrenner doesn't want to be loved, and he doesn't want to be hated," the man said. "George Steinbrenner wants to be feared." If that assessment is accurate, Steinbrenner has succeeded—because the source of the remark obviously feared having his name used.

Critics who paint Steinbrenner as an ogre often illustrate their thesis with a reference to how often he fires his secretaries. Pearl Davis, who worked for the Yankees for ten years, most of them pre-Steinbrenner, claimed that in his first five years with the team he went through twelve secretaries. "He's a direct, mean man," Pearl Davis said. "He has no feelings for other people. He wants what he wants when he wants it." Her impressions might be correct, but her math could be wrong, judging by the stories that have been published detailing Steinbrenner's passion for firing his secretary.

In *The New York Times,* Tony Kornheiser said that once, when Steinbrenner got to an airport and found out that his ticket was not waiting for him, he called his office and told his secretary, "You're through." The secretary, according to Kornheiser, ignored the order, and the next day Steinbrenner said to her, "I've made arrangements to send your kid to camp this summer."

In *Cleveland* magazine, a team of writers reported that once, when Steinbrenner boarded an airplane and found out he did not have a first-class seat, he got off the plane, called his office and told his secretary she was through. An official of American Ship, according to the magazine, told her to ignore the order, and a few days later Steinbrenner told her that he had made arrangements to send her and her husband on a vacation for a week.

In *Newsday,* the Long Island newspaper, interviewer Len Katz allowed Steinbrenner to tell his own version of the firing. "I got out to the airport—she was supposed to have made reservations for me—and they weren't there," Steinbrenner said. "I called her and told her, 'You're fired! You can't even make a simple reservation!' Then I felt bad about it. So the next time—she didn't leave, she knows me—the next time I came back, I arranged to send *her two kids* to summer camp with all expenses paid. *And* she and her husband on a trip."

The odds are infinitely good that all three stories, despite the slight differences in detail, were about the same single incident, which may or may not be essentially apocryphal. It is fitting, of course, that the most elaborate, most generous version came from Steinbrenner himself. The best variation on the theme came from a gentleman in the sporting goods business who said, "I once saw Steinbrenner fire a girl for not bringing him a tuna fish sandwich on time." When Steinbrenner gets around to repeating that story, it will be, at the least, pheasant under glass.

Steinbrenner makes no secret of the fact that he demands of his secretaries, and of his vice-presidents, efficiency, extra effort and total dedication, but none of these traits is his top priority. "We have found in searching for people," Steinbrenner said, before he ever got into the baseball business, "the people that have been most appealing to us, have been people, number one and most important of all, that we knew we could count on their loyalty.

That's the supreme quality that a top business executive can ask from his people. I would trade, in my corporation, all of the degrees, all of the business expertise, all of the financial expertise and all of the technological expertise for that one quality, loyalty."

Loyalty, hard work, in fact all of the qualities Steinbrenner so admired and demanded, might have gone to waste at American Ship without a much more practical consideration—a boost from the government, a factor that thrust George Steinbrenner onto the national political scene, an arena that provided him with immense influence, immense ego gratification and, in time, his most damaging and painful experience.

At about the time Steinbrenner took over American Ship, Congress began to consider amending the Merchant Marine Act of 1936. "From the start," Steinbrenner said, "I knew the secret for American Ship was to get the Great Lakes included in the Maritime Act—to get the Great Lakes in there so that they could get their share of assistance." By assistance to the Great Lakes, Steinbrenner meant tax benefits to the shipping industry. "I saw that the whole Great Lakes fleet had to be rebuilt," he said, "and the only way this could be done was with help."

George Steinbrenner promptly descended upon Washington, collecting people of power and charming them, getting to know congressmen and senators, and their administrative and legislative assistants, mastering the key political art of trading favors. "I was in business a half dozen years before I even found out what the name of the game was," Steinbrenner said. "It's Washington. The name of the game is Washington, D.C."

Steinbrenner played the game with zest and avoided one great trap: He was never afflicted by the urge to run for public office. When Steinbrenner jumped into the game, Richard M. Nixon was President, but Nixon's opposition, the Democratic party, controlled both houses of Congress. Not surprisingly, when Steinbrenner was approached to be

chairman of the 1969 Democratic Congressional Dinner, a major fund-raising affair in Washington, he eagerly accepted—despite his family's Republican background, despite his statement that he was neither a registered Democrat nor a registered Republican and despite the fact that a handful of other men, some more prominent than he, had already rejected the honor. The others had shied away, reportedly, because they feared the displeasure of the Nixon administration. Steinbrenner received similar warnings, that the Nixon administration believed fervently in getting even, but, partly because he liked a challenge, partly because he wanted to be important in Washington, partly because he admired individual members of the Democratic Congress, and largely because he needed the votes of the Democratic Congress, he decided to run the dinner. As chairman, Steinbrenner solidified his relationships with powerful Democrats, particularly with Senator Edward M. Kennedy of Massachusetts. The two men, less than two years apart in age, became such good friends that whenever Steinbrenner had a private jet at his disposal, Ted Kennedy knew he had a private jet at his disposal. There were even rumors that if Senator Kennedy could achieve the presidency, George Steinbrenner could count on a cabinet post. By 1972, Steinbrenner and Kennedy were so close that they flew together to the Democratic National Convention in Miami. A few years later, after Kennedy's son, Teddy, lost a leg to cancer, Steinbrenner invited the young man to throw out the first ball at an Opening Day at Yankee Stadium. Steinbrenner developed a friendship, too, with Thomas P. "Tip" O'Neill, the majority leader of the House of Representatives and an incorrigible Boston Red Sox fan. O'Neill loved to recall that, in the first game he ever attended, in 1920, the great Walter Johnson pitched a no-hitter, and he was as proud that Carl Yastrzemski was his friend as he was that Lyndon Johnson and Jack Kennedy had been his friends.

Steinbrenner's Congressional Dinner raised a record

sum, eight hundred three thousand dollars, which meant that the Democrats thought the dinner was terrific, and so was Steinbrenner. They asked him to run the dinner again in 1970, and he did, raising one million dollars, breaking his own record. In 1981, during the last month of the baseball season, Steinbrenner, still raising political funds, used the executive dining room at Yankee Stadium and his own private box for a five-hundred-dollar-a-plate dinner to help pay off the debts from Ted Kennedy's frustrated campaign for the presidency. The senator—and the Yankees against the Baltimore Orioles—attracted fifty guests who contributed among them a quarter of a million dollars.

In 1970, the Democratic-dominated Congress, after considering the sworn testimony of interested citizen George Steinbrenner, revised the Merchant Marine Act of 1936 to include benefits for Great Lakes shippers, tax inducements to build new carriers, to stimulate shipping on the Lakes. The Merchant Marine Act of 1970 inspired more than three hundred million dollars worth of new ship construction on the Great Lakes. Not all of that three hundred million went to American Ship, but enough to make George Steinbrenner pleased, powerful and more wealthy. *Fortune* magazine, the *Sporting News* of capitalism, named Steinbrenner one of the country's twelve "Movers and Shakers."

At the same time, as the 1970s began, Steinbrenner was not totally ignoring the Nixon administration. He could not afford to. He had to be concerned about four specific problems that involved American Ship and the administration. First, Amship had built an oceanographic survey ship called the *Researcher* and, in the process, had encountered a ninety-nine-week construction delay and had incurred a $5.4-million cost overrun. In 1971, Amship was negotiating with the government for a settlement on that overrun and was meeting strong resistance. Second, Amship was examining the possibility of purchasing, for seven million

90

dollars, the Great Lakes Towing Company, the largest tugboat company on the Great Lakes. Amship knew the negotiations were being monitored by the antitrust division of the Justice Department. Third, on June 29, 1971, a fire broke out aboard the *Roger Blough,* a huge twenty-million-dollar iron-ore carrier being built for U.S. Steel in Amship's Lorain shipyard, and four workmen died (Steinbrenner, incidentally, immediately established scholarships for their children), a tragedy that triggered a Labor Department investigation into safety standards and working conditions at Amship. And fourth, the Justice Department knew that Amship was considering paying $4.3 million to Litton Industries for a shipyard in Erie, Pennsylvania, plus the Wilson Marine Transit Company, an acquisition that would give Amship a virtual monopoly on grain-shipping on the Great Lakes.

Steinbrenner had already taken one significant step toward establishing friendly relations with the Nixon administration. A man named Thomas W. Evans had been chief legal counsel to candidate Nixon in 1968; in 1972, Thomas W. Evans was deputy finance chairman of Nixon's re-election campaign. In between, Thomas W. Evans became legal counsel to Amship and a director of the company. Evans was also a managing partner in the prominent New York firm of Mudge, Rose, Guthrie and Alexander, which had been Nixon, Mudge, Rose, Guthrie, Alexander and Mitchell before Richard Nixon and John Mitchell turned to more prestigious jobs in Washington.

Naturally, Steinbrenner did not acknowledge publicly that he had hired Evans because Evans provided a direct line into the Nixon administration. Instead, Steinbrenner implied that he hired Evans because he knew him from their college days at Williams. They were classmates, with at least one close tie. In the Class of 1952 yearbook, in the same class elections in which Steinbrenner drew so many votes, Evans drew many more. He was, by an overwhelming margin, voted both "Class Politician" and "Funniest," an

unusual parlay, hinting (in 1952) at a Stevensonian Democrat much more than at a Nixon Republican. Evans also finished far in front in "Shovels It Fastest," the category in which Steinbrenner tied for a distant second. Evans, a Renaissance man, apparently, also drew votes as "Class Griper," "Thinks He Is [Handsomest]," "Biggest Weekender," "Class Tightwad," "Social Light," "Woman Hater," "Class Wolf," "Most Original," "Laziest" and "Most Likely to Succeed," a mind-boggling collection of antonyms.

To impress, and perhaps infiltrate, the Nixon camp, Steinbrenner did more than hire Thomas W. Evans. He contributed, in 1972, a hundred thousand dollars to CREEP (Committee to Re-Elect the President), seventy-five thousand dollars directly, out of his own pocket, and twenty-five thousand indirectly, and, as it turned out, illegally, criminally, a stunning blow to a man who had wrapped himself in good causes.

George Steinbrenner's civic and charitable activities in his Cleveland years defied tabulation they were so numerous, so varied. He ran the Cleveland March of Dimes one year, and the contributions rose thirty-seven percent over the previous year, the greatest gain in the country for any health-fund drive; another year, he concentrated on the campaign to sell Bonds for Israel, and he was Cleveland's Man of the Year. He was a director of Cleveland Now and of the Greater Cleveland Growth Corporation, he led Cleveland's Little Hoover Commission, which studied the area's harbors and airports, and he helped organize Group 66, a collection of Cleveland businessmen whose intentions to improve the city were admirable, even if their impact was small. He was chairman of the Junior Olympic Games, which financed track and field competitions for youngsters, and one year, when the qualifiers in the Ohio Special Olympics, an athletic competition for the retarded, came up thirteen thousand dollars short of funds to go to the international Special Olympics in California, Steinbrenner

supplied the thirteen thousand.

When the Huntington Playhouse burned down in Bay Village, he put up ten thousand dollars to rebuild it, and when he discovered that a couple of predominantly black Cleveland high schools couldn't afford scoreboards at their football fields, he bought them each a four-thousand-dollar scoreboard. The *Call & Post,* a newspaper aimed at the black community in Cleveland, wanted to sponsor an annual dinner to honor young black athletes; George Steinbrenner paid the bill. The students at Bay Village High School weren't needy, but one year, to celebrate the success of "good kids at a good school," he took the whole basketball team to New York City, put the kids up at the Hotel Carlyle and treated them to the National Invitation Tournament, a Broadway musical and a chartered bus tour of the city. His funds seemed as boundless as his energy, and, obviously, he accomplished an enormous amount of good, even if *Cleveland* magazine did point out that his thirst for power was combined with "a certain philanthropic nature that would give the characteristics of a modern-day benovolent despot." He was a ubiquitous benevolent despot. The Ohio Board of Regents was short a member? Tap George Steinbrenner. A church in Lorain faced a financial crisis? Tap George Steinbrenner. He was doing so many good deeds, aiding so many good causes, raising and donating so many dollars, casual observers had to lose track of all his activities. Even Steinbrenner himself might have lost track, but not likely. "George is torn between wanting to do things anonymously, and wanting them to be known," his friend, Barbara Walters, once said. "He's always fighting that war within himself." Usually, but not always, the second impulse won, after a struggle. For instance, almost as soon as he reached a position where he could use some of his money to help other people, Steinbrenner chose to help needy young people attend college. Almost every major

article ever written about Steinbrenner has alluded to this admirable inclination with specific numbers, and invariably the source was Steinbrenner, the number generally confided quietly, reluctantly, as close as he could come to self-effacingly. But the number was consistent—always rising. In a 1974 article, he confessed he had helped fifty-six students gain a higher education; in 1975, "almost" sixty; in 1976, precisely fifty-nine; in 1977, seventy; and in 1981, seventy-nine.

Few of the names of the students Steinbrenner helped ever became public, but the ones that did slip out confirmed his commitment. He took a special interest in Glenville High School, one of Cleveland's predominantly black inner-city schools. In the early 1960s, Frank Perez was a student at Glenville High and a sprinter on the state championship track team. His father, who was blind, worked in a factory and earned five thousand dollars a year. Frank was one of five children. His father certainly could not afford to send him to college, and neither his athletic skills nor his grades were spectacular enough to earn him a full scholarship. Perez had two teammates at Glenville who were exceptional athletes, and Purdue University wanted Steinbrenner, who was recruiting for the school in the Cleveland area, to offer them scholarships. Steinbrenner met the two track stars, and also met Perez and his family, and took a liking to them. Steinbrenner told Purdue that if it wanted the other two Glenville athletes, Frank Perez had to get a scholarship, too. Purdue agreed to the package deal. "I got a ten-thousand-dollar scholarship," said Perez in 1981, when he was assistant principal of Bedford (Ohio) High School, "and as far as I'm concerned, George Steinbrenner gave me that ten thousand dollars. I never would have gone to college without him, never. And he never asked for anything in return. All he wanted was for me just to be successful and do well. I

think that's what he gets his jollies, his kicks, out of, seeing people he helped do well." Occasionally, as a teacher and coach in the Cleveland area, Perez would tell another teacher, or another coach, that George Steinbrenner had helped him get to college, and the other person would smile and shake his head and say, "That's funny. He helped me, too."

Perez grew to love Steinbrenner, but he always recognized there was more than one side to the man. Like so many people who knew Steinbrenner, Perez described him as "a fierce competitor," a man who hated to lose, at anything. "A few years ago, when I was coaching at East High in Cleveland," Perez said, "he came over to the Arena in the middle of an afternoon to watch a citywide track meet that was going on. He sat down with me for a while. He had a few people with him who didn't know much about sports, and we were watching the sprints and the hurdles, and George asked me how do you know who were the fastest runners in the early heats, and I told him the ones with the best times were all put in lane three. He turned to the men he was with, and he said, 'Hey, let's have a little bet on these races. I'll give you even money, and in each race I'll take the guy in lane three, no matter who he is, or what school he comes from, and you guys can have all the rest of the field. How's that?' The other guys thought they had a terrific bet. They couldn't believe it when George won almost every race. They thought he was a genius. He just kept smiling and collecting. They were betting like five dollars a race."

When Perez was a freshman at Purdue, another Glenville graduate, Dave Mills, was a senior. Dave Mills was one of the first young people Steinbrenner helped get to college, but Dave Mills did not love George Steinbrenner. Mills not only had accepted help from Steinbrenner; he had accepted a job. "Don't never ever work for him," Mills

warned Frank Perez. "As much as I respect him, I wouldn't," Perez said many years later. "It's almost like he feels, 'If I pay you, I own you.'"

Herman Alexander was an assistant track coach at Glenville High, and he got to know Steinbrenner well. "We had kids who couldn't afford shoes, couldn't afford food," Alexander said, "and every time I asked George, he would send me a check to take care of a problem. He never said no." In the 1960s, Alexander coached a high jumper named Stanley Albright, who came from a large and poor family. He could jump seven feet in high school. Steinbrenner hired Albright's mother and sister as housekeepers, gave the youngster a nominal job and overpaid all of them. In effect, he put the groceries on the Albright table; he paid the rent. When Albright had a chance, as a high school student, to make the United States team that would compete against the Soviet Union, Steinbrenner paid to send him and Alexander on at least half a dozen trips around the country to compete in major track meets. "There were no strings attached," Albright said. "Those trips cost George at least seven hundred dollars apiece, and he insisted that we fly first class and stay at the best hotels." Albright qualified for the United States team. Then Steinbrenner helped him get into Ohio State, but Albright, even though he was bright, was not a student. He couldn't adjust to college life and left Ohio State after one year. Steinbrenner was disappointed, but he didn't turn his back on Albright. He continued to help the family.

Steinbrenner helped Herman Alexander, too. When Alexander was not made head coach of track and field at Glenville, Steinbrenner suspected that Alexander was the victim of racial prejudice. Steinbrenner encouraged him to leave the school, arranged for him to get a job working for the mayor of Cleveland and urged him to continue his education. Alexander earned his doctorate in education and became evening and weekend director of Cuyahoga

Community College. "George Steinbrenner changed my life," he said.

Sometimes Steinbrenner helped young people get to college with gifts of money, sometimes with loans, sometimes with influence and sometimes simply with encouragement. Jim Holland, for instance, came from Bay Village, which meant he didn't need any financial assistance. But he did get moral support from Steinbrenner, and a sense of purpose, and, in time, a job, working as a lawyer for the Yankees. Holland's experience in working for Steinbrenner was not painful; he left on good terms to accept a job with greater potential, working for Bowie Kuhn in the commissioner of baseball's office.

Other young men aided by Steinbrenner went on to become doctors, actors and soldiers, and even if most of the students he chose to help were male, and most of them were athletes, still Steinbrenner deserved credit, for his interest, for his effort, for his generosity. One of Steinbrenner's generous acts in Cleveland, however, earned him more criticism than acclaim. In the early 1970s, when a strike closed down the two major Cleveland newspapers, Steinbrenner gave ten thousand dollars to the Board of Education to pay out-of-work newspapermen to deliver lectures on journalism at various schools. The newspapermen were to receive five hundred dollars a week for five lectures a week. Steinbrenner considered the fees enlightened generosity. Some journalists considered them lifesavers. But some journalists rejected the fees as bribes. They thought it was no coincidence that many of the reporters selected for the program worked in fields in which Steinbrenner had a vested interest; business, labor, sports and the theater.

Steinbrenner's financial interest in the theater began in a small way, in 1964, when, between his shipbuilding and his civic works, he found time to invest in a road company production of Arthur Miller's play, *After the Fall*. For a few

years, Steinbrenner contented himself with road companies, of such shows as *On a Clear Day, You Can See Forever, Funny Girl* and, most notably, *George M.,* a show whose title and star-spangled story line George M. Steinbrenner could not possibly resist. "George put that show in every city in the country," said Tip O'Neill, his congressional friend, "not so much to make money, but to get people waving the flag again. He did it right after Vietnam." Steinbrenner absorbed a sizable loss to bring *George M.* into Cleveland on the Fourth of July, a touch that was inevitable. Gradually, working with a producer named Jimmy Nederlander, who was bred for the theater business the way Steinbrenner was bred for the shipping business, George began to put his money on Broadway, to gamble on picking hits. Nederlander and Steinbrenner, at first, were not exactly Ruth and Gehrig, Mantle and Maris, or even Winfield and Jackson. The two producers' first venture, in 1967, *The Ninety-Day Mistress,* starring Dyan Cannon, did not last long enough to justify the title; it folded after three weeks. Their next production, *Not Now Darling,* collapsed just as quickly, living up to its title. But their next effort became their first hit, *Applause,* which won the Tony Award as the best musical of 1970 and earned a Tony also for its star, Lauren Bacall. The Playbill for *Applause* carried the weighty credit: "Joseph Kipness and Lawrence Kasha in association with Nederlander Productions and George M. Steinbrenner III present . . ." Joe Kipness, a Broadway character as well as a Broadway producer, found working with Steinbrenner an absolute delight. "To me," Kipness said, "he was the sweetest guy in the world. He never interfered." Actually, Steinbrenner did interfere—once—and effectively. In *Applause,* the character played by Lauren Bacall loses the man she loves, a director, to a younger woman. When *Applause* began its pre-Broadway run, in Baltimore, the younger woman was played by an eighteen-year-old girl so beautiful that even a

decade later, when Kipness recalled her, his eyes misted over. But the play didn't work. Kipness knew something was wrong, but he didn't know—or wouldn't admit to himself—what it was. "Then," Kipness said, "George saw the show and said, 'A girl like her could never take the man away from Lauren Bacall. She's too young. She's too sweet.' George was right." Kipness reluctantly replaced the beautiful teenager with an older and more gifted actress, and from then on, the show was a smash.

One night during the highly profitable run of *Applause,* Steinbrenner found himself in an orchestra seat next to Barbra Streisand. He introduced himself as one of the producers. Streisand checked the program, saw that his name was George M. Steinbrenner III and, for the rest of the evening, called him "The Third." Steinbrenner was not terribly amused.

Despite brushing elbows with fame—*Applause* was his first, and only, genuine hit—Steinbrenner was not quite ready to abandon Cleveland for the bright lights of Broadway. In Cleveland, he could have had a regular table at the Union Club, the traditional headquarters for the industrial establishment, but Steinbrenner preferred to hang out at Mushy Wexler's Theatrical Grill, with its faded pictures of jazz musicians, and at the Pewter Mug, run by Al Bernstein, one of the investors in the Cleveland Pipers, who still calls George "the sweetest man in the world." In the Theatrical, men argued and lied about football, and horses, and gambling, and in the Pewter Mug, men like John Minco, who did the advertising for the Cleveland Browns, and Daniel McCarthy and Edward Rosenthal, both of whom later invested in the Yankees, crowded around table fourteen and, once in a while, enjoyed the sight of George Steinbrenner finishing a drink. His friends outdrank him, some of them by miles, and often they kidded him for his Prussian manner—"Ja, General, ve vill eat and ve vill like it." Once, Steinbrenner presented Mushy Wexler, a gradu-

ate of the streets, with a Culver school tie; at table fourteen, the regulars needled George for being taken by his older son. George had promised Henry G. Steinbrenner III any entertainer he wanted for a prom at Culver, and the son had asked for Barry White, who traveled with a huge orchestra, and Steinbrenner ended up paying something like fifty thousand dollars to keep his promise. The best part, his friends kept reminding him, was that he didn't even know who Barry White was. Steinbrenner mixed camaraderie and commerce easily. When he and Jimmy Nederlander got the closed-circuit rights in Ohio for the first Ali-Frazier fight, a dramatic bout between two unbeaten champions, George offered several of his friends a piece of the action; they didn't even have to put up any capital; they could simply relax and share in the almost inevitable profits.

George's generosity, and his compassion, toward friends he considered loyal, was remarkable. When several of his cronies got caught in a financial disaster called Hill Properties, a land-speculation company based in Dallas, Steinbrenner used his money and his word to help bail them out. Of course not every investment Steinbrenner touched turned to dollars. He and his friends lost money on a Marriott Hotel near San Francisco. Al Rosen, the former baseball star, a member of Cleveland's Group 66, lost money both in Hill Properties and in the Marriott, but did not lose faith in Steinbrenner. "The only thing that would keep me out of a deal with Steinbrenner," said Rosen, not long after those two unhappy experiences, "is a lack of funds. No one would ever question one of George's deals. You just deal with him through trust. He inspires confidence and loyalty. The guy's a genius. He's got a mind like a steel trap." Rosen's faith, and friendship, never wavered until he made a critical mistake. He went to work for Steinbrenner. He served for two years as president of the Yankees, in between Gabe Paul, who later sued

Steinbrenner for $3.1 million, and Lou Saban, who would rather have been coaching a football team. When Rosen quit, his confidence and his loyalty had been severely tested.

Steinbrenner, after his unhappy experience with the Pipers, managed to stay out of professional sports for almost a decade. But at the end of the 1960s, his finances unmistakably healthy, he plunged into a different sport. He bought an 860-acre horse farm in Ocala, Florida, named it Kinsman Stud Farm, then formed a syndicate called Kinship Stables, with himself as majority stockholder, to race horses. He started off with a limited knowledge of the sport, but he quickly embarked on a cram course to make himself an expert. He spent hours talking horse racing with Mushy Wexler and John Minco, his expert friends, and then he read every book he could find on the subject. He learned bloodlines. He learned configuration. He learned about claiming races and allowances, about rating a horse and raising a foal. He made one of his first investments in a nondescript nineteen-hundred-dollar mare, and when her first foal came along, he named the colt Big Whippendeal, a euphemistic version of what some of his Pewter Mug buddies thought he considered himself. In 1974, as a four-year-old, Big Whippendeal won the Hialeah Turf Cup, one of Steinbrenner's more significant victories. But George's finest day in horse racing came on the first Saturday in May in 1977, Derby Day at Churchill Downs in Louisville, Kentucky. Steinbrenner's filly, Sweet Little Lady, who was, as he liked to point out, not sweet or little or much of a lady, won the Debutante Stakes, a prestigious event for two-year-olds, and then, in the Kentucky Derby itself, Steinbrenner's colt, Steve's Friend, was fourth at the quarter pole and, under Ruben Hernandez, apparently ready to make a move, when he suddenly jumped a shadow on the turn, broke his stride and finished fifth in a field of fifteen. The winner, Seattle Slew, went on

to become the first undefeated Triple Crown champion. Steve's Friend faded after the Derby, and Sweet Little Lady, who won four of her five races as a two-year-old, did little as a three-year-old. "Horses are great," Steinbrenner was heard to observe, as he looked at Sweet Little Lady one day. "They never complain, and they can't talk to sportswriters and tell them what a bum the owner is."

Steinbrenner never needed anyone to tell on him. He didn't hide his vices. In 1978, Tony Kornheiser, the writer, accompanied him to the race track one day to watch one of his horses run, a filly named Jenny's Lady. "In the ninth race," the race-track announcer intoned, "Jenny's Lady, three pounds over." Steinbrenner knew the announcement meant that Jenny's Lady, who was scheduled to carry 119 pounds on a muddy track, the kind of track that didn't favor her come-from-behind style, would now carry 122 pounds, because her jockey was three pounds overweight. Steinbrenner calculated that the extra weight would cost his filly one length in the race, a length she could hardly afford. The owner made no effort to conceal his anger. He slammed his program against a wall. "Trainer's fault," he said. "Sure, the boy should come in at weight, but it's the trainer's fault for not knowing about it."

When the jockeys came out to claim their mounts for the ninth race, Kornheiser suggested that one of them looked as if he had come straight from a police lineup. "That yours, George?" the writer asked.

"He's the one," Steinbrenner said. "I wanted him because he's a veteran, and I thought this little girl needed a veteran." Then Steinbrenner glared at the overweight jockey and said, "He'll never ride for me again."

Jenny's Lady finished next-to-last.

In the late 1970s, Steinbrenner's interest in *racing horses* diminished. His syndicate, Kinship Stables, vanished from the record books, and the horses he raced in his own name won only $84,967 in 1978, $83,518 in 1979 and

$73,123 in 1980, probably not even enough to pay the feed bills at Kinsman Stud Farm. But Steinbrenner's interest in *horse racing* did not fade. In 1980, he purchased an aging race track called Florida Downs, put hundreds of thousands of dollars into renovations, renamed the track Tampa Bay Downs, dressed the mutuel clerks in Yankee blue-and-white and reopened with the theme: It's a Whole New Ball Game. Only one thing went wrong on opening day. The programs did not show up at the race track until after the first race. The printing presses had broken down the night before. The printer was the stepson of the general manager of Tampa Bay Downs, Eddie McKinsey, a veteran racing man Steinbrenner had lured away from Hialeah only a few months earlier. When the programs did not arrive on time, Steinbrenner walked into McKinsey's office with Sam Davis, a former general manager of the track. "From now on," McKinsey said Steinbrenner said, "Sam will tell you when to jump and how high."

McKinsey could take a hint. He offered to resign. Still, at the end of the day, he went to a meeting to discuss what had happened. "I volunteered an opinion," McKinsey said, "and George said, 'I don't want to hear your opinions.' I told him nobody could stop me from giving an opinion in a free society. He stood up and we were very close together. He said, 'If you were a little bigger, I'd punch you out.' I said, 'You don't have the heart to punch me out.' I resigned and he gave me a check for nineteen thousand dollars and said, 'This is the least I can do.' He never even said, 'Good luck in whatever you do.' I had given my blood to the man and my loyalty. He tried to dehumanize me. Even if the programs hadn't been the problem, something else would have been." The story, of course, was vintage Steinbrenner.

Earlier the same day, Steinbrenner had announced, "No, I will not be involved in the day-to-day operation of Tampa Bay Downs. With the Yankees and the American Ship Building Company, I just have too much to do. I can't

spread myself too thin." Almost no one believed him.

Not long after he got into horse racing, Steinbrenner entered another sports business. He returned to professional basketball, this time into the NBA, which had rejected him in 1962. Ten years later, he was part of a group of men who purchased the Chicago Bulls. He owned eleven percent of the team, and, atypically, he never did get involved in the day-to-day operation of the Bulls, perhaps because, by the time he invested, he already had made up his mind that he wanted to own a baseball team. The most likely candidate was his hometown team, the Cleveland Indians.

The Indians were owned by Vernon Stouffer, who had made his millions in the restaurant business, and Steinbrenner had grown up with his son, Jim Stouffer. George's mother and Jim's mother, both Christian Scientists, were good friends, and when Vernon Stouffer, pressed for cash, decided to sell the Indians, his son Jim set up the deal. Jim Stouffer outlined the terms, and George Steinbrenner agreed to them, and everything seemed settled. But, somehow, when the deal was presented to Vernon Stouffer, something went awry. Al Bernstein, the owner of the Pewter Mug, suggested later that Vernon Stouffer was known to be anti-Semitic, and that when he discovered Al Rosen might be among Steinbrenner's partners, he backed out. Other people discounted that story— after all, Gabe Paul, the Indians' general manager under Stouffer, was also Jewish—and said that Vernon Stouffer was drinking heavily, which he was known to do, and irrationally turned down a deal he should have accepted. Either way, George Steinbrenner stepped out of the Pewter Mug one night convinced he had bought the Cleveland Indians and found out, a short time later, he was wrong.

Later the same year, 1972, Steinbrenner learned through Gabe Paul, whom he had met in Group 66, that the New York Yankees were up for sale.

A few months later, when George Steinbrenner purchased the New York Yankees, a Cleveland newspaperman asked Henry Steinbrenner what he thought of his son's investment in sports this time. "It's the first smart thing he's ever done," said George Steinbrenner's father, finally impressed.

3

When the Columbia Broadcasting System, seeking to diversify, purchased the New York Yankees in 1964 for $13.2 million, CBS took over a team that was flourishing on the field and at the box office, a team that had won twenty-nine American League pennants and twenty World Series in forty-five years, a team that had not had a losing season in thirty-nine years, a team that had drawn more than 1.3 million fans each season for nineteen straight years, a team that had Mickey Mantle in the outfield, Whitey Ford on the pitching mound and Yogi Berra as its manager, all three of whom enjoyed excellent seasons in 1964 and all three of whom would, within a decade, be elected to baseball's Hall of Fame. In other words, CBS bought pure gold.

But by the end of 1972, CBS had performed perfect alchemy—in reverse. In eight years under CBS, the Yankees won no pennants and played in no World Series,

suffered through four losing seasons, finished higher than fourth only once, finished tenth once with the worst record of any Yankee team in fifty-three years, never drew as many as 1.3 million fans in a season, slipped below one million in attendance in 1972 and, on that 1972 team, had no one who batted .300, only one player who was able to make the All-Star team and no one who was likely ever to end up in the Hall of Fame. No wonder William S. Paley, the chairman of the board of CBS, was ready to sell the Yankees. They were an embarrassment.

The man who had advised CBS to purchase the Yankees in 1964 was a vice-president, in charge of investments, named Michael Burke. In 1966, as a reward, or possibly a punishment, Burke was made president of the Yankees, a job he thoroughly enjoyed. Burke had also thoroughly enjoyed his job during World War II, going behind enemy lines as an OSS intelligence agent. Burke was a charming and unfailingly cheerful man, immensely well-known and well-liked in New York, and even as he presided over the decline and fall of the Yankee empire, he managed to maintain his good humor and his popularity. He was not a good loser. He was a great loser.

William S. Paley thought highly of Michael Burke, and when Paley decided CBS should sell the Yankees, he wanted to see Burke remain part of the Yankee management. Paley suggested that Burke put together an organization, a syndicate to purchase the team, and he told Burke, in effect, if not in so many words, that a group including Burke would get the team for a much better price than a group that did not include Burke.

At first, Burke sought to find people in New York to buy the Yankees, but perhaps because they knew too well that the team was struggling and that the area in which Yankee Stadium was situated was decaying, no New York investors showed interest. Then Mike Burke happened to

speak to Gabe Paul, who had spent the previous decade being general manager, vice-president and president of the Cleveland Indians, and mentioned that he was hoping to assemble a syndicate to buy the Yankees. Gabe Paul mentioned, in return, that a group of men who had just tried, and failed, to buy the Indians might be interested in the Yankees. The leader of the group, Paul said, was a Cleveland businessman named George Steinbrenner. Burke had never heard of him. Paul said he could bring them together, and he did.

On January 3, 1973, at Yankee Stadium, Mike Burke announced that a twelve-man group headed by two "general partners," himself and George M. Steinbrenner III of Cleveland, Ohio, had purchased the Yankees for $10 million in cash, $3.2 million less than CBS had paid for the team, $3 or $4 million less than another syndicate, put together by a former baseball manager named Herman Franks, was considering paying for the team and $5 million less than the "intrinsic value" of the team, calculated by National Economic Research Associates.

"It's the best buy in sports today," George Steinbrenner said, well aware that the Indians, a team with a poorer record and considerably less commercial potential, had just been sold for $10.8 million. "I think it's a bargain," Steinbrenner added, "but they [CBS] feel the chemistry is right. They feel they haven't taken a loss on the team." Steinbrenner himself had bought twenty percent of the Yankees, a share that would climb, by 1981, as he bought out several of his partners, to fifty-five percent. By then, the team would be valued at $35 million.

"CBS substantially broke even on this deal, taking account of interest and depreciation and things like that," Michael Burke said in 1973.

"The purchase price," said CBS, in a corporate state-

ment, "is well in excess of the value carried on the CBS books."

Burke and Steinbrenner were the only members of the syndicate who appeared—and the only ones who were identified—at the news conference announcing the sale. Burke, long-haired and lean, said that he would continue to run the team as its president. Steinbrenner, who favored short hair and ice cream, spoke for himself and the other investors and said, "We plan absentee ownership. We're not going to pretend we're something we aren't. I'll stick to building ships." Steinbrenner struck the same theme repeatedly. "I won't be active in the day-to-day operations of the club at all," he added. "I can't spread myself so thin. I've got enough headaches with the shipping company."

Ironically, Steinbrenner's major headache was just beginning. Only a few months before the purchase of the Yankees, a reporter in Washington named James Polk had started an investigation that would lead to Steinbrenner's conviction as a felon, which would, in turn, lead to a moderate fine and to his suspension from baseball for a period of fifteen months.

Among the spectators at the Burke-and-Steinbrenner news conference were two former Yankee stars, Phil Rizzuto and Elston Howard, each once the Most Valuable Player in the American League and each still with the Yankees in 1973, Rizzuto as a broadcaster, Howard as a coach. With them stood Lee MacPhail, the general manager of the Yankees, perfectly bred for the job. He was the son of Larry MacPhail, who had been general manager of the Cincinnati Reds and the Brooklyn Dodgers, had introduced night baseball to the major leagues and had in the late 1940s owned one-third of the New York Yankees. Lee MacPhail had just signed a new three-year contract with the Yankees. The field manager, Ralph Houk, who also had a new three-year contract, was not present. Houk was a

World War II hero, a Ranger in the Battle of the Bulge, a major by the age of twenty-five—when Steinbrenner was a freshman at Culver Military Academy.

One week after the Yankee Stadium gathering, the other investors were introduced to the media at the "21" Club, one of New York's more expensive, and exclusive, restaurants. The original team of twelve, including Steinbrenner and Burke, had swelled to fifteen, including the attorney Thomas W. Evans, fresh from the successful campaign to re-elect the President; Jimmy Nederlander, whose Steinbrenner-backed production of *Seesaw* was about to open on Broadway; Nelson Bunker Hunt, a horse breeder and racer, son of oilman H. L. Hunt and brother of Lamar Hunt, who owned football's Kansas City Chiefs; John DeLorean, who had not yet left General Motors to bring out an automobile bearing his own name; a quartet of Cleveland attorneys, Edward Ginsberg, Sheldon Guren, Daniel McCarthy and Edward Greenwald, one of whom had been born in Brooklyn and one in Manhattan, and all of whom had participated in earlier business ventures with Steinbrenner; Lester Crown, one of the owners of the Chicago Bulls; Jess Bell, the president of Bonne Bell, a cosmetics firm; Marvin K. Warner, a former member of the United States delegation to the United Nations, a job that may have prepared him for the size of the syndicate; Francis J. O'Neill, who had previously owned a share of the Cleveland Indians; and, the surprise of the group, giving up his job with the Indians, Gabe Paul, who was rejoining Graig Nettles, the third baseman he had traded to the Yankees only six weeks earlier, a deal that, because of Paul's shift in allegiance, was questioned and then affirmed.

On the chartered plane that carried several members of the syndicate from Cleveland to New York for their unveiling, George Steinbrenner had confided that Gabe Paul, the newest member of the syndicate, added only a

few days earlier because of his baseball expertise, was going to be introduced as the new president of the Yankees. This came as news to the Cleveland *Press,* which dutifully reported the item in its early editions, and it came as news, too, to Mike Burke, who thought he was going to continue as president. Somewhere between the airport and the "21" Club, perhaps at a breakfast gathering of the syndicate at the Hotel Carlyle, Burke reminded Steinbrenner that the team already had a chief executive officer, and Steinbrenner and Paul, for the time being, acquiesced, which made the Cleveland *Press* a liar and made Burke understandably nervous. "This may be the largest partnership ever to run a baseball club," Burke said at "21." "But I don't expect to have fifteen voices telling me what to do. Gabe Paul will join the Yankees in a major post within the context of not throwing out my present organization." Burke's sentence was a bit convoluted, but not nearly so convoluted as his brief term, not even four months, as president of the Steinbrenner Yankees.

In theory, the two men, Burke and Steinbrenner, should have gotten along quite well—both charming (one most of the time, the other whenever he wanted to be), both with football backgrounds (Steinbrenner as a coach, Burke as a halfback at the University of Pennsylvania), both obviously delighted by recognition. At the time, Burke was certainly the more famous of the two, and he knew more famous people. Once, at the end of World War II, on the cobblestone streets of Montmartre, Ernest Hemingway, fired by wine and *machismo,* tried to tackle Mike Burke, who lugged an empty bottle under his arm as a football. Burke sidestepped, Hemingway hit the cobblestones and ripped the knees off his pants and both men recuperated at the bar. Steinbrenner had to love that story; he loved American authors. And Burke's OSS exploits inspired a movie called *Cloak and Dagger,* in which Michael Burke,

who assisted as a screenwriter, was portrayed by Gary Cooper, the same man who had portrayed Lou Gehrig. Steinbrenner loved Lou Gehrig. But, somehow, the combination of the long-haired New Yorker and the close-cropped Clevelander didn't click. When they walked down the street together, in those early days, passersby, the little people, the cabbies and the cops, called out, "Hiya, Mike," and "Howyadoin', Mike," and "Watcha say, Mike?" and Burke grinned, and waved, and shook hands, and Steinbrenner steamed. He wanted that attention too. He wanted "21" to treat him the way the Pewter Mug did; he wanted to be as big a man on Park Avenue as he was on Superior. Burke recognized Steinbrenner's need immediately. Asked what drew the members of the syndicate to the Yankees, Burke said, "There's a romanticism in the ownership of the Yankees. It means a higher visibility for these guys in New York. There is undeniable public prestige for them in owning the Yankees, and they all know that."

Steinbrenner was clearly in command at the news conference, the other investors, the "limited partners," posing and nodding not precisely at his command, but definitely at his suggestion. Some of the New York sportswriters took an instant dislike to Steinbrenner, a negative gut reaction. "My first impression was this guy's full of shit," recalled one baseball writer, who was still covering the Yankees eight years later. "He had no credibility. My second impression was that he was stuffed into his shirt, it was too small for him, and my third was that he must have just taken a haircut, it was so short, so neat."

During spring training of 1973, Steinbrenner seemed to concentrate on the shipping business, as he had promised, maintaining a very low baseball profile, possibly because he was just starting to sense the seriousness of his emerging legal problems. But Steinbrenner would not have

caused much of a stir at the training camp, anyway. There was too much excitement already, created by the recent decision of two of the team's pitchers, Fritz Peterson and Mike Kekich, to trade wives and families, a dramatic event that tended to obscure everything else, including a new owner. Steinbrenner made no public comment about the Peterson-Kekich swap, but he did make an appearance at the camp, and so did his parents. At one game, Michael Burke asked Henry G. Steinbrenner if he would throw out the ceremonial first ball. The elder Steinbrenner was delighted, but a little more than a month later, in a less cheerful ceremony, the younger Steinbrenner threw out Mike Burke. "Forced out" would be a pleasanter phrase, but no more accurate.

Steinbrenner was motivated at least in part by unhappiness with Burke's financial management of the Yankees. In 1973, to Steinbrenner's dismay, the Yankees were giving away the radio rights to their games, in fact were paying the station that carried them, and, even worse, the Yankees were collecting only two hundred thousand dollars for the television rights. In contrast, their intra-city rivals, the Mets, were getting two million dollars for television rights. Even if the Mets had won a pennant in 1969 and would win another in 1973, the disparity struck Steinbrenner as obscene. Steinbrenner, too, could not have been pleased by the way the season started. The Yankees lost their first four games, by a combined score of thirty-two to fourteen, and the fourth game, which was Opening Day at Yankee Stadium, drew only seventeen thousand fans. The next two crowds were considerably smaller. To stimulate attendance, Steinbrenner imported a baseball clown, Max Patkin, for pregame entertainment. Burke, a baseball purist and a New York sophisticate, was appalled. The Yankees, on the playing field, were funnier than Patkin; they stumbled into last place after

sixteen games. Steinbrenner was appalled.

Late in April, the two men announced that their marriage of convenience had failed, that Gabe Paul was, as promised, moving into a "major post" in the Yankee organization. He was replacing Burke, as president, and the team was going to have just one "general partner," George M. Steinbrenner III. Mike Burke was sinking back among the army of "limited partners," even though he would be designated a "consultant" to the team, on a ten-year contract.

"A lot of times making someone a consultant is putting him out to pasture or a settlement," Steinbrenner said. "This isn't the case here." Steinbrenner's credibility declined a little further.

Mike Burke did not say that Steinbrenner was lying. Burke, the consummate New Yorker (as *Cleveland* magazine called him), instead quoted mildly from William Butler Yeats' "An Irish Airman Foresees His Death." "I balanced all, brought all to mind," said Burke, explaining the process that had led him to surrender the presidency. He could have quoted further:

> Nor law, nor duty bade me fight,
> Nor public men, nor cheering crowds,
> A lonely impulse of delight
> Drove to this tumult in the clouds.

The tumult in the Bronx continued without Burke, and if his services as a consultant were ever called upon, he received no credit, at least not publicly. Burke, of course, was hurt, but the pain was soothed when he was soon named president of Madison Square Garden; his training in defeat at Yankee Stadium prepared him well to preside over the New York Knicks and the New York Rangers during frustrating periods for both those teams. Perhaps

because he remained a limited partner and a stockholder in the Yankees, perhaps because he commanded a handsome fee as a consultant, perhaps because he still enjoyed sitting in a front-row seat behind the Yankee dugout at the big games, perhaps because he suspected that Gabe Paul orchestrated the rift between him and Steinbrenner or perhaps because he was too much a gentleman to be vindictive, Burke never openly struck back at Steinbrenner.

Once, however, in an interview with *Cleveland* magazine, Burke did not completely disguise his feelings. "No, there was no intention on George's part to mouse-trap me," he said. "I don't think that either of us started out anticipating that this would be the outcome, ah, but it just emerged . . . simply that we two were incompatible . . . for chemical or whatever reasons.

"But perhaps it's in George's nature, perhaps once he's involved in any situation, that he has a compulsion to take charge . . . rather, ah, aggressively."

Burke paused. "And, ah," he continued, "there is a kind of compulsiveness about him that makes me question his . . . his, ah, judgment in certain circumstances."

The interviewer pressed Burke for an example of Steinbrenner's compulsiveness. "Well," Burke said, "the way he just *propelled* himself into the Yankee situation, making decisions and judgments right and left before he really had an understanding either of baseball or the city . . . which I think caused, ah, resulted in certain mistakes."

Supposedly, oe evening not long after his demotion, Burke happened to dine in a restaurant where Gabe Paul and his wife were also eating. "How are you?" Mary Paul asked, brightly, and Mike Burke was said to have responded, "I'll feel a lot better as soon as I get this knife removed from my back."

At the same time Steinbrenner shook up the front office, the Yankees, perhaps only coincidentally, reversed them-

selves on the field. After losing ten of their first sixteen games, the Yankees won forty of their next sixty-four and woke up on the morning of George Steinbrenner's forty-third birthday, July 4, the traditional halfway mark of the baseball season, in first place, four full games ahead of the next-best team. The Yankees had not been in so lofty a position in nine years. One of their players, Ron Blomberg, was batting .400—no one had been hitting as high as .400 in July since Ted Williams and Stan Musial in 1948, a quarter of a century earlier—and their pitching staff had been strengthened by the addition of two men, Sam McDowell and Pat Dobson, who between them won seven of their first nine games. The Yankees had paid $150,000 for McDowell even though his skills were fading, a sizable sum in those days and a fair indication of George Steinbrenner's desire to build a winning team. McDowell's presence, plus Dobson's, meant that the Yankees' annual payroll shot up to $1.2 million, or approximately what one player alone, Dave Winfield, would be earning only eight years later. The organist at Yankee Stadium took to playing, "It Seems Like Old Times," and the Yankees and their fans began dreaming about a pennant, perhaps even a subway Series between the Yankees and the Mets.

Then the dream died. The Yankees celebrated George's birthday by losing a doubleheader, and although they managed to cling to first place for the rest of July, they slipped to second on the first day of August, then plummeted straight down, winding up in fourth place, seventeen games behind Baltimore. Steinbrenner, of course, did not suffer silently. He had started the season off by noting, during the playing of "The Star-Spangled Banner," which of the Yankees had hair he considered too long. He wrote down the offenders' uniform numbers and sent the list to the manager, Ralph Houk, suggesting that Houk send them to a barber, a maneuver that prompted one sportswri-

ter to liken Steinbrenner to Lewis Carroll's Queen of Hearts: "Off with their hair . . . off with their hair!" Mike Burke, contemplating his own tresses in the looking glass, must have realized that he was in trouble.

Later, after hearing that the Yankees had traded for Pat Dobson, Steinbrenner caused some amusement by announcing, "We needed a lefthanded pitcher, and we got one," at best a lefthanded compliment to Dobson, who pitched righthanded. Steinbrenner stories began to spread, fueled by his eagerness to promote his own version of the Yankee image, which was based mostly on countless viewings of Gary Cooper as Lou Gehrig. One day, Gene Michael, who had a well-known fear of snakes, picked up his glove on his way to his position, stuck his hand in, then suddenly ripped off the glove and rattled it furiously—until a hot dog fell out. Relieved and embarrassed, Michael tossed the hot dog toward the dugout. The frankfurter landed in front of Steinbrenner, who was sitting in his box seat. The owner was offended, and told Houk to find the man who had planted the hot dog in Michael's glove and punish him. "He's got to be kidding," said Houk, who obviously did not know his employer well. A few days later, when outfielder Johnny Callison committed an error, Steinbrenner told Houk and Lee MacPhail, "I will not have that man on my team." Within hours, Callison was an ex-Yankee. (The fact that he was batting .176 made Callison more expendable. "In fairness to George," Lee MacPhail said later, "any time that Houk and I were opposed to making a move, the move wasn't made.") More and more often, as the Yankees dropped out of the pennant race, Houk found postgame notes waiting for him: "Call George Steinbrenner immediately." Houk, accustomed to being left alone, even when his team finished tenth, did not take kindly to Steinbrenner's concern. On the final day of the season, Houk resigned, the second World War II hero to

surrender to Steinbrenner in his first year as owner.

Soon after the season ended, the Yankees moved out of Yankee Stadium and across the East River to the Borough of Queens, into temporary headquarters in the Parks Administration Building, across the street from Shea Stadium. For the next two seasons, the home of the New York Mets would be the home-away-from-home of the New York Yankees.

The Yankees, who did not own their own field, had been displaced from the Bronx because their stadium was getting a facelifting. The City of New York had bought both the ground under Yankee Stadium (from the Knights of Columbus) and the stadium itself (from Rice University in Houston), had promised to renovate both the structure and the surrounding parking and access facilities at an estimated cost of twenty-four million dollars, then in 1972 had given the Yankees a thirty-year lease on the upgraded stadium, a very favorable lease that permitted the Yankees, among other benefits, to deduct maintenance costs before paying tenant taxes. Mike Burke might not have done a brilliant job of selling radio and television rights, but he had negotiated masterfully with his good friend, John V. Lindsay, the mayor of New York.

Ultimately, the extra cost of remodeling the stadium, the parking garages and the approach roads, including the Major Deegan Expressway, the direct connection to the New York State Thruway, soared to more than one hundred million dollars, four times the original estimate. The city absorbed the extra cost—and a great deal of abuse. Steinbrenner eventually shared the abuse. He was accused more than once of raping the city, but he was absolutely innocent. He didn't even know the lady at the time of the incident.

In the winter following Steinbrenner's first Yankee season, the face of the team, on the field and off, changed

119

perceptibly. Lee MacPhail, the last survivor of the Burke-Houk-MacPhail triumvirate that had guided the Yankees through their darkest years, resigned and accepted a more prestigious post, president of the American League. And the Yankees engineered the first trade of the Steinbrenner era that would have a lasting impact on the team. They gave up an aging relief pitcher named Lindy McDaniel to acquire outfielder Lou Piniella, a key to the Yankees' future pennants. Then Steinbrenner thought he made an even bigger deal. The Yankees rented the Terrace in the Park, a restaurant high above the heart of the World's Fair grounds, and called a massive news conference to announce the signing of a new manager, Dick Williams, who had just guided the Oakland A's to two straight World Series championships. The only problem was that Dick Williams was still under contract to the Oakland A's, and the Oakland owner, Charles O. Finley, was not about to set him free—not unless the Yankees gave him two of their most promising young prospects. The Yankees rejected the deal, gave up Williams and, in his place, a few weeks later, hired Bill Virdon, a young and earnest man who had won a divisional title for Pittsburgh in his only full season as a major-league manager.

The Williams fiasco was embarrassing, but by then George Steinbrenner was preoccupied by more pressing problems. Suddenly, he was a part of Watergate, part of a scandal that was dragging down a government, and both his business empire and his career were threatened. He wasn't Haldeman or Ehrlichman, or even Liddy or Hunt. He hadn't authorized any break-ins or sanctioned any wiretaps. But George Steinbrenner, in his own relatively small way, had been caught up in the atmosphere of Watergate, had stretched the law to his own convenience. Steinbrenner's minor role in Richard Nixon's major disaster could be traced back to long before the Watergate

break-in, back, in fact, to April, 1970, when Steinbrenner—convinced that, as he said, "The name of the game is Washington, D.C."—met with Robert Bartlome, the secretary of Amship, and with Stanley J. Lepkowski, the treasurer, and told them, "We need to make political contributions." The way to do it, Steinbrenner suggested, without breaking the federal laws against corporate contributions, was to award bonuses to certain loyal employees who would, in turn, make personal contributions to political candidates and committees. Lepkowski wondered if such subterfuge were legal. Steinbrenner assured him that many companies resorted to such a system and that it was, he had been advised, within the letter of the law. In 1970 and 1971, Amship, using bogus bonuses, made a wide variety of political contributions, to members of both major parties. Most of them were reasonably modest, one thousand dollars, for instance, to support Senator Vance Hartke, a Democrat from Indiana, five hundred dollars to support Representative Frank G. Bow, a Republican from Ohio. The foundations of the republic did not tremble.

Then, on February 11, 1972, an incident occurred that may have encouraged George Steinbrenner to make more significant contributions. Secretary of Commerce Maurice H. Stans flatly turned down Amship's bid to be compensated for the $5.4-million cost overrun on the building of the oceanographic survey ship *Researcher*. Steinbrenner, and other more objective observers, suspected that his fine work on behalf of the 1969 and 1970 Democratic Congressional Dinners had not helped his case.

Four days after the cost overrun was rejected, Stans left his Cabinet post and became finance director of Richard Nixon's campaign for re-election. The deputy finance director was Thomas W. Evans, Steinbrenner's classmate at Williams and, of course, in 1972, a member of the board of directors of American Ship Building. Steinbrenner men-

tioned to Evans how unhappy he was with Stans' decision. George also mentioned that he was not too happy with the state of the Democratic party, or with the possibility of Senator George McGovern running for President. Evans suggested that it might be a very good idea for Steinbrenner to meet Herbert W. Kalmbach, Richard Nixon's personal attorney and fundraiser. By great good fortune, the Committee to Re-elect the President (CREEP) and the law firm of Mudge, Rose, Guthrie & Alexander happened to have offices in the same building on Pennsylvania Avenue in Washington, which made it remarkably convenient for Evans to contact Kalmbach. In the middle of March 1972, George Steinbrenner sat down with Herb Kalmbach and, for a few minutes, talked politely about football. Then Kalmbach got to the point. "I understand from Tom Evans that you're interested in contributing to the campaign," he said.

"Yes," said Steinbrenner, "I am."

"Well if you're thinking of coming in here for under a hundred thousand dollars," Kalmbach said, "don't bother." Anything less would not be "meaningful." The stakes settled, Kalmbach then took out a list of some sixty committees that had been established to funnel contributions to the President's campaign: The Loyal Americans for Government, the Stable Society Council, Dedicated Americans for Effective Government—all branches of CREEP. At the top of the list, Kalmbach wrote, "33 @ 3, 1 @ 1," which translated quite easily to thirty-three checks for $3,000 and one check for $1,000, a total of $100,000 in relatively inconspicuous checks. "As he escorted me to the door," Steinbrenner said later, of his audience with Kalmbach, "he said that, 'It would be wise for you to get with the right people.'"

Kalmbach had not picked the $3,000 figure arbitrarily. Existing federal law required the disclosure of the names

of all people who made political contributions in excess of $3,000. The law was going to be amended on April 7, 1972, to reduce the limit drastically, so that the names of virtually all political contributors would have to be disclosed. On April 6, George Steinbrenner had bogus bonus checks made out to eight loyal employees, checks totaling $42,325.17. After taxes, and other mandatory deductions, the employees were left with precisely $25,000 among them. Six wrote out personal checks to the Nixon campaign for $3,000 apiece, and two wrote out personal checks for $3,500 apiece. Steinbrenner himself wrote out twenty-five personal checks for $3,000 apiece, each to a different pro-Nixon committee. The same day, an Amship vice-president delivered all thirty-three checks to Herb Kalmbach on Pennsylvania Avenue.

Significantly, Kalmbach's directions had not been followed exactly. Instead of thirty-three checks at $3,000, and one at $1,000, there were thirty-one at $3,000 and two at $3,500. That discrepancy would play a large part in exposing Amship's illegal corporate involvement.

One of the mysteries of the whole elaborate procedure was: Why did Steinbrenner risk breaking the law for a mere $25,000? If he could afford to contribute $75,000 of his own money, in twenty-five checks, he very likely could afford to contribute $100,000, in thirty-four checks. Why didn't he make the whole contribution personal—and legal? Steinbrenner's answer, not entirely satisfying, was that his lawyers had told him that the bonus plan was viable. "If I hadn't believed it was legal, I'd have been a perfect idiot to give $75,000 of my own money and $25,000 of company money," he once said. "If I hadn't believed it was legal, I'd have given all personal funds." That argument, however, seems flawed. If Steinbrenner believed the bonus plan to be legal, why didn't he give all $100,000 through the company? After all, the idea of the contribu-

tion was to protect and promote the company in its dealings with the Nixon administration, not to help Steinbrenner personally gain favor among the Republicans. In other words, if any of the money was a legitimate business expense, then all of it was. To compound the mystery, Steinbrenner himself did receive from Amship two bonuses of $37,500 each, but he received those bonuses back in 1970, long before he displayed any interest in investing in the political career of Richard Nixon, and neither Watergate investigators nor witnesses ever established any direct connection between Steinbrenner's $75,000 bonuses and Steinbrenner's $75,000 personal contribution to CREEP.

Steinbrenner never really cleared up the mysteries. When confronted by questions regarding his part in Watergate (in many interviews, he simply ruled Watergate questions off-bounds), he responded with references to poor counsel, with admissions of unintentional guilt, with reminders that he had taken the punishment himself and had not pushed it off on subordinates, with hints that the Nixon administration took vengeance on him because he would not reveal damaging gossip he had learned about congressional Democrats, with intimations that other companies and other executives had done far worse things and with suggestions that the law he violated was unknown and antiquated and, when you came right down to it, not one of the more important laws. "I must say honestly," Steinbrenner once wrote, trying to make himself perfectly clear in response to a Cleveland *Press* series about his involvement with Watergate, "that in some ways I believe the matter of illegal political campaign contributions concerning not only my company, but many, many bigger and more well-known corporations has been blown somewhat out of proportion due to its identification with the Nixon Presidency. In this country, we are plagued as never

before with murder on our streets, narcotics and drugs in our schools, crime and violence everywhere, and yet those who have knowingly or unknowingly violated an election contribution law that lay dormant for over forty years are suddenly treated like public enemies #1 of this nation. In a way, it's really unreal."

Steinbrenner, clearly, was trying to shine a soft blue light on his role in Watergate. He was trying to say that since no one had been harmed physically, no one had been beaten or robbed or shot or knifed, his crime was a minor one, hardly worth noting. He completely ignored the argument students of criminology had been making for years, that even white-collar crime, bloodless crime, Watergate and Abscam, for instance, breeds more crime, creates the atmosphere in which someone can say, "If those guys can knock off the government, why can't I knock off a candy store?" Steinbrenner didn't want to hear that argument. "I wanted to do things that I thought were needed for the Great Lakes, for Cleveland, and I knew that if I had some pop, or whatever you want to call it, I could do the things that I knew had to be done for the people, and that's the truth," Steinbrenner told Tony Kornheiser, the writer who formulated "The Blue Spotlight Theory." In the case of Watergate, Kornheiser suggested, George "doesn't have enough amps."

If Steinbrenner expected the hundred-thousand-dollar contribution to alter dramatically Amship's relations with the Nixon administration, he was soon disillusioned. Only six days after the money went to Kalmbach, the Justice Department requested details of Amship's seven-million-dollar purchase of the Great Lakes Towing Company, raising the specter of antitrust action. Within a month, the Labor Department, as a result of its investigation into the *Roger Blough* fire, fined Amship ten thousand dollars for violating federal safety laws, and Maurice Stans' successor,

Secretary of Commerce Peter Peterson, not only reaffirmed that the cost overruns on the OSS *Researcher* were disallowed, but also announced that Amship had to pay the government two hundred eight thousand dollars for late delivery and another twenty-two thousand dollars in lesser penalties.

Bruised, but still bold, Steinbrenner communicated to Maurice Stans his desire to acquire for his brother-in-law, Jacob Kamm, an ambassadorship, preferably to Denmark, or a seat on the President's Council of Economic Advisers. Kamm, who had taught economics at Case Western Reserve and had served as president of American Ship, was not unqualified. But not surprisingly, considering the difficulties Steinbrenner was having with the Departments of Commerce, Labor and Justice, Jacob Kamm did not become an ambassador or a presidential adviser. Steinbrenner must have been wondering why he had allowed himself to be pressured into contributing to CREEP. If he needed further proof that his hundred thousand dollars had not gained him favored treatment, in August of 1972, the day after Amship purchased the Wilson Marine Transit Company and the Erie (Pennsylvania) shipyard from Litton Industries, the Justice Department obtained a temporary restraining order halting the sale. After a month of delicate negotiations, the sale was sanctioned, but Amship was forced to divest itself of three of nine newly acquired boats and to scrap two others.

A few weeks later, reporters for the Cleveland *Plain Dealer,* with no idea that Steinbrenner had orchestrated illegal campaign contributions, began examining his antitrust problems with the Justice Department. Steinbrenner told the reporters of "Gestapo tactics," and insisted that the settlement, forcing Amship to surrender boats, was unjust. Queried about his politics, he conceded he leaned toward Nixon in the presidential race, but mentioned that he had

rejected an offer to lead an Ohio branch of Democrats for Nixon. During the interview, Steinbrenner was noticeably uneasy, and occasionally angry, and when the *Plain Dealer* ran a front-page story, just before Election Day, detailing the antitrust settlement and Steinbrenner's reaction, he complained to the newspaper's executive editor. "Word was sent to reporters from the newspaper's front office," *Cleveland* magazine noted. "There was to be no further investigation into Steinbrenner's affairs and two related stories on the deal were killed."

But another study of Steinbrenner's affairs had begun, conducted by James Polk of the Washington *Star-News,* who specialized in investigative political reporting. "Sometime in the fall of '72," Polk recalled almost a decade later, "I heard that Steinbrenner had told some people in Washington that he had been a victim of extortion on his cost overrun claim, that Herb Kalmbach shook him down for a contribution and then the Nixon people double-crossed him."

Polk did not know if the story was true. Steinbrenner may have been spreading it simply to justify to his Democratic friends his contributions to the Nixon campaign. Or he may just have been angry because his overrun claim had been rejected. Still, the story intrigued Polk, and he flew to Cleveland to see Steinbrenner. "We sat in a conference room at his company headquarters," Polk said, "and George gave me a song and dance." Steinbrenner admitted he had met with Kalmbach, but said they had talked mostly about football, about the Rose Bowl, to be exact, and when Kalmbach had brought up the subject of a contribution to the Nixon campaign, he had turned Kalmbach down. No pressure, no threats, no extortion, Steinbrenner said, and not a penny in tribute. Polk didn't believe Steinbrenner's denial, but he couldn't disprove it. He went back to Washington and did not write a story.

Instead, Polk turned his attention to the milk-fund scandal. The Nixon administration had granted an increase in the government price support for milk; the milk producers, in turn, or perhaps independently, made sizable contributions to the Nixon campaign fund. One day, investigating the milk story, Polk was looking through microfilm records of contributions to the Nixon campaign, and two checks caught his eye. Each was for thirty-five hundred dollars; Polk had rarely seen contributions of more than three thousand dollars, the old disclosure limit. Polk looked at the checks and noticed that one was made out to Supporters of Good Government, the other to Active Volunteers for Improved Government, typical CREEP fronts. He also noticed that both checks came from banks in the Cleveland area, one from the account of Roy Walker, the other from the account of Daniel Kissel. Polk decided to take a look at a Dun & Bradstreet list of the officers of American Ship Building. The treasurer of the marine transport division was Daniel Kissel. Polk soon determined that Roy Walker, too, worked for Amship.

On January 4, 1973, the day after Steinbrenner and his associates bought the New York Yankees, Jim Polk flew to Cleveland and, using the home addresses imprinted on the checks, called on Roy Walker and Daniel Kissel. Walker, recruited by Steinbrenner, had played fullback for Purdue a decade earlier, then had been drafted by the Baltimore Colts, but had failed to make the team. Steinbrenner had brought him to Amship to supervise security. His home, Polk said, looked "moderately well off." Questioned by Polk, Walker insisted that his $3,500 contribution was personal. He said he had asked Robert Bartlome, the Amship secretary, to pass the check on to Washington, but the money was his own. He was adamant.

Polk went next to Kissel's home. "As soon as he opened the door," Polk said, "I was convinced his contribution was

a corporate one. A man with a dinette in his home instead of a dining room simply can't afford to throw thirty-five hundred dollars into a political campaign."

Polk asked Kissel how he could afford the contribution. "I won't answer," Kissel said. Was it a company bonus? "I can't answer that. I won't answer." Polk rephrased the question, and Kissel said, "I don't want to comment."

As certain as Polk was that Kissel's contribution came from the corporation, he couldn't prove it. The next day, he called a real-estate agent and found out what the homes were worth in Kissel's neighborhood; the house across the street had sold the previous year for twenty-two thousand dollars, strengthening Polk's conviction that Kissel could not afford a thirty-five-hundred-dollar contribution. Polk also went to the Amship office in Lorain and talked to Robert Bartlome, who conceded he had forwarded Walker's check, and a few others, but insisted that all the contributions were personal.

Again, Polk did not write anything about Steinbrenner or Amship. He was diverted by the dealings of Robert Vesco, the financier. Late in the winter, while he was covering the Vesco hearings in New York, Polk made an appointment to see Steinbrenner again, at "21." Polk let Steinbrenner know he was convinced the company had made illegal campaign contributions. Steinbrenner flatly denied any corporate involvement, then told Polk that he had more important things to worry about, that his son was going into Massachusetts General Hospital for major surgery. Steinbrenner implied that an unfavorable story might set back his son. "I kept checking Mass General patient information for a month," Polk said, "and no Steinbrenner ever showed up there."

The conversation at "21" turned to baseball, and Polk told Steinbrenner what a fan he was, how he used to ride the bus a hundred miles to watch the Yankees play the

Browns in St. Louis, how as a youngster he saw Satchel Paige pitch five and a third perfect innings against the Yankees, how he was sitting deep in the left-field stands the day Bill Veeck hired a pinch-hitter named Eddie Gaedel, who came to bat only once, the first midget to play in the major leagues. "We talked about that," Polk remembered, "and then George magnanimously said, 'Why don't you bring your boy down to spring training with the Yankees?' And then I knew he was guilty because I didn't think George considered me that much of a newly found good friend. I did it, on a weekend, making sure everything was at my personal expense—still, the opportunity was the closest thing to a bribe I've ever taken—and from that moment on, I was committed to making damn sure we did a story on George Steinbrenner."

Polk, not yet ready to write, kept gathering more material. A citizens' group called Common Cause was demanding that a secret list of two thousand contributors to the Committee to Re-Elect the President be made public. Common Cause was almost thwarted; every copy of the list had been destroyed, except one. Rose Mary Woods, the President's secretary, the woman who had accidentally erased more than eighteen minutes of a controversial White House tape, had kept a copy of the list. The copy became known as Rose Mary's baby, and the list became known to the public, and George Steinbrenner's name was on it.

Then Polk sat down with Herb Kalmbach, and Kalmbach recounted the story of his meeting with Steinbrenner. He did not remember any mention of cost overruns. He did remember Steinbrenner pledging one hundred thousand dollars. The pieces of the puzzle were falling into place, and then Polk saw a story in *The New York Times* saying that Tom McBride of the Watergate special prosecutor's office was going to be investigating company contributions. The

story mentioned "cost overruns," a veiled reference to Amship, Polk figured. He assumed the special prosecutor's office had found out about Steinbrenner. Polk went to McBride, the assistant special prosecutor, and began asking questions. McBride didn't have the answers. In fact, the special prosecutor's office had no information about Amship's illegal contributions. But Polk's inquiries aroused McBride's curiosity, and moved the assistant special prosecutor to start looking into political contributions made by employees of the American Ship Building Company.

Polk decided to take one more crack at Steinbrenner. He flew to Cleveland and met Steinbrenner for lunch, armed with Rose Mary's baby and with Kalmbach's cooperation. "George acknowledged a hundred-thousand-dollar contribution this time," Polk said, "insisted it was personal money and offered me a job down the line in the Yankees' front office because he could use a good man like me. Maybe if he had offered me first base, I would have seriously considered it, but he didn't. He told me some more woes about family illness—his wife this time, rather than his son—and said how much a story would hurt her."

But then, in the summer of 1973, while Polk concentrated on the latest Spiro Agnew revelation, the special prosecutor's office had the Federal Bureau of Investigation exploring Amship's financial relations with CREEP. And at Amship, a cover-up was well under way. A few fortunate Amship employees actually benefited from the company's precarious position. They received legitimate bonuses, with no strings attached, to help camouflage the false bonuses that had been converted into political contributions. One day Bartlome showed Steinbrenner the records he had kept of each of the "political" bonuses—the amounts, the dates, the recipients—and Steinbrenner immediately summoned Lepkowski to his office and asked the

131

treasurer to bring all the records pertaining to the false bonus payments. Bartlome later testified in front of the Senate Watergate Committee that Lepkowski told him that Steinbrenner then destroyed all the dangerous documents. Bartlome also testified that he was instructed to replace those records with a counterfeit memorandum backdated to April 5, 1972, stating that the company's board of directors had, in November 1971, approved bonuses for those loyal employees who, coincidentally, later made contributions to the Nixon campaign. And if that wasn't enough, John Melcher, corporate counsel to Amship, prepared statements for each of the loyal employees to sign, statements testifying, falsely, that the company had not encouraged or advised them to turn their bonuses into political contributions. Those statements, too, were backdated, to December 30, 1972.

When the FBI came to Ohio to question Amship employees who had made sizable political contributions, Matthew Clark, the director of purchasing, got very specific advice from attorney Melcher. "He told me that I would be questioned by the FBI," Clark told the Senate Watergate Committee, "and to tell them that my wife and I had decided on our own to donate the money to re-elect the President. I mentioned to Mr. Melcher that I did not want to involve my wife and would not. But I would say that *I* had decided to do this." Bartlome said he got similar advice from Steinbrenner himself, who, according to Bartlome's later testimony, created his own version of how the contributions happened to be made. "The group in Lorain [the political contributors] had met, had determined that they wanted to make contributions to the Committee to Re-elect the President [and] had approached Mr. Steinbrenner, asking him the best manner in which we could make a contribution," said Bartlome, recalling Steinbrenner's synopsis of the situation. "We were told that if it was a small

contribution to do it locally, and if it was a large contribution he would furnish us the names of committees and that the money would be delivered in Washington." For a man who had written a thesis on Thomas Hardy, the plot was neither very imaginative nor very convincing.

Matthew Clark recalled that Melcher "mentioned that we should say that we gave the donations because of President Nixon's involvement in the shipping industry . . . he had helped the shipping industry."

Bartlome and Clark, "were under extreme pressure by the prosecutors," Steinbrenner said five years later, suggesting that their recollections might not have been totally accurate. "I never asked them to lie," Steinbrenner has always maintained, even though his loyal employees had testified that he did.

They also testified that, in 1973, Steinbrenner had directed other executives to submit fictional expense accounts, which would be reimbursed in cash. Steinbrenner expected them to place that cash in a fund for political gifts. One such gift went to Senator Daniel Inouye, a Democrat from Hawaii who was serving, along with Steinbrenner's Culver classmate, Senator Lowell Weicker, on the Senate Watergate Committee. Senator Inouye, embarrassed when he learned of the $5,650 gift, ordered it returned.

While Steinbrenner was, at the very least, condoning the cover-up efforts, he apparently still felt his own position was safe. He said later that his lawyers, Evans and Melcher, advised him that, in the first place, he probably hadn't violated the law, and in the second, if he had, he certainly wasn't going to get into any serious trouble. Their advice proved disastrous.

In the summer of 1973, when American Airlines voluntarily disclosed its illegal corporate contributions, which had been funneled rather exotically through an agent in

Lebanon, Archibald Cox, the special prosecutor, urged other companies to do the same. By the fall, six other major companies—Ashland Oil, Braniff Airways, Goodyear Tire and Rubber, Gulf Oil, Minnesota Mining and Manufacturing and Phillips Petroleum—had admitted making illegal contributions. (Coincidentally, Phillips and Goodyear had been among Steinbrenner's basketball rivals when he bought the Cleveland Pipers, which was his last large error before Watergate.) Not one of the executives from the companies that had confessed was even indicted on a felony charge, much less convicted of one. Steinbrenner, too, could have gotten off with nothing worse than a misdemeanor conviction if he had stepped forward in mid-1973 and admitted his company's complicity.

But Evans and Melcher, according to Steinbrenner, counseled him to admit nothing. In fact, Evans went so far as to tell him not to worry about the Watergate special prosecutor. "He said the President didn't like Archibald Cox at all," Steinbrenner stated in federal court. Melcher, Steinbrenner added, claimed to be connected to a "mystery man" in Washington who was going to fix everything. "There's nothing to worry about," Steinbrenner claimed Melcher said. Melcher later maintained that he never alluded to a "mystery man" or to influential connections in Washington. Eventually, Melcher pleaded guilty to helping cover up Amship's illegal contributions and was fined twenty-five hundred dollars. He also resigned from the bar because of what he called "this mess."

On Labor Day, 1973, in a motel near the Cleveland airport, Steinbrenner sat down with a group of his attorneys and advisers, including Timothy McMahon, a member of the same Cleveland law firm as Melcher, and Charles Cusick, a former FBI agent who had become an Amship executive. McMahon looked at some of the FBI reports on the investigation into Amship and, according to Steinbren-

ner's court testimony, threw the papers across the desk and said, "That's it. That's the ball game. You'd better get down to Washington quick. You've got a problem." Cusick apparently agreed. "I remember looking over at Cusick, who had his head in his hands and was obviously disgusted," Steinbrenner said. Again, Steinbrenner was ready to go to Archibald Cox, to admit his involvement, and again, according to his own recollection, he was dissuaded.

The house of cards that had been built to shelter the Amship contributions was perilously close to collapse. The employees who had allowed themselves to be used as conduits for the political contributions and who had lied to FBI investigators had been summoned to appear before a grand jury in Washington, and now, either because they were very fearful or because they were very courageous, they were determined to tell the truth. They were not going to risk prosecution for perjury; instead, they would risk their employer's displeasure. Bartlome testified that when he told Steinbrenner he was not going to lie to the grand jury, "Mr. Steinbrenner was distraught." He put his head down on his desk, Bartlome reported, and said, "I'm ruined, the company's ruined," and threatened to leap off a bridge. Later, Steinbrenner disputed one part of that testimony; he said he never had any intention of jumping off a bridge and endangering the investments of his business associates.

On September 5, 1973, the link between Amship and Watergate finally became public. The eight Amship employees who had been subpoenaed to appear before the Watergate grand jury went into open federal court and asked for a delay. The next day, despite last-minute pleas from George Steinbrenner, Jim Polk's long-delayed story appeared in the Washington *Star-News:* "The Watergate grand jury is probing a secret $100,000 Nixon campaign donation made by officials of a Cleveland ship company

while the firm was trying—without success—to win payment of a $5 million cost overrun on a government contract."

Within the story, Polk gave Steinbrenner the opportunity to deny that any of his employees had been given corporate bonuses to be used as political contributions: "Never once have we said, 'Here's a bonus. Give it politically.'" And Steinbrenner also denied that there was any connection between the acknowledged hundred-thousand-dollar campaign contribution and the cost overruns on the OSS *Researcher:* "There was no thought in my mind connected to the *Researcher*—my God, may I be struck down if there was one."

The day Polk's story was published, several of the subpoenaed Amship employees met with Steinbrenner, and out of the meeting came one of the few genuinely funny moments of the entire episode. At one point, Matthew Clark later testified, Steinbrenner said to him, "Don't worry about it," and Clark replied, "I wish you'd stop using that phrase." Then Clark explained to Steinbrenner his objection. "Mr. Melcher told me not to worry about the FBI report," Clark said. "Mr. Melcher told me not to worry when I was subpoenaed. He told me not to worry because I did not have to answer a grand jury subpoena, and he told me not to worry about having to go down at all. All I can see is me standing behind bars, and Mr. Melcher telling me not to worry about it."

Even Steinbrenner laughed, and just then the phone rang. George answered it. John Melcher was calling. Steinbrenner cupped his hand over the mouthpiece and turned to Clark. "Matt, it's your friend," George said.

"Tell him not to worry about anything," said Clark.

Eventually, the eight Amship employees did go before the Watergate grand jury, and told the truth, and in November, Clark and Bartlome were questioned on na-

tional television by the Senate Watergate Committee, and again told the truth, and by then neither Melcher nor Evans, who had resigned from the Amship board of directors, could say anything to convince Steinbrenner he was not in deep trouble. George had already turned for help to an attorney with a national reputation for defending people in deep trouble, and for rescuing them, one of the country's most skilled criminal lawyers, Edward Bennett Williams. But Williams, as gifted as he was, could not perform miracles.

In the first three months of 1974, as a measure of the mood Watergate had created, the House of Representatives began impeachment proceedings against President Nixon, Herb Kalmbach pleaded guilty to running an illegal campaign committee and promising a potential contributor an ambassadorship for a hundred thousand dollars (Kalmbach was later sentenced to six to eight months in prison, plus a ten-thousand-dollar fine), and Ehrlichman, Haldeman and former Attorney General John Mitchell, among others, were indicted for their parts in the Watergate cover-up (each was convicted and sentenced to a minimum of two and a half years in prison). Steinbrenner, even if he was a relatively small target, had to be very nervous.

On April 5, 1974, the opening day of the baseball season, George M. Steinbrenner III was indicted by a grand jury in Cleveland acting on the basis of information provided by Thomas McBride and John Koete, aides to Leon Jaworski, Archibald Cox's successor as special prosecutor. Steinbrenner, the first corporate executive to be brought up on felony charges related to illegal political contributions, was indicted on five counts of violating campaign contribution laws, two counts of aiding and abetting false statements to the FBI, four counts of obstruction of justice, two counts of obstructing a criminal investigation and one count of conspiracy. If Steinbrenner were convicted on all fourteen

counts, he faced a maximum penalty of fifty-five years in prison and one hundred thousand dollars in fines.

Steinbrenner promptly announced he would plead innocent. He said also that Jaworski's office had offered him a deal, that if he had agreed to plead guilty to one felony charge of conspiring to violate election laws, he could have avoided the fourteen-count indictment and a possible trial. But, Steinbrenner insisted, he felt compelled to reject the offer. "There was no way I could plead guilty," he said, "on a charge involving willful conspiracy to violate [the election law] or willful conspiracy on any other charge . . . because I just am not guilty of any such violations.

"No one wants to go through the agony of a trial," he added, "but I feel strongly that I must stand and fight for what I believe is right. I am confident that I will be found innocent of the charges."

The next day, Steinbrenner's Yankees played their first game in Shea Stadium, against Cleveland. Mel Stottlemyre pitched a shutout, and more than twenty thousand fans showed up, but Steinbrenner himself did not attend. He could not enjoy the opener, or even the drama of a tight pennant race, a race so tight in its early days that the Yankees went from first place on May 11 to last place only ten days later. From then until late in August, the Yankees never rose above third place in a six-team division.

Steinbrenner's legal concerns had to take precedence over baseball, but both his team and its stadium were remodeled during the 1974 season, certainly with Steinbrenner's approval, if not his direction. The first major move came late in April, when Gabe Paul traded four pitchers to the Cleveland Indians—Steve Kline, Fred Beene, Tom Busky and Fritz Peterson, who found this swap less traumatic than his earlier one with Mike Kekich—for two pitchers, Dick Tidrow and Cecil Upshaw, and a young

first baseman, Chris Chambliss. The trade was ridiculed, at first, by Yankee fans, and cursed by Yankee players, but the move was, in fact, a brilliant one: Tidrow and especially Chambliss played major roles in bringing Steinbrenner his first pennant in 1976 and his first World Series championship in 1977. Paul, originally condemned for making the trade, was eventually praised, by fans and by Steinbrenner. "Gabe knows how to get talent, he knows where to get it," Steinbrenner said a few years later. "He'll fly to Timbuktu in the middle of the night if he thinks he can get a ballplayer who'll help us."

The Yankees' second-choice manager, Bill Virdon, also made a bold and controversial move that paid off in 1974. He took Bobby Murcer, the heir-apparent to DiMaggio and Mantle, only the third Yankee ever to earn a hundred thousand for a season, and moved him out of his hallowed turf, out of center field, and into right field, and replaced him in center with Elliott Maddox, an unusual athlete, an articulate college graduate, a black who was studying to convert to Judaism. Maddox had come to the Yankees only a few weeks before the season began, joining his fourth team in five years. He responded to Virdon's move by batting .303, coming in eighth in the balloting for Most Valuable Player in the American League and leading the Yankees back into first place in early September.

By then, George Steinbrenner was a felon. He had changed his mind, had decided not to go to trial, and on August 23, 1974, precisely two weeks after Richard Nixon surrendered the presidency, Steinbrenner pleaded guilty to one felony count of conspiracy to violate the campaign contribution laws and one felony count of aiding and abetting obstruction of an investigation. Appearing with Steinbrenner, in front of Federal Judge Leroy Contie, Edward Bennett Williams endeavored to make his client appear more victim than perpetrator. Steinbrenner, Wil-

liams said, had received "the most incompetent professional advice that it has been my experience to know of in my time at the bar . . . He was told by his counsel not to go in—although he wanted to come in and lay the facts before the special Watergate prosecutor—he was advised, counseled urgently not to do it."

Addressing the cover-up story Steinbrenner had invented for his loyal employees, Williams turned his own blue spotlight on the facts. "At a point when this investigation was launched, he did talk to his employees," Williams said, "and he did recount to them his recollection of the facts, and that recollection was not a full and adequate disclosure, and not in conformity with objective reality." *Not in conformity with objective reality*—an inspired phrase, an absolute masterpiece of euphemism.

"I think 'false' is an easier and more accurate way of describing it," suggested Tom McBride, the assistant special prosecutor. McBride said the whole scheme "can be laid solely and properly at the door of Mr. Steinbrenner." McBride jabbed, too, at Williams' contention that Steinbrenner was the misguided victim of bad legal advice. "The evidence makes clear, in my judgment," McBride said, "that Mr. Steinbrenner concealed the true facts surrounding these contributions from his counsel, and without commenting on the competence or incompetence of Mr. Melcher, I know no lawyer who can give proper advice if a full and adequate disclosure of the facts is not made to him by his client."

Steinbrenner could have been sentenced to up to six years in prison. Judge Contie, however, was reportedly deluged with letters and phone calls testifying to Steinbrenner's good character, to his civic and charitable commitments, to his financial and political achievements, and when he was sentenced, one week after his guilty plea, Steinbrenner was not given even a token jail term, and was

fined merely fifteen thousand dollars, hardly a slap on the wrist by his standards. Amship, for its corporate part in the conspiracy, was fined an additional twenty thousand dollars. "The only contributions I'm going to make from now on will be to United Appeal," Steinbrenner said as he left the courtroom, sufficiently relieved by the sentence to joke.

A year later, a special committee set up by the Securities and Exchange Commission recommended that Steinbrenner personally reimburse American Ship the $42,325.17 that had been spent on the false bonuses. Steinbrenner accepted the recommendation without complaint.

Steinbrenner, of course, was not delighted with the felony conviction, but he did not seem particularly bitter. Rather, he acted almost as if he had played a game, and had lost to a better team. "All things considered, I can't be critical [toward the prosecutors] because what happened happened, and it was a tough situation," Steinbrenner wrote in the Cleveland *Press*. "They were fair and tough. I'm not sure I'll invite them to my next party, but thank God the country ha guys like that. As for my sentencing, I know that I faced one of the toughest judges on the federal bench. I guess the bench felt that the sum of the good things I have done in my life exceeded the mistakes, willful or non-willful, made in this matter." Steinbrenner sounded very much like the good loser, congratulating the winners, which could not have been easy for him, considering his attitude toward defeat. He might have been expected to react harshly toward those employees who had finally told the truth to the grand jury and to the Senate Watergate Committee, but he did not. Robert Bartlome, the most visible and probably the most damaging witness against him, certainly did not suffer. By 1980, Bartlome was a vice-president of American Ship Building.

There were two things about his conviction that seemed to gnaw at Steinbrenner. The first was that the conviction

linked him to the Nixon presidency, while he would much rather have been associated with Ted Kennedy or with Tip O'Neill, his friends. The second was that the felony conviction made him ineligible to run for President, an unlikely idea, or even to vote for a President. Being disenfranchised had to be painful to a man who placed so much stock in the American system, a man who enjoyed thinking of himself as a true patriot. Not surprisingly, on December 28, 1978, so quietly that the event was not noted in newspapers or in magazines, on radio or on television, George Steinbrenner applied for a presidential pardon. The office of the pardon attorney in the Department of Justice eventually passed the application on to President Carter—with its recommendation that the pardon be granted or denied. Two years and two weeks later, Steinbrenner got his answer. On January 15, 1981, Jimmy Carter, caught up in a furious attempt to win the release of the American hostages in Iran before the end of his presidential term, denied Steinbrenner's application. Once again, the action went unreported. Steinbrenner was free to apply again for a presidential pardon—but not before January 15, 1983.

The day Steinbrenner was sentenced, August 30, 1974, the Yankees started a four-game winning streak that lifted them into first place. On September 6, the commissioner of baseball, Bowie Kuhn, asked Steinbrenner not to contact any of his baseball employees for a period of one month, pending the outcome of an investigation into his felony conviction. The owner acceded, and for the next three weeks, as the Yankees battled Boston and Baltimore for first place, he kept his word. When the Yankees won a doubleheader in Cleveland on September 28, to stay within half a game of first-place Baltimore with only three games to play, Steinbrenner carefully waited outside the Yankee locker room after the game. "I can't go in," he said. "I just want to be near the players." He did invite all the members

of the Yankees' entourage, players, coaches, even sports-writers, to have a postgame dinner at his expense at Mushy Wexler's Theatrical Grill.

Three days later, when the Yankees lost in Milwaukee and were eliminated from the pennant race, Steinbrenner ignored the commissioner's request and entered the locker room. "I don't care what they do to me," he said. "I want to be with these guys."

Three weeks later, Gabe Paul announced one of the most spectacular trades in Yankee history, sending Bobby Murcer, the successor to DiMaggio and Mantle, a member of the All-Star team for four straight years, to San Francisco, for Bobby Bonds, another twenty-eight-year-old outfielder with enormous skill. In 1973, in fact, Bobby Bonds had almost become the first major-league baseball player to hit forty home runs and steal forty bases in one season. He stole forty-three bases, but fell one home run short of forty. With his rare blend of speed and power, Bonds had the potential to become baseball's dominant player.

But before Steinbrenner could fully appreciate the acquisition, Commissioner Kuhn did something for which he was not known: He made a decision. On November 27, 1974, he suspended George Steinbrenner from baseball. "Attempting to influence employees to behave dishonestly is the kind of misconduct which, if ignored by baseball, would undermine the public's confidence in our game," Kuhn said. Since George Steinbrenner had pleaded guilty to attempting to influence employees to behave dishonestly, "I have decided to place Mr. Steinbrenner on the ineligible list for a period of two years. In accordance, he is declared ineligible and incompetent to manage or advise in the management of the affairs of the New York Yankees."

Sports Illustrated applauded Kuhn's "finest hour"— "THE COMMISSIONER HOMERS," read the headline—

while Steinbrenner's immediate reaction was sarcasm. "It is certainly a wonderful Thanksgiving present," he said. Then he added, "It's impossible to understand how the commissioner of baseball could call *me* incompetent." But after brief thoughts of a lawsuit, Steinbrenner quickly assumed one of his favorite roles, the good soldier, accepting the orders of his commanding officer, even if he did not completely agree with them. "Let me be perfectly frank," Steinbrenner wrote. "I don't agree with the commissioner's decision. I felt it was too harsh in view of the facts, the federal bench's decision, and in view of action or lack of action he took in other cases which I considered far more injurious to baseball. I feel that Bowie believed that what he was doing he had to do, and I respect him for that. I probably think more of him as a commissioner than he does of me as an owner. There will not be any lawsuit. The only thing that really matters is that the Yankees win a pennant and hopefully a World Series for the people of New York. To involve myself, the Yankees and baseball in a lawsuit would detract from that goal."

That goal appeared much closer a month after Steinbrenner was suspended. The Yankees lost an owner, temporarily, but they gained a star. The star's name was James Augustus Hunter, and his nickname was "Catfish," or, among teammates, "Cat."

Catfish Hunter pitched for the Oakland A's in the first half of the 1970s, and in those five years he won 106 games and lost only 49 during the regular seasons. He also won four out of four World Series games while the A's were winning three straight world championships. In 1974, at the age of twenty-eight, prime time for a pitcher, he won the Cy Young Award as the Americn League's best pitcher; he had the best earned run average in the league (2.49), the most victories (twenty-five) and the most fortuitous contract. The contract provided Hunter with a

hundred thousand dollars for the year, fifty thousand dollars in straight salary and fifty thousand dollars to be paid on a deferred basis, through an insurance company. The owner of the Oakland A's, Charles O. Finley, was obligated to pay the fifty thousand dollars to the insurance company by a specific date; in 1974, Finley carelessly missed the deadline. Hunter promptly filed a grievance, claiming that, because Finley had breached the contract, he should be declared a free agent, free to negotiate a new contract with any team. Peter Seitz, the arbitrator in the case, ruled in Hunter's favor, making him, suddenly, the most coveted and available human being in baseball history.

Twenty-three of the twenty-four major-league teams indicated an interest in signing Hunter—all except the San Francisco Giants; San Franciscans, by nature, try to ignore people who spend any appreciable amount of time in Oakland. Commissioner Kuhn ruled that the bidding could begin on December 18, 1974. The auction was conducted by the law firm of Cherry, Cherry and Flythe in Ahoskie, North Carolina, a very small town some sixty miles from Hunter's home in Hertford, North Carolina, an even smaller town. At the time, the highest-paid player in baseball was earning $250,000 a year, but it quickly became apparent that Hunter would shatter the record. Eleven teams chased Hunter only by telephone; twelve sent representatives to North Carolina. The Yankees dispatched their president Gabe Paul, and a scout named Clyde Kluttz, who knew the target well. Ten years earlier, Kluttz had signed Hunter for the A's. But on December 30, despite the relationship, Hunter and his attorneys informed Paul and Kluttz that they had decided to reject the Yankees' handsome offer. Paul retreated to New York, but he left Kluttz behind, with instructions to change Hunter's mind.

Somehow, in the next day and a half, Kluttz succeeded, and on Tuesday afternoon, December 31, 1974, Hunter and his attorneys agreed to a Yankee contract that promised the pitcher, for five years of work, a total of $3.35 million—$100,000 a year in salary for five years, $50,000 a year in deferred salary for five years, $100,000 as a signing bonus, $100,000 a year for fifteen years (from 1980 through 1994) as a deferred bonus, $750,000 in life insurance, $25,000 in life insurance for each of his two children and $200,000 in lawyers' fees—all of which had to be promised, according to Commissioner Kuhn's ruling a month earlier, without George Steinbrenner's advice or consent. "Gabe knew what the philosophy was," Steinbrenner said later. "That decision was made without checking with me. The only checking was with our bank."

If you believe that Steinbrenner had nothing to do with the decision to promise Catfish Hunter $3.35 million, to be paid over the next twenty years, then you will also believe his explanation for the fact that late Tuesday afternoon, December 31, 1974, his own private jet, a five-hundred-thousand-dollar Jet Commander bearing the registration number N101GS, carrying Edward Greenwald, a partner in the Yankees and a tax attorney, flew from Cleveland, Ohio, to Suffolk, Virginia (not far from the North Carolina border), picked up Catfish Hunter, Clyde Kluttz and a lawyer from Ahoskie named J. Carlton Cherry and transported them all to LaGuardia Airport, not five minutes away from the Yankees' temporary offices, site of a New Year's Eve party celebrating the arrival of the new Yankee. According to Steinbrenner, the reason N101GS—the plane's registration number had been N101TH until GS purchased it—was used for the occasion was that it was the only plane the Yankees were able to charter in the whole country. "Gabe called me," Steinbrenner explained, innocently, "to see if my plane was available. I told him to call

146

Kinsman Aeronautical, to keep me out of it."

Paul, of course, corroborated the story. "George didn't give us his plane," he said. "It cost us twenty-eight thousand dollars. We tried to get another plane."

When the Yankees' annual Press-Radio-TV Guide was published on February 14, 1975, the Valentine's Day brochure featured Catfish Hunter and Bobby Bonds on the front cover. On the inside cover, with no mention of any suspension, George Steinbrenner was listed as the sole general partner. The group of limited partners had grown to fifteen; four of the originals were gone, having sold out to Steinbrenner, but there were five new ones, including a woman, Charlotte Witkind, and a former baseball star, Al Rosen, plus a consulting partner and a legal counsel. The legal counsel was Patrick J. Cunningham, to whom Steinbrenner nominally delegated his suspended authority. Cunningham, a charming politician, was New York State's Democratic chairman, a position of influence that did not save him, several years later, from being indicted on federal charges of income-tax evasion.

At about the same time the Yankees were publishing their guide to the team, the Cleveland *Press* was publishing its guide to George Steinbrenner, a four-part series detailing George's political, financial and legal problems. Steinbrenner fought the series in almost every conceivable way. He did grant an interview that lasted eight hours, but he set the condition that he not be quoted directly, and he bathed himself in so many soft blue lights that Roy Meyers, one of the coauthors of the series, said, "I came out with the feeling that the guy was a saint." Meyers got over that feeling when Steinbrenner began putting pressure on the reporters, and on their superiors. "It wasn't so much he wanted the series killed," Bill Tanner, then the city editor of the *Press,* later recalled. "He wanted it slanted. He was disturbed that it wasn't a puff job. I can't remember exactly

why, but I think before we ran it we turned it over to him to see if we had any serious errors. If we had something wrong, we wanted to know about it. We weren't going to let him edit it. He said, 'Would you delay it?' We said, 'Why?' And he said, 'Because my wife is ill. She's in the hospital.' We were a little concerned, but we decided to go ahead and use it. She'd read worse about him."

The series appeared, considerably watered down. By 1981, Roy Meyers was working as press secretary to Ohio Senator Howard Metzenbaum, but Meyers still sounded frustrated when he spoke of the way his series had been emasculated. "You know," Meyers said, "right after he mentioned the thing about his wife being ill, I talked to Jim Polk in Washington, and Polk said to me, 'He lay the Tiny Tim story on you yet?'"

The day the first part of the series ran in the *Press,* Tanner got a phone call from Steinbrenner. "He wanted me to make some small change," said Tanner, after he had left Cleveland to become editor of the Albuquerque *Tribune.* "I thought, 'Why is he calling me? The owner of the Yankees, the Chicago Bulls, has shows on Broadway, owns a big shipping company, why is he calling the city editor of some pissy-ant local paper and whining?' Which is what he was doing. He was whining."

Herb Kamm, associate editor of the *Press* in 1975 and later the editor, said in 1981 he had only a vague memory of what happened with the series. "I think I took the initiative in giving George a chance to respond," Kamm said. "I knew him very well. I still get invited to the World Series."

The day after the four-part series ended, the *Press,* in a most unusual journalistic gesture, permitted Steinbrenner to frame both the questions and the answers for a front-page Q-&-A response to the series. In other words, Steinbrenner interviewed himself for his views on his

148

conviction, his suspension from baseball and his shipping business. He included the news that he was moving to Florida. "You have decided to leave Cleveland," he stated. "What are your thoughts about Cleveland, a city in which you were so heavily involved and committed?"

Steinbrenner answered almost belligerently, as if he were replying to an objective reporter: "Look, Cleveland has been my home, and we'll continue to have a residence here. You can't begrudge me a little sunshine now and then during the winter." Then he took a few shots at his hometown critics. "Cleveland is only going to be as great as its leadership," he said. "Cleveland can't have the attitude that every time someone does something, he's got an angle. And the newspapers, at the risk of getting you mad at me a little, I'd say that is where the leadership must start . . . They've got to lead by building, not tearing down."

Steinbrenner was at least hinting at the real reason he was fleeing Cleveland for Tampa. He had confided to friends that he was tired of being abused, distrusted and misunderstood, tired of not being appreciated. He wanted to protect his children from a curious press, and he wanted to protect his wife, too, even though the media in Cleveland had always treated Joan Steinbrenner most tenderly. In one interview, describing life with Cleveland's most famous entrepreneur, Joan Steinbrenner revealed nothing more dramatic than the fact that George was a fanatic about neatness in the home. "We might vacuum two or three times a day," Joan said. George, of course, had faced slightly more probing questions. If the Cleveland papers wanted to snipe at him, he would cancel his subscription, just as he had done in the days of the Pipers, and he would start getting the Tampa *Tribune* instead. The *Press* and the *Plain Dealer* weren't going to have George Steinbrenner to kick around anymore.

Steinbrenner was, coincidentally, one of three very

prominent Clevelanders to abandon the Great Lakes city in the first half of the 1970s. The others were Carl Stokes, the former mayor, and Don King, a former executive in the "numbers" game, and a convicted felon himself, on a charge of manslaughter. (One of King's runners had once made the mistake of trying to swindle him.) Both Stokes and King, like Steinbrenner, decided to test their talents in New York. Stokes, who had a sensational smile and a gift for glibness, went into television, as a newsman, and King, who had unlimited gall and a dazzling arsenal of multisyllabic malaprops, into boxing, as a promoter. Stokes, for all his charm and intelligence, never quite conquered New York and eventually returned to Cleveland to resume an interrupted law practice. King, however, succeeded as spectacularly as Steinbrenner. He promoted fights for Ali, and for Larry Holmes, and for Roberto Duran, and he became, with his tower of hair and his constant cigar, the quintessential showman, rarely caught in an unvarnished truth. Stokes, King and Steinbrenner were living proof of Cleveland's strength as a training ground.

In 1975, despite Steinbrenner's suspension, Yankee fans had every reason to expect a great season. After all, the 1974 team had come closer to a pennant than any Yankee team in a decade, and the addition of Hunter and Bonds had strengthened the lineup considerably. The Yankees were supposed to win in 1975, but the Boston Red Sox moved into first place in June and stayed there the rest of the season. After the All-Star break in mid-July, the Yankees were never even a threat to Tip O'Neill's favorite team.

Steinbrenner, as commanded, stayed away from his team, most of the time. Once in a while, he couldn't resist sending a tape recording to the clubhouse, a football-style pep talk, intended to inspire the players, who were, more often, merely amused. He must have communicated with

Gabe Paul occasionally, and with Pat Cunningham, but to the lesser executives in the Yankee office, he was invisible. In fact, when the team's young publicity director, Marty Appel, underwent surgery, and the owner of the Yankees called to see how he was feeling, Appel did not recognize Steinbrenner's voice. "It was the only time I spoke to him during his suspension," said Appel, who had been given his job by Steinbrenner late in 1974.

During Steinbrenner's suspension, the Yankees made three monumental moves. The first was the signing of Hunter, an event that altered the salary expectations of all baseball players. The other two occurred on August 2, 1975. With the Yankees out of the pennant race, manager Bill Virdon was fired, and a fiery former Yankee named Billy Martin was hired to replace him. Steinbrenner, of course, had nothing to do with either decision.

4

Neither Billy Martin nor Reggie Jackson was a virgin when he met George Steinbrenner. Each had lived at the heart of controversy, and each had thrived under extreme pressure. Martin began as a fiercely competitive and inventive ballplayer, a journeyman during the regular season who turned into a giant during the World Series. Drummed out of the New York Yankees when his twenty-ninth birthday party at the Copacabana nightclub erupted into a brawl and headlines, he later became a big-league manager, for Detroit, Minnesota and Texas, building a winning team in each city, then getting himself fired, never lasting as many as three full seasons in one job, cultivating a reputation as a man with a lightning base-ball mind and a matching temper, a temper that drove him to arguments with employers and to fistfights with almost anyone. Managing Minnesota, he even punched one of his own players; managing Texas, he swung at his team's traveling secretary, a sixty-year-old ex-sportswriter.

153

Jackson, who was much quicker with words than punches, spent his first eight major-league seasons on the Oakland A's, performing brilliantly while feuding bitterly with his employer, Charles O. Finley, baseball's most notorious owner until George Steinbrenner came along. Jackson grew famous for long home runs and longer speeches, so articulate and so egotistical that one Oakland teammate, a pitcher named Darold Knowles, once said, "There isn't enough mustard in all America to cover that hot dog." Jackson was the most outrageous player in baseball, Martin the most outrageous manager. It was probably inevitable that they would, in time, join forces with the most outrageous owner.

If a sociologist had set out to illustrate different levels of American society, he could not have chosen three more diverse case studies than Martin, Jackson and Steinbrenner. Martin was the tough kid off the streets of Berkeley, California, fighting his way up from lower-class welfare, lean and wiry, barbed wiry. Jackson was the educated son of a tailor, rising out of the growing black middle class, out of the suburbs of Philadelphia, muscular and majestic, the prototypical stud. And Steinbrenner, of course, was the upper-class heir, born wealthy of a father who was born wealthy, not idle rich, but ambitious rich, a moneyed manipulator. Yet as different as their backgrounds were, the scrappy Italo-American, the proud black-American and the imperious mid-American had much in common. All three of them were winners, Steinbrenner in commerce, the other two in baseball. In the early-to-mid-1950s, during the three years that Billy Martin was the New York Yankees' fulltime second baseman, the Yankees won three world championships; twenty years later, when Reggie Jackson was playing right field and batting cleanup for Oakland, the A's won three straight world championships. Each of the three men demanded the spotlight, and not one of them ever underestimated his own ability, his own

wisdom, his own virtue, his own contributions to victory. And each of the three was a man's man, committed to his own brand of *machismo*.

Perhaps the most significant trait the three men shared was an ability to inspire, among their friends and enemies, among their fans and critics, and especially among themselves, the extremes of emotion. The three of them formed a perfect triangle: Billy loved/hated and was loved/hated by George who loved/hated and was loved/hated by Reggie who loved/hated and was loved/hated by Billy. Or, as one Yankee employee who loved/hated all three once said, "The three of them deserve each other," a variation on a line that would, eventually, get Billy Martin into great trouble.

The presence of Martin or Jackson or both virtually guaranteed the Yankees, from the middle of 1975 through the end of 1981, the kind of atmosphere Steinbrenner needs the way other people need air: constant turmoil. "George lives in a world of turmoil," Gabe Paul once said. "He couldn't survive in any other." As long as either Martin or Jackson was around, there would be no peace among the Yankees, which suited Steinbrenner, who, like his hero Patton, was wasted in peacetime, but flourished in war. There were perhaps a dozen Yankees who, at one time or another between 1975 and 1981, upstaged their teammates—Catfish Hunter, Thurman Munson, Graig Nettles, Sparky Lyle, Chris Chambliss, Ron Guidry, Lou Piniella, Mickey Rivers, Willie Randolph, Bucky Dent, Goose Gossage and Dave Winfield each had his moment or moments—but in the end they were all supporting players, all spearcarriers for the superstar player, the superstar manager and the superstar owner.

Martin, of course, joined Steinbrenner a year and a half before Jackson, in the summer of 1975, when the dictates of federal law plus the dictates of Bowie Kuhn were still combining to keep Steinbrenner "ineligible and incompetent to manage or advise in the management of the affairs

of the New York Yankees." Eligible or not, Steinbrenner decided, a week after Martin was fired by the Texas Rangers, to send Gabe Paul to Denver to persuade the tempestuous former Yankee infielder to take the job that had once been held by Casey Stengel. Martin looked upon Stengel almost as a surrogate father; he had played for Casey in the minor leagues and in New York. "Your temperaments aren't compatible," Gabe Paul warned Steinbrenner the first time the owner mentioned Martin as a managerial possibility, but Steinbrenner dismissed the warning. He wanted Martin because Martin was a personality. Martin was box office, and the incumbent manager, Bill Virdon, a decent human being, was bland. Steinbrenner weighed Virdon's decency against his blandness, and elected to go for Martin.

According to *Number 1*, Martin's autobiography—the gist of the book was that not since Joan of Arc had a saint been so misunderstood—Martin declined the Yankee job the first two times Gabe Paul offered it to him. Then, according to Martin, Paul said, "Billy, don't be so hasty. Why don't you talk to George?"

At which point Paul called the defrocked owner and put Martin on the phone. "Billy, I would like to have you as our manager," Steinbrenner supposedly said.

"I'd like to be the manager of the Yankees," Martin supposedly said, continuing the snappy dialogue.

Then, Martin recalled, he told Steinbrenner that he didn't like the offer. He didn't object to the money— seventy-two thousand dollars a year, precisely what he had been earning in Texas—but he did object to the small print. He was offended by the clause that said he was to conduct himself at all times "so as to represent the best interests of the New York Yankees," the clause that said he could not criticize the Yankee management, the clause that said he had to make himself available to consult with the Yankee management and, most of all, the clause that said that if

he didn't adhere to the other clauses, he could be fired without compensation.

"If you don't take the offer now," Steinbrenner supposedly said, "you will never get it again. C'mon, Billy, be the manager."

Martin responded to the threat just as Steinbrenner had hoped. After a day of reflection, he took the job, clauses and all, and on August 2, 1975, which was Old Timers' Day at Shea Stadium, after Mantle, Ford, DiMaggio and the lesser of the former Yankees had been introduced, Billy Martin was introduced as the team's new manager. If the Yankees had suddenly produced Jimmy Hoffa, who had vanished three days earlier, the crowd's reaction could not have been more enthusiastic. Martin always was a favorite of the fans in New York, the little people. The introduction was pure theater, book, music and lyrics by George Steinbrenner. Of course Bowie Kuhn had ordered Steinbrenner not to take such a direct hand in the workings of the Yankees, but Steinbrenner, in this instance, elected to ignore the ban, or at least, so Martin recalled in his autobiography.

Steinbrenner, incidentally, was not delighted by *Number 1*, which was published in 1980, when Martin was safely ensconced in a new job, managing the Oakland A's for Charles O. Finley. In fact, Steinbrenner found the book so disturbing he filed a brief in New York State Supreme Court asking the publisher to withhold the book because of potential legal action. The publisher declined to withhold the book, and Steinbrenner withdrew his objections after persuading Martin, and the publisher, to delete from the text four small sections that the Yankee owner felt reflected poorly upon his character and integrity. When the second printing of the book came out, those four sections had disappeared, leaving strange and unexplained blank lines on several pages. The references to Steinbrenner courting Martin on the phone, then orchestrating his introduction on Old Timers' Day, were neither deleted nor

altered, leaving the strong implication that the essence of Martin's account of those happenings must be accurate.

The first section of the Martin book that Steinbrenner found objectionable concerned a conversation that took place in December 1975 on Curaçao, a Dutch island in the Caribbean. Yogi Berra, Elston Howard, Ford, Mantle and Martin had come to Curaçao to conduct a baseball clinic, set up by Steinbrenner. "George had been trying to build a shipyard there or he was trying to get something else for his ships from the government," Martin wrote, "and I guess he figured the clinic would help him get it, and so he asked us all to do this for him, and we agreed."

Steinbrenner did not object to that portion of Martin's recitation. He objected, instead, to this dialogue about the forthcoming 1976 season:

Steinbrenner: "You know, we have a lot of holes."

Martin: "George, don't worry about it. We're going to win the pennant."

Steinbrenner: "You are like heck."

Martin: "What do you want to bet?"

Steinbrenner: "Tell you what. I own some tugboats. If you win the pennant, I'll give you a tugboat."

Martin: "A tugboat is worth about three hundred thousand dollars, right?"

Steinbrenner: "You win, you got it."

Martin then related that after the Yankees won the 1976 pennant, but lost the World Series, he reminded Steinbrenner about the promise of the tugboat, and Steinbrenner reneged, claiming, "I promised it to you if you won the World Series, not just the pennant."

"So far as I'm concerned," author Martin insisted, "George still owes me a tugboat."

The whole tugboat episode vanished from the second printing after a meeting between Steinbrenner and Martin's attorney, New Orleans Judge Eddie Sapir. "We had an excellent meeting," Sapir announced. "George was most

appreciative of my coming to see him on Billy's behalf. Perhaps I can help set the record straight . . . With respect to the so-called 'tugboat incident' in the book, George regarded it as a joke and [now] Billy does too."

Just as Steinbrenner, even at his revisionist best, did not deny that he had joined Martin and the other former Yankee heroes at the clinic in Curaçao, while he was still suspended from baseball, he never denied that he played a part in the three major trades Gabe Paul engineered in the fall of 1975. The Yankees, a distant third in the American League East when Martin became manager, were still a distant third when the season ended, and the lineup clearly needed improvement. The first trade sent Pat Dobson to Cleveland for outfielder Oscar Gamble; the second sent Bobby Bonds to California for outfielder Mickey Rivers and pitcher Ed Figueroa; and the third sent Doc Medich to Pittsburgh for two pitchers, Dock Ellis and Ken Brett, and a young second baseman, Willie Randolph. Each of the trades was, to a certain extent, risky. Bonds had enormous talent, Medich had enormous potential and Dobson had won more than one hundred games in the major leagues. Still, the trades turned out magnificently for the Yankees. They gave up one regular, Bonds, and two pitchers, Dobson and Medich, who between them had won twenty-seven games and lost thirty in 1975, and received in turn three regulars, Gamble and Rivers and Randolph, and two pitchers, Figueroa and Ellis, who between them won nine more games than Dobson and Medich had, and lost twelve fewer. The instigator of those trades had to be a genius. Martin confessed in his autobiography that it was his idea to get rid of Dobson, for questioning his authority; and Medich, for griping about his teammates; and Bonds, for refusing to play while hurting. Paul admitted that while he had hesitated to give up Bonds and Medich, he had anticipated great things from Figueroa, Ellis, Rivers, and, especially, Randolph. Steinbrenner, naturally, had the

final word, which was delivered after Paul quit the Yankees at the end of the 1977 season. "I don't mind Gabe leaving with his image intact," Steinbrenner said. "But he was in baseball for forty years, twenty-five as a general manager, and did he ever win a pennant before? You think he made all those moves with this team himself? You think all of a sudden he got brilliant?"

When an interviewer reminded Steinbrenner he had himself used the word "brilliant" to describe Paul, when Paul was still in his employ, the owner changed direction like a bear in a shooting gallery. "A brilliant baseball man, yes," Steinbrenner said. "But he was getting old. Look, let him have his image if he wants it. I won't say anything bad about Gabe. Maybe I was too hard on him. Maybe I hurt him. If I did, I'm sorry."

To another sportswriter, Steinbrenner said, in a less conciliatory mood, "Gabe hasn't got the guts to put a winner on the field. I made all those trades."

Not long after Steinbrenner made the Bonds and Medich trades, not long after Steinbrenner pulled the old tugboat joke on Martin, an impartial arbitrator made a decision that would have a tremendous impact on all baseball players, and a special impact on George Steinbrenner's Yankees. The arbitrator was Peter Seitz, the same man who had ruled a year earlier that Charles Finley had violated Catfish Hunter's contract. Two days before Christmas, 1975, Seitz handed down historic rulings in the cases of Andy Messersmith and Dave McNally, a pair of pitchers who were challenging baseball's traditional structure. Seitz supported their challenge. He ruled that the option clause in baseball contracts, the standard clause that gave a team an option to retain a player's services for one year after his contract expired, meant *for one year*, not for one year plus one year plus one year ad infinitum, the way the option clause had long been interpreted. Seitz said that a ballplayer could play out or even sit out his option year and

then become a free agent, free to offer his services on the open market to the highest bidder. The baseball owners challenged the arbitrator's decision in the courts, and lost, then asked for mercy on the grounds that a completely free market might enable the wealthiest of owners to buy up all the good talent and create a competitive imbalance that could destroy the game. The Major League Baseball Players Association, the ballplayers' union, not out of any legal obligation, but perhaps out of a sense of enlightened self-interest, developed with the owners a formula to determine which players would qualify to become free agents, so that the number of free agents would be limited.

A year after Seitz's decision, at the end of 1976, baseball's first crop of free agents would be put up for auction, each player going not necessarily to the highest bidder, but to the offer the player himself found most attractive. At that time, the Yankees, thanks to George Steinbrenner's initiative and money, would use the system to strengthen themselves greatly. But at first, the chief beneficiaries of Peter Seitz's ruling were Catfish Hunter's former Oakland teammates, almost all of whom felt they had been underpaid by Charles Finley and the best of whom were eligible to become free agents. Reggie Jackson, in particular, was certain to command a high price on the open market; to a slightly lesser degree, so was pitcher Ken Holtzman. A few days before the 1976 season began, Finley, aware he was likely to lose them anyway, traded Jackson and Holtzman to the Baltimore Orioles for a pair of players with less imposing records and less expensive expectations. The trade brought Reggie Jackson from West Coast to East, close to his Philadelphia roots and within two hundred miles of George Steinbrenner's domain.

On March 1, 1976, nine months ahead of schedule, Commissioner Bowie Kuhn pardoned George Steinbrenner, ended his suspension, presumably giving him time off for good behavior, meaning that during the fifteen months he was adjudged ineligible and incompetent, although

Steinbrenner certainly flouted Kuhn's decree, he did not commit a single crime of violence. Perhaps not coincidentally, Kuhn's original seven-year contract as commissioner expired in 1976; rumors persist that Steinbrenner, to show his gratitude for an early pardon, supported the rehiring of the commissioner. (Kuhn's contract expires again in 1983, and the rumors now are that if Kuhn is counting upon Steinbrenner as a friend, he will not need enemies.)

Steinbrenner celebrated his return during spring training in Fort Lauderdale, the Yankees' Florida base, by going out on the town one night with perhaps ten members of his court, including Martin, Ford, Mantle and Berra, all of whom had played in a World Series before George graduated from Williams. The entourage drifted from saloon to saloon, a raucous and sometimes raunchy group, everybody drinking and hollering and carrying on, everybody except the man who picked up the tab at each stop. The owner sipped at a soft drink. He observed. He did not participate. He was with employees, not with friends.

"George Steinbrenner doesn't have a friend." The man who offered that opinion, in 1981, was a man who had often been identified, in stories about Steinbrenner, as one of George's friends. He requested anonymity because he wanted to continue to be identified as one of George's friends.

Another acquaintance said the same thing in a kinder way. "George Steinbrenner can't cope with friendship," he said.

"George's friends?" Bill Fugazy, Steinbrenner's frequent companion, and occasional messenger, once said. "Lee Iacocca. Terence Cardinal Cooke. Gerald Ford." If Fugazy had said, "I'm his friend," or, "Mike Forrest is his friend," then he would have been utterly believable. But Fugazy was such a loyal "friend" he felt compelled to assign Steinbrenner more famous friends. Iacocca, from Chrysler.

Cardinal Cooke, from St. Patrick's. Ford, from the White House. Those men, no matter how accomplished and admirable they might be, were too busy for real friendship. Iacocca was trying to save an automotive giant from financial disaster. Cardinal Cooke was concerned with the spiritual welfare of millions of Roman Catholics in the Archdiocese of New York. President Ford was having problems with his golf game. Not that they weren't friendly toward Steinbrenner, but there was a distinct gap between being "friendly" and being a "friend," a distinction that often became blurred in print. For instance, in one *New York Times Magazine* article analyzing the rebuilding of the Yankees, the author wrote, "Steinbrenner brought in a friend from Cleveland, Gabe Paul." In the same magazine eighteen months later, after Paul had been replaced as president of the Yankees by Al Rosen, a different author wrote, "In Rosen, Steinbrenner has a good and true friend, the devoted ally he never had in Paul."

By 1981, Paul had stopped referring to Steinbrenner as a "friend"—Paul's $3.1-million suit against George did tend to strain the relationship—but he did accept Steinbrenner's hospitality at pre-World Series dinners, and he did say, "George and I were an excellent team. He provided what I lacked, and I provided what he lacked." Paul spoke very cautiously, very gingerly, but Al Rosen, who also was among Steinbrenner's World Series guests, offered more illuminating thoughts. "George treats me as a dear, dear friend whenever he's around me," said Rosen, who had become president and general manager of the Houston Astros. "I'm not sure what he says when I'm not around." Rosen said he considered himself a friend of Steinbrenner's before he went to work for him—and after he quit working for him. "The day you go to work for him," Rosen said, "it becomes a whole different relationship." But, Rosen pointed out, he knew what to expect when he took the job;

he had been warned—by Steinbrenner himself. "He doesn't fool you," Rosen said. "He tells you what he's like." Forewarned, in this case, was not sufficiently forearmed. Rosen, who quit when he could not stand being demeaned and pressured any further, would never work for Steinbrenner again. But he *could*. "Almost everyone who has ever worked for George could go back," Rosen said. "He has an affinity for wanting to maintain those relationships. Just look at what he does with managers." Rosen laughed. "George is as complicated as the baseball contracts have become," he said.

In spring training, 1976, when Steinbrenner was not yet the ubiquitous owner, his influence was felt only mildly, in two specific ways. First, one of the new Yankees, Oscar Gamble, reported with an Afro hairdo that turned him from an almost–six-footer into seven-feet-plus, and manager Martin, well aware of the owner's feelings about long hair, sent the newcomer straight to the barber, prompting Gamble to label Steinbrenner "the Yankee Clipper," a nickname that had earlier been applied, more reverently, to Joe DiMaggio. Second, Steinbrenner tried to persuade Martin to drive the Yankees through two workouts a day, but Martin insisted that one workout a day, organized perfectly, the way he intended to organize it, would be more productive. Martin got his way, and when the season began, back in the comfort of refurbished Yankee Stadium, the Yankees won fifteen of their first twenty games, moved into first place and never fell out, freeing Martin from considerable pressure even if he didn't earn a tugboat. Steinbrenner, of course, did not remain entirely aloof; he did send word, through Gabe Paul, that he wanted one of his tape recordings to be played in the clubhouse "to motivate the players." Martin refused. "I told him that I didn't need his tapes to motivate my players, that I could do my own motivating," Martin boasted.

Still, even though the Yankees quickly built a big lead

in the American League East, not everything went smoothly. On June 15, for instance, the deadline for intra-league trades, the Yankees and the Baltimore Orioles consummated a ten-player deal, five for five. Of the five players the Orioles received, three were still contributing significantly to the team five years later; of the five players the Yankees received, only one was still a Yankee even two years later, and that one, Ken Holtzman, whose skills had atrophied, managed to win only one game for the 1978 Yankees before he was dispatched to the Chicago Cubs. Obviously, the trade was not a good one for the Yankees, and, naturally, no one, not Steinbrenner nor Paul nor Martin, rushed to take credit for it. Martin did, however, assign blame. In *Number 1*, Martin said of the ten-man swap: "George made a trade that I couldn't believe . . . one of the most ridiculous trades I had ever seen or heard of." Then Martin explained why George made the deal: "I heard that George's little boy, who was about twelve at the time, saw Holtzman pitch for Baltimore, and he told George, 'Dad, get him, he'll win the pennant for you,' and George went out and got him." The story did have a basis in truth—when Holtzman scored his first victory as a Yankee, Steinbrenner did brag that his older son, Hank, had spotted him—but in 1975 and 1976, the only years Holtzman pitched for Baltimore, Hank was sixteen and seventeen years old. The exact age of Steinbrenner's son certainly was not significant in itself, but if Martin could be that far off on a very simple fact, when he had time to do research and a collaborator to guide him, imagine how far he could stray from the truth when he spoke in haste, or in anger. (Ages weren't the only simple facts that confounded Martin in his autobiography; names troubled him, too. Jimmy "Butsikaris" turned into Jimmy "Busakeris" only eleven pages later, and he wasn't just a casual acquaintance; he was the owner of one of Martin's favorite saloons. The correct spelling of his name, incidentally, was neither

Butsikaris nor Busakeris, but Butsicaris.)

Curiously, in his book, Martin neglected to mention the deal Steinbrenner made, or almost made, the same day as the ten-man trade with Baltimore. This was a one-man deal, with Charles O. Finley, for another of his players who was on the brink of abandoning him, the gifted young lefthanded pitcher Vida Blue. The Yankees agreed to pay Finley $1.5 million for Blue, a price that Gabe Paul, negotiating the purchase, had to clear by telephone with the Yankee owner. Steinbrenner gave his blessing, Finley gave his, and then the commissioner of baseball intervened. Bowie Kuhn decreed that cash-for-stars deals, involving huge sums, were detrimental to baseball, that they, like unlimited free agency, could create a dangerous imbalance of talent. The same day Finley thought he sold Blue to the Yankees, he thought he sold Joe Rudi and Rollie Fingers to the Boston Red Sox for $1 million apiece. Commissioner Kuhn vetoed all three deals, but for a short time, on June 15, 1976, Steinbrenner thought he possessed the three pitchers—Hunter, Holtzman and Blue—who started seventeen of the nineteen World Series games Oakland played from 1972 through 1974.

Hunter, who had won twenty-three games in his first year as a wealthy Yankee, tapered off in 1976, winning seventeen and losing fifteen. One of his defeats came in a night game against Baltimore at Yankee Stadium. Earlier the same day, in the same stadium, Hunter had filmed a chewing-tobacco commercial. After the defeat, Steinbrenner attacked Hunter publicly, arguing that a man earning as much as Hunter did not have to make commercials, and certainly not on a day when he was going to pitch. Steinbrenner had witnessed the filming from his office. "I couldn't believe that was [Hunter] down there," the owner said later. "There must have been sixty people down there, different script people, everything under the sun surrounding him around the mound." Steinbrenner suggested that

the commercial had weakened Hunter, so that he pitched poorly against the Orioles. Stung by Steinbrenner's criticism, which came through the press, Hunter defended himself, insisting that he had not put as much energy into the commercial as he would have put into his yard had he stayed at home all day. He went on to assail Steinbrenner's method of criticizing him. "Why doesn't he call me like a man?" Hunter demanded. The pitcher threatened the most terrible revenge; he was going to let his hair grow long. "On the field, they can tell me to do anything they want," Hunter said. "But I'm not gonna let 'em control my life off the field, too. We're not kids. No one has to hold our hands."

Steinbrenner soon made up with Hunter, possibly because he realized he could not intimidate the pitcher. Hunter did trim his hair, but he did not become subservient. "He's a man of his word," Hunter once said of Steinbrenner, "even though a lot of times you have to get it in writing to make sure of it." And when Steinbrenner eventually persuaded Martin to permit him to deliver inspirational clubhouse speeches in person, Hunter was not stirred. "Once you've heard the first one or two, you can almost sleep through the others," he said. "He means well, but they always sound the same. It's always how we're embarrassing ourselves and embarrassing New York and baseball and the country. George tells us how he was a football coach, and how he was in locker rooms before we were born. It's always 'I' this and 'I' that. The way he talks, you think he thinks he could do a better job than the manager. He tells us that he never makes a mistake, and that we can't either; he tells us that if he made mistakes, he wouldn't be as successful in business as he is."

Two days after the massive trade with Baltimore and the aborted deal with Oakland, the Yankees happened to encounter the Orioles in the lobby of a Chicago hotel, the Yankees checking in, the Orioles checking out. "Tell the man to save some money," Reggie Jackson said to a

reporter traveling with the Yankees. "I'll be there next year." Then Jackson shouted to Thurman Munson, "Hey, Thurman, don't be too nasty. We might be teammates next year."

Munson, a marvelously talented but mildly misshapen athlete, disproportioned enough for his teammates to call him "Squatty Body," was the captain of the Yankees, anointed at the start of the 1976 season by Steinbrenner, who felt, based on his football background, that a team needed a leader, a captain. The Yankees had survived without one for almost forty years, since the death of Lou Gehrig, the Yankees' only previous captain. When Steinbrenner decided to appoint Munson captain, Marty Appel, the team's director of public relations, a Brooklyn-born Yankee fan since the age of seven, appointed himself protector of Yankee traditions. "When Gehrig died," Appel told Steinbrenner, "Joe McCarthy [then the manager] said no one else would ever be captain of the Yankees." Steinbrenner dismissed the argument by saying, "If Joe McCarthy had known Thurman Munson, he would have approved." On Opening Day, however, Steinbrenner himself disapproved of his new captain. Munson had lined up without his cap on for the playing of "The Star-Spangled Banner." Steinbrenner promptly phoned the dugout and demanded that Martin fine Munson. Steinbrenner said neatness counts. Martin, no diplomat, told the owner what he could do with neatness.

Martin never was a great admirer of Steinbrenner's values—except for the value he placed on winning. "What does George know about being a Yankee?" Martin once demanded of a reporter. "I'm a Yankee. I've worn the uniform. What the hell does he know?" Martin never discouraged stories that made Steinbrenner appear ignorant of baseball's niceties. One such story was that, at a game early in his ownership, when the Yankees had a runner on third base with two out, and the batter hit a slow

ground ball to shortstop, and the runner on third crossed home plate before the batter was thrown out at first base, Steinbrenner stood and cheered, believing wrongly that the run counted. Another was that, during his first spring training, he jumped on a young Yankee for wearing his cap backwards and did not stop chewing him out until someone told him that the player was a catcher and catchers wore their caps backwards so that the catcher's mask would fit properly. That echoed a story which was told about George Steinbrenner's role model, George Patton. The general once was driving around an army base he commanded when he spotted a young man in sloppy fatigues working atop a telephone pole. Patton, too, demanded neatness in his troops. He ordered his driver to stop, climbed out of his jeep and shouted at the man to come down immediately. "Screw off," the man in the fatigues replied. "Can't you see I'm busy?" Stunned that a young soldier could be so disrespectful, Patton exploded in such fury that the man stopped his work and climbed down the pole. "What's your name and what's your company," Patton snapped, ready to pounce on the company commander. "My name's Smith," the man replied, "and my company's the Bell Telephone."

Steinbrenner had a matching experience. Riding the elevator up to his office at Yankee Stadium one day, he found himself standing next to a young man, apparently a messenger, with uncommonly long hair. "Get a haircut," the Yankee Clipper suggested.

"I don't work for you," the messenger said.

"Who do you work for?" Steinbrenner said.

"The New York Times."

"Then," said Steinbrenner, suitably impressed, "you certainly ought to get your hair cut."

By the beginning of September 1976, the Yankees had virtually clinched first place in the American League East, and Martin was rewarded with a new three-year contract raising his salary to $92,000 the first year, $100,000 the

second and $110,000 the third. Still, Martin did not feel secure. "I began to feel that George was acting jealous of me," Martin later wrote. "He seemed to feel that he wasn't going to get enough of the credit. It bothered him that I was getting so much publicity."

Martin protested that publicity was the last thing in the world he wanted, but when the American League championship series began, the Yankees facing the winners in the West, the Kansas City Royals, Martin promptly generated more publicity. He got into a name-calling contest with George Brett, the Kansas City star whose brother Ken had been traded away by the Yankees, and with Larry Gura, a Kansas City pitcher who had himself been traded away by the Yankees. Brett said that Martin had lied to his brother. Gura said that Martin had lied to him. Martin denied both charges and stopped just short of insisting that he could not tell a lie. By the time the championship series ended, Brett and Gura and Martin and Steinbrenner and all the more vocal principals had been drowned out by the Yankees' quiet first baseman, Chris Chambliss. In the bottom of the ninth inning of the fifth and decisive game, with the score tied at six runs apiece, and the series tied at two victories apiece, Chambliss led off with a game-winning home run.

The Yankees were in the World Series for the first time in twelve years, and in a wild and frightening demonstration, a savage minority of fans flooded the field, forcing Chambliss to stiff-arm his way to the safety of the dugout. The more sensible fans stood and cheered, obviously delighted. Strangely, Steinbrenner himself displayed no sense of exhilaration, nothing more than a sense of satisfaction. "Winning isn't *fun* for George," Marty Appel, who was then the Yankees' publicity man, once suggested. "Nothing is *fun* for George. He takes everything so seriously."

But a couple of days later, when the World Series opened

170

in Cincinnati, Steinbrenner did enjoy what he later called his "greatest moment" in baseball. "They were playing the national anthem," he said, "and I looked around and I said, 'My God, we're here. In three years. It's the World Series, and we're here.'" Actually, it took Steinbrenner's Yankees four seasons to get to the World Series, almost four full years, but in that proud moment, the owner was entitled to mild exaggeration.

Four games later, Billy Martin was in tears, and George Steinbrenner did not feel at all proud. The Yankees had lost the World Series to Cincinnati in four straight games, a humiliating experience. Steinbrenner reacted predictably. Furious, he summoned his staff. "The morning after we got wiped out, after that fourth game," Steinbrenner said, "my people were at work at eight-thirty. We were getting ready. That was never going to happen again." And never again was George Steinbrenner going to be so *uninvolved* in the day-to-day running of the Yankees as he felt he had been in 1976.

Two weeks after the World Series ended, Steinbrenner and his staff carefully began constructing the team that would represent the Yankees in 1977. Baseball's first re-entry draft, the first auction of veteran free agents, was held at New York's Plaza Hotel, and the Yankees declared an interest in nine of the available players. "Grich, Gullett, Baylor and Jackson are the players we're most interested in," Steinbrenner said.

Bobby Grich was the Yankees' prime target. He was an infielder, a second baseman primarily, who could play shortstop, the weakest position in the Yankee lineup, or, at least, the only position at which the Yankees could not field a proven All-Star. Don Gullett was the most successful young pitcher in baseball, winner of the opening game of the 1976 World Series against the Yankees, gifted but fragile. Don Baylor was an outfielder with great power and promise, and Reggie Jackson was Reggie Jackson. The

Yankees, for a time, thought they had Grich, but he opted for California, his home state. Baylor, too, elected to take Gene Autry's money—Autry, the old cowboy star, owned the California Angels—and the Yankees quickly signed Gullett to a six-year contract worth slightly more than two million dollars. Under the rules of the re-entry draft, the Yankees were limited to signing one more free agent. Billy Martin didn't want Reggie Jackson. George Steinbrenner did. But before he set out personally to persuade Jackson to become a Yankee, Steinbrenner talked to Thurman Munson, to see how the players would react. "Go get the big man," Munson said. "He's the only guy in baseball who can carry a club for a month. And the hell with what you hear. He hustles every minute on the field."

Steinbrenner pursued Jackson, flew him to New York, sent his personal limousine with the "NYY" plates to pick him up at the airport, escorted him to "21," pointed out the most elegant shops and the most luxurious apartment houses, and told him he could own the city. Then Jackson moved on to Chicago, settled into a hotel suite and began to weigh his choices, offers from Montreal, San Diego and Baltimore, as well as the Yankees. Montreal and San Diego offered considerably more money. Steinbrenner offered something more valuable. He offered affection. He followed Jackson to Chicago. The day before Thanksgiving, at seven-thirty in the morning, Steinbrenner visited with Jackson briefly, then waited anxiously while the other teams made their final presentations. That evening, he was summoned back to Jackson's suite. "You're it, George," Jackson said, and handed Steinbrenner a four-paragraph note hand-written on a piece of hotel stationery, summarizing the terms of the agreement, adding up to almost three million dollars for five years. At the end of the note, Jackson wrote, "We are going on this venture together. I will not let you down. Reginald M. Jackson." George M. Steinbrenner preserved the note under glass in his home.

Alfred M. Martin, better known as Billy, simmered.

"I like George's style," Jackson said, explaining his decision. "He hustled me like a broad." Jackson's assessment was colorful, but wrong. Two well-known women, one a writer, the other a former athlete, both of whom said they were hustled by Steinbrenner, both reported no serious trouble getting him to give up the chase. Steinbrenner hustled Jackson much better than he hustled broads.

A few days later, the Yankees held a news conference to announce the signing, and Jackson, wearing a World Series ring and a gold bracelet with the name "Reggie" spelled out in diamonds, positively beamed. "The reason why I am a Yankee," he reiterated, "is because George Steinbrenner outhustled everybody. George Steinbrenner dealt with me as a man and a person . . . It will be exciting hitting a home run in Yankee Stadium as a Yankee. For me to get applause from the crowd or slaps on the back or have George Steinbrenner say to me that he felt he wanted me to play here and always wanted me here, that's something I never had. I never felt wanted like that." Reggie Jackson, who wanted desperately to be wanted, was so delighted to be free of Charles Finley he thought he had found paradise.

But trouble was already brewing in paradise, or, at least, in New Jersey, where Billy Martin was making his temporary home. "George was taking Reggie to the "21" Club for lunch all the time, and I was sitting across the river in my hotel room the entire winter," Martin said later, "and George hadn't taken me out to lunch even once."

"It's going to be great with the Yankees because George and I are going to get along real good, and that's very important," Jackson told a reporter, and when Martin read Jackson's words, he progressed from simmering to steaming. "I said to myself, 'You're going to find out that George isn't the manager,'" Martin said.

173

Even Jackson had one misgiving as he waited for his first spring training as a Yankee. "I can't understand it," he said. "Here he's gotten the best player in the whole world, and Billy Martin hasn't called me up even once." Of course Jackson did not call Martin, either, and once, when both of them happened to be in the same restaurant in Manhattan, each waited for the other to make the first overture, and neither did. The two of them were living proof that monumental egos could also be incredibly delicate.

If George Steinbrenner really enjoyed constant turmoil, he must have loved the Yankees' spring training camp in 1977. Mickey Rivers showed up a few hours late, and Sparky Lyle a few days late. Fred Stanley was miserable because his job, at shortstop, was being given to a rookie, Mickey Klutts, and soon the rookie, too, was miserable, because he broke his hand, which made Oscar Gamble miserable because he was being offered in exchange for a shortstop to replace Stanley and Klutts. Dock Ellis was furious because he expected a handsome new contract after his fine 1976 season, and faced instead a cut in pay, and Graig Nettles was equally furious because he had had the poor timing to sign a multi-year contract midway through the 1976 season, after a mediocre first half, and not at the end of the season, after a brilliant second half. Roy White, who had played an average of 150 games a year for the Yankees for nine seasons, was unhappy with his contract negotiations, and Chris Chambliss, the hero of the Yankees' greatest victory in 1976, was just as unhappy with his. Captain Thurman Munson, voted the Most Valuable Player in the American League in 1976, was angry because he had been promised that no Yankee would receive a salary greater than his, and he had discovered that Jackson was outearning him, not in salary alone perhaps, but in salary plus deferred income. ("Just a misunderstanding," said Steinbrenner later. "Misunder-

standings happen in business; they are not lies.") Many of the players took out their financial unhappiness, not surprisingly, on Jackson, on the theory that he had taken their share of Steinbrenner's millions. "George Steinbrenner talks about loyalty," Sparky Lyle said. "He told us to be loyal to him, and he would be good to us. His loyalty went out the window. I'm not using any specific player as an example, but as soon as a good player becomes available, there goes two or three million dollars."

Jackson wanted to be greeted by his new teammates, if not as the second coming of Babe Ruth, at least the way ancient Greek cities greeted a returning Olympic champion: The hero would enter through a hole cut in the city's protective wall, he would receive a free home and free meals for the rest of his life and, often, he would have a street renamed in his honor. Jackson would have settled, cheerfully, for Park Avenue, or Fifth. But he found himself, instead, treated more like a leper. Many of the Yankees didn't want to touch him, not even conversationally. Jackson's feelings were wounded, and after a couple of days of workouts, so was his elbow, which, at first, made throwing painful and, in time, made batting equally painful. Jackson's powers of speech, however, were not affected. "You never met anyone like me, I'm not just a ballplayer, I'm a multi-faceted person, a myriad of personalities," he told reporters soon after his arrival, and a few days later, he dwelled on one of his facets. "I think Reggie Jackson on your ball club is a show of force," Reggie Jackson said. "It's a show of power. I help to intimidate the opposition, just because I'm here." His ego was not quite sturdy enough to repel all doubts ("I don't know if I'm going to fit in," he admitted at one point; "Maybe I can have a rotten year," he confessed at another), but most of the time, Jackson simply counted his blessings, out loud. He counted his money the same way. He flashed fat rolls of bills and spoke of his three-million-dollar contract so often

one observant reporter, Murray Chass of the *Times,* was moved to comment, "Reggie is obsessed with money. Amateur psychologists view him as a tremendously insecure person who feels that money gives him instant status and importance far beyond his standing as a baseball player." One of the few Yankees who had good things to say about Jackson was Catfish Hunter, who, recalling their Oakland days together, spoke glowingly of Jackson's ability, especially under pressure. But even Hunter could not resist a gentle needle. "Reggie's really a good guy, down deep he is," Hunter once said. "I really like him. I always did. He'd give you the shirt off his back. Of course, he'd call a press conference to announce it." Rebuffed by most of his teammates, Jackson was embraced by writers, particularly those with a good ear and a fondness for metaphor. A writer named Robert Ward, on assignment from *Sport* magazine, offered Jackson his good ear, and Jackson responded with hundreds of good words, quotable and provocative. "This team, it all flows from me," Jackson said. "I've got to keep it going." Then he hit the metaphorical jackpot: "I'm the straw that stirs the drink. It all comes back to me. Maybe I should say me and Munson. But really he doesn't enter into it. He's so damned insecure . . . Munson thinks he can be the straw that stirs the drink, but he can only stir it bad." Ward recorded Jackson's words carefully, to use them in an article that would not be printed for more than two months, an article that would eventually promote fresh turmoil and headlines, the red and white corpuscles of George Steinbrenner's lifeblood.

Steinbrenner himself kept a reasonably low profile during the early weeks of training camp. Still, his presence was noted, even by some opponents. Bill Lee, a lefthanded pitcher for the Boston Red Sox and a man with an unusually fertile and bizarre mind, had been injured during a 1976 free-for-all between the Red Sox and the Yankees. He struck back during spring training. A poetry

lover with far-ranging tastes (his favorite poets, he said, were T. S. Eliot and Ogden Nash), he attacked the Yankees with the sort of outrageous rhetoric Jonathan Swift might have enjoyed. "I was assaulted by George Steinbrenner's Nazis, his Brown Shirts," Lee modestly proposed. "He brainwashes those kids over there, and they're led by Billy Martin—Hermann Goering the Second. They've got a convicted felon running the club, what do you expect?"

Lee's overstatement did not disturb Steinbrenner so much as Billy Martin's quiet statement, a few days later, that during the season he would probably bat Chris Chambliss fourth in the Yankee lineup, and Reggie Jackson fifth—a clear case of provoking the owner. Steinbrenner never was much of a Chambliss fan—Chris had been Gabe Paul's find, first at Cleveland, then as a Yankee—and that Chris was cut from the Bill Virdon mold, bland and decent, did not thrill the owner. Also, from a practical standpoint, Reggie Jackson had hit more home runs in *one* season than Chris Chambliss had hit in his *four* best seasons, and traditionally, home-run hitters batted fourth. But Billy Martin did not resent Chris Chambliss' presence and Chris Chambliss was not, as Martin would phrase it, George's boy, and so, in the manager's eyes, Chambliss had all the qualifications to bat cleanup.

Irritated by Martin's independence, which bordered on mutiny, Steinbrenner had another upsetting experience a couple of days later. He walked into the locker room and found Dock Ellis wearing an earring. If Ellis had been wearing a low-cut dress, Steinbrenner could not have been more caustic. Ellis, an intelligent and fiercely outspoken black, had been the first major leaguer to have his hair done corn-row style, which led him to wear rollers in the locker room and sometimes in the dugout. For him, an earring was mild. When Steinbrenner objected, Ellis said that if the owner didn't shut up, he would wear the earring on the field. "The only reason I don't do it is because I don't

want to rock your little boat," Ellis shouted. Steinbrenner shouted back, working himself into shape for the season.

The Yankees stumbled through the exhibition season, losing more often than winning, Jackson nursing his elbow and sharpening his batting eye, and Catfish Hunter searching for vanished skills. In the last week of March, when the Yankees barely beat the University of Florida, 10–9, under lights donated to the university by George M. Steinbrenner, the owner erupted, mildly by his standards, ordering two pitchers hit hard by the collegians, Ken Clay and Randy Niemann, demoted to the minor leagues. A few days later, when the Yankees lost to the Mets, 6–0, in a game televised back to New York, a game in which Jackson's aching arm limited him to a pinch-hitting role, and Martin rested most of his regulars in the late innings, Steinbrenner really exploded. He was livid about the defeat, about Jackson, and about the substitutes, and he blamed the man who was both box office and belligerent, Billy Martin. He was angry with the manager anyway for not living in the team's Fort Lauderdale headquarters, but in Boca Raton with his buddy, Mickey Mantle, who was not one of Steinbrenner's favorite people. (George considered Mantle crude, and thought his behavior off the field tarnished the Yankee image; he probably wouldn't have liked Babe Ruth, either.) But Steinbrenner was more angry because he had insisted that the manager travel to each game on the bus with the team, and after the Mets' victory, George had spotted the manager's car in the stadium parking lot. Fuming, Steinbrenner charged into the clubhouse. Miraculously, no one was gored. "I want to see you now!" Steinbrenner demanded of Martin. "I want you to ride on the team bus!"

"You don't tell me where to ride, you sonuvabitch!" Martin responded.

"Hey, watch yourself," said Gabe Paul, caught, by force of habit, in the middle.

"You lied to me!" Steinbrenner yelled.

"You're a lying sonuvabitch!" Martin retorted.

"I ought to get rid of you!" Steinbrenner threatened.

"Why don't you fire me right now?" Martin suggested.

Martin slammed his fist against an ice bucket and splashed ice on Steinbrenner and Paul, accidentally, and soon all three cooled off. The next day, over breakfast, Steinbrenner made one of his rare apologies, for triggering the confrontation in the clubhouse, and the owner and the manager declared a truce, a very temporary truce.

A few days later, the owner was at war again, this time with Graig Nettles, the third baseman who was feeling economically depressed. Nettles had signed a contract that not only paid him less than he believed he was worth, but also paid him in the most costly way, from a tax viewpoint. Nettles wanted to renegotiate the numbers, and the method of payment. Steinbrenner flatly refused. Less than two weeks before the start of the season, Nettles walked out. Steinbrenner did not panic. "If Graig's not there on Opening Day," the owner said, "we'll go after damages to our ball club. A contract is a contract. A player has to realize that."

The following day, Nettles was still missing, and Steinbrenner still adamant. "He made a business deal, and he's going to be made to abide by his contract," the owner said. "He's going to understand the facts of life." Then Steinbrenner offered his player an opening. "If Graig realizes he made a mistake leaving the team, and learns from it, I'm willing to sit down and help him, within the confines of his existing contract. But he has to stand up like a man and admit he made a mistake."

The next day, Nettles returned to camp. "I understand Graig feels badly, and feels he made a mistake," Steinbrenner said. "That's the only positive thing to come out of this, and it will make a better man of him."

Nettles responded with a printed statement: "The prob-

179

lem I have is a personal one. I now realize it should be settled at the conference table, and not on the field. I want to apologize if I have caused any embarrassment or inconvenience to the Yankees. All I want to do now is get ready for the upcoming season."

Steinbrenner could not have phrased it better if he had dictated the statement himself. "I was really itching for this battle," the owner said, "and I really licked their tails. These guys can't go through life walking through obligations." Steinbrenner said that three other owners of baseball teams had called him to congratulate him upon his firmness, and upon its success. "What was going to happen if I had backed down," he said, "is that a lot of players get this idea in their head that a contract is a unilateral document: If he has a bad year, the club has to make good on it; if he has a good year, he wants to come in and negotiate."

The owner's syntax was flawed—he kept switching back and forth between singular and plural, between past and present—but he had logic on his side, and more. He could not be accused, like many other baseball owners, of being cheap. He had negotiated new contracts with Chambliss, White and Lyle, each for a minimum of one hundred twenty-five thousand dollars a year, a salary none of them could have conceived of earning when he broke into the major leagues. Steinbrenner was not paying big salaries because he was altruistic, but because he was realistic. He expected his players to be the same, to strike for the big money when they could, not when they legally couldn't.

Remarkably, with all the skirmishes that kept breaking out during the Yankee training camp, the festering antagonism between Martin and Jackson never quite burst into open conflict. But no one could miss the tension. Not long before the regular season began, Phil Pepe of the *Daily News* asked Jackson about his busy exhibition schedule.

"You're playing almost every day," Pepe said. "What's the purpose?"

"Don't ask me," Jackson said. Then he nodded toward Billy Martin's office. "I don't know what he's trying to prove."

When Pepe repeated Jackson's remark to Martin, the manager seemed stunned. "He said that?" Martin said. "I'll be a sonuvabitch. He asked to play. He told me he likes to play a lot of innings in spring training."

Finally, spring training came to an end, "the worst spring training in my whole history in baseball," Martin said. But the regular season was going to be even more frustrating for the manager. Steinbrenner was just beginning to play.

The Yankees won their opening home game before 43,785 fans, a crowd four times larger than the one that had turned out for the last pre-Steinbrenner opening in 1972. But then the Yankees lost eight of their next nine games, and sank into last place in the Eastern Division of the American League. Their slump was punctuated by a series of ominous events, the first confrontation between Martin and Jackson (who was benched because he told a group of reporters he had a sore elbow, a violation of Martin's Secrecy Act), the first reconciliation of Martin and Jackson (after a conference in a hotel bar, Reggie returned to the lineup), Jackson's first enthusiastic attempt to fit in with his teammates (he joined in a favorite clubhouse sport, needling Munson, which pleased Munson), Steinbrenner's first vote of confidence in Martin ("I have every confidence Billy is going to turn it around"—with the "or else" unspoken) and Steinbrenner's first locker-room speech of the season, a predictable ode to pride and pinstripes, to valor and victory. Dock Ellis skipped the pep talk—"I'm not going to listen to that high-school Charley shit"—and soon afterward skipped the Yankees, traded to

the Oakland A's, but not before he was credited with a rather vicious line that appeared, anonymously, in *The New York Times:* "The more we lose, the more often Steinbrenner will fly in. And the more he flies, the better the chance there will be of the plane crashing."

The source of the remark, actually, was not Ellis, but Graig Nettles, but it was much more practical to blame, and to trade, Ellis. Less than a year later, Steinbrenner was able to needle himself in a similar vein. Driving in Fort Lauderdale one day, he spotted a hang-glider floating over the beach. "You wouldn't get me up on one of those for all the money in the world," Steinbrenner said to the man with him.

"It's just a ride," the man said. "The guy is being towed by a boat. It's nothing scary."

"Don't kid me," Steinbrenner said. "I'll tell you what. I bet you could get every guy on the team to put up one thousand dollars each to get me up there, and then one of them would stand there with a rifle and—bang—shoot the glider." Steinbrenner laughed; the joke was his own.

After the tenth game of the 1977 season, when the Yankees had the worst record in baseball, behind even Toronto and Seattle, both of which had just joined the American League, Steinbrenner called a meeting of his top executives and, during the meeting, Gabe Paul suffered what appeared, at first, to be a stroke. The ailment turned out to be less serious, a cerebral spasm, which hospitalized Paul, but did not prevent him from persuading Steinbrenner not to trade Mickey Rivers, the moody outfielder, or Ron Guidry, a young pitcher who was just beginning to harness his skills, a pair of moves that might have destroyed the Yankees' pennant chances.

The day after Paul's attack, Billy Martin had Reggie Jackson pick the Yankee batting order out of a hat, and the resulting lineup, a remarkably strong one, with only a couple of players obviously out of their normal order,

promptly started a six-game winning streak. "If the manager says I picked the lineup out of a hat," Jackson said, "then I picked it out of a hat." By early May, the Yankees would be in first place, and even though they slipped as low as third in early August, they then won forty of their next fifty games, an incredible pace, a surge that coincided with the long-delayed enshrinement of Reggie Jackson as the cleanup hitter in the New York Yankees' lineup. Jackson, finally, was where George Steinbrenner had always wanted him to be, and the Yankees also wound up where he wanted them, in first place in the American League East.

But between the early slump and the closing rally, the Yankees lived a life that never once threatened to become dull. For instance, Sparky Lyle and Ed Figueroa were fined one hundred dollars apiece for sleeping through one of Steinbrenner's locker-room speeches, and Lyle and Rivers were fined five hundred dollars apiece for skipping an exhibition game in Syracuse. Lyle may have had trouble off the field, but on the pitcher's mound, during games that counted, he was magnificent. He appeared in seventy-two games, won thirteen and saved twenty-six other victories, lost only five times and became the first relief pitcher in the American League to win the Cy Young Award, presented annually to the league's best pitcher. Don Gullett was equally magnificent when he was free from injuries; after losing his first two decisions as a Yankee, Gullett won fourteen of his next sixteen and finished with the best won-lost percentage of any pitcher in the American League. Steinbrenner was delighted with his investment in Gullett, whom he still considered an All-American boy, an image that was not damaged when someone, without Gullett's knowledge, began growing marijuana on his Kentucky farm, a crop that was harvested, in headlines, by the authorities. Not all of the pitchers flourished. Catfish Hunter struggled with injuries, and Ken Holtzman, who

did not win a game after May 1, was called upon so rarely he called George Steinbrenner "a fool" for paying him one hundred sixty-five thousand dollars a year. But these were mere diversions compared to the continuing soap opera starring the owner, the manager and the straw that stirred the drink.

In early May, soon after the Yankees moved into first place, Billy Martin, with his gift for self-destruction, precipitated another crisis in his career. The manager decided that he desperately needed a third catcher and an extra lefthanded hitter to keep the Yankees winning, and that the perfect man for both roles was Elrod Hendricks, a veteran who had recently been farmed out to Syracuse. Martin mentioned his pressing need to Gabe Paul, who had returned to work only two weeks after the cerebral spasm. Paul said that if Martin would come into his office the next day, just before the Yankees left on a trip to the West Coast, the two of them would discuss the Hendricks situation. But Martin didn't show up for the meeting, a violation of one of the clauses of his contract: Thou shalt consult with the principal owner and the president. Instead, he took off for the West Coast without talking to Paul.

The first game of the trip, the Yankees lost to Seattle, and Martin, who had not had a lefthanded pinch-hitter to use when he needed one, complained to reporters afterward, "I want Elrod Hendricks. I've been asking for Elrod for a week and a half. But George and Gabe think I'm kidding. Why are we going with twenty-four players? It cost us tonight's game, as far as I'm concerned."

Martin's remarks had violated a second clause in his contract: Thou shalt not criticize the principal owner or the president. The second game of the trip, the Yankees again lost to Seattle, and Thurman Munson, who permitted three stolen bases and then left the game with a cramp in his leg, seconded Martin's call for Elrod Hendricks. "I can't visual-

184

ize a major-league team without three catchers," the aching Munson said. "His legs have been bothering him for a whole week," the bellyaching Martin said.

Martin, clearly, was not being a good soldier. Nor was he being spectacularly loyal. He was going to have to be disciplined. Steinbrenner and Paul discussed the possibility of firing Martin, and decided not to. Steinbrenner let it be known that he had protected Martin, which was probably true, because if he and Paul had a difference of opinion, that Paul's opinion was not likely to be the one that would not prevail. By the same reasoning, Steinbrenner must have been the one who decided that Martin, instead of being fired, would be publicly humiliated.

Paul, of course, had to do the dirty work. He telephoned Mickey Morabito, the Yankees' third public relations director under Steinbrenner, keeping pace with the number of managers, and dictated a statement for Morabito to release to the press. The statement revealed that Dell Alston, a lefthanded-hitting outfielder, was being promoted to the Yankees from Syracuse, where he was batting .338. The statement also revealed that Elrod Hendricks, who was not being promoted, was batting .105. "Frankly," said Paul, "if we have to depend on a player batting .105 at Syracuse to enable us to beat an expansion team [Seattle], we are indeed in bad trouble." The statement also revealed that Martin was in bad trouble. "Certain comments directed at Mr. Steinbrenner, the team's principal owner, by manager Billy Martin, concerning the alleged failure to add a twenty-fifth player, are totally inaccurate and unfounded," Paul said. "Martin was asked to report to my office on May tenth prior to leaving for Seattle, and at such time the determination of the twenty-fifth player was to be made. He agreed to be there. However, Billy failed to show up for the meeting with me. If we had had that conversation as scheduled, the twenty-fifth player would have been added and the matter would have been settled then

and there." The statement did not reveal that Billy Martin was being fined twenty-five hundred dollars, the largest fine any team had ever imposed on its manager.

Martin muted his displeasure, and while the Yankees concluded their West Coast tour in Oakland, which was once the home of Gertrude Stein ("There's no there there," she said), Steinbrenner, Paul and Whitey Ford went off on a trip of their own. Theirs was a secret trip to another literary landmark, Havana, Cuba, the former home of Stein's friend, Ernest Hemingway ("Gertrude was always right," he said). Steinbrenner, however, was not furthering his literary education in Havana, but visiting Fidel Castro, a former college pitcher who was studied, but not signed by major-league scouts, one of the very few events in baseball history that may have had lasting international significance. Castro, like many of his followers, was anti-U.S. Yankee, but pro-N.Y. Yankee, and he had asked Steinbrenner down to explore the possibility of having the Yankees play an exhibition or a series of exhibitions in Cuba. While they were in Havana, the three Yanquis went to see a Cuban all-star baseball game. Steinbrenner did not spot a future Yankee player at the Cuban ball park, but he did find a future friend.

A couple of days before Steinbrenner and company landed in Cuba, Barbara Walters and an ABC News crew arrived there to interview Castro. Fidel recommended that Walters and her crew take in a baseball game, and at the game, the ABC cameraman, who was more of a sports fan than Barbara, suddenly called out, "Hey, look, there's the Yankees!" He pointed to Ford, Paul and Steinbrenner.

Walters, who had heard of Whitey Ford, but not of the other two, decided it would be a good idea to get a few pictures of the Yankees who had invaded Cuba. "We began to film them," Walters recalled four years later, "and George got furious. I had never heard of him. I didn't have the slightest idea who he was. He lit into me. 'We came

down here secretly. Castro promised us secrecy. We're going to stop you from using this.' I probably wasn't going to use the story till he said that. The story was on the air the next night."

The ABC team and the Yankees trio retreated from the ball park to the Havana Libre Hotel, formerly the Hotel Nacional, one of Hemingway's favorite hangouts. The Americans all ended up at the bar, talking, and Walters and Steinbrenner ended up confidants at a time when each very much needed a confidant. Walters had come to ABC, from NBC, in 1976, with a much-publicized five-million-dollar, five-year contract that made her, in a sense, the Reggie Jackson of broadcasting, the most expensive free agent in the business. ("I never heard of her till she got all that money," Reggie Jackson once said. "I don't want to hurt your feelings," his companion said, "but she never heard of you till you got all that money." Reggie was not to be topped. "That's bullshit," he said. "Everybody's heard of me.") She had been installed as one of the anchors on ABC's evening news, an almost disastrous misuse of her talents as an interviewer. Her tour as an anchor lasted little more than a year, and her detractors, especially those who simply resented her success, had a field day. By the time she met George Steinbrenner, she was conditioned to abuse.

George was no stranger to the subject, either, but even he was shocked by the severity of an attack upon him that appeared in *New York* magazine during the summer of 1977. The author was Jeff Greenfield, a bright young man who had worked for both Bobby Kennedy and John Lindsay, and the title of his article was certainly not ambiguous: "George Steinbrenner, Get Out of Town!" Greenfield started off by attacking Cleveland for spawning Steinbrenner and for inflicting him upon New York, then attacked Steinbrenner for stripping the Yankees of their "most enduring trait"—class. "It is the ultimate irony,"

Greenfield wrote, "a big-league team in a big-league town in the hands of a bush-league owner." Then he really got nasty. "Billy Martin was helping the Yankees win titles when Steinbrenner was dreaming of his first polyester suit," said Greenfield, a Yankee fan since childhood. The article, not Greenfield at his most reasoned, stung Steinbrenner so much that he suspected Michael Burke of planting it. Burke was innocent, although he never denied that he had enjoyed reading the article.

"We were being pummeled by the press," Barbara Walters said. "We were both getting awful publicity. Everything we did was wrong. One night we walked home together after dinner, and we talked about our lives, and we told each other secrets. I like George very much. He's funny. He's thoughtful. He's touching. He's like the hooker with the heart of gold. He's a bully with a heart of gold."

Of her "long and funny relationship" with Steinbrenner, Walters said, "We have an *insult* relationship. When he's in the news every day, I'll call him up and I'll say, 'What's the matter? I never hear about you.' We are so different. I once asked him, 'Who's the president of France?' and he didn't know it was Giscard. I asked him if he knew who Margaret Thatcher was, and he said, 'What position does she play?' But he's very well-informed about the U.S. He knows the capitals of every state. He's a superpatriot." (Ironically, the trip on which Steinbrenner met Walters was one of his very few outside the United States. Despite his wealth, he has never visited Europe, and he has insisted, "I have no plans to travel anywhere until I've seen everything there is to see in this great country." He told me that Europe is more tempting now, now that he can rarely escape recognition in the U.S., but he still seems likely to resist the temptation.)

Walters then offered a reporter's string of random insights: "He's consumed with having to be tough . . . He talks about his father all the time . . . He's very shy, goes

to no dinner parties, very few cocktail parties . . . There's a difference between the way he treats men and the way he treats women . . . With women, he's more gentlemanly, old-fashioned . . . When I see him, I go as part of the crowd, and the crowd is almost always the same, Bill Fugazy, Mike Forrest, a few others, all inside humor, putdown humor, mostly about his ice cream and his weight . . . He's very much the boss, and they're the supporting cast."

Steinbrenner enjoyed speaking of himself and Barbara Walters as sort of an East Coast version of Spencer Tracy and Katharine Hepburn, a notion both romantic and self-aggrandizing. He also enjoyed coming out of P. J. Clarke's saloon with Barbara, seeing which of them would be recognized by more passersby. "I swear," Steinbrenner once recalled, "we went one-to-one," a truly remarkable feat considering that Barbara Walters was the most famous television newswoman in the United States back when George Steinbrenner wasn't even one of the better-known shipbuilders. Of course, Steinbrenner also recalled singing with Stephen Sondheim in the Williams Glee Club and picking the winner of the Kentucky Derby in the Williams *Record.*

If Steinbrenner, in truth, in 1977, was not quite so major a celebrity as Barbara Walters, he certainly wanted to be. "George's principal reason for buying the Yankees," Michael Burke once said, "was to cease being anonymous and to become a celebrity." One of Steinbrenner's first steps toward becoming a celebrity was collecting celebrities, governors and mayors, actors and actresses, athletes and entrepreneurs. He even had a weakness for writers. Gay Talese, who wrote books on subjects as diverse as *The New York Times* and sex; Kurt Vonnegut, who wrote novels ridiculing many of the values Steinbrenner prized; Jimmy Breslin, a New York *Daily News* columnist who actually knew the kind of little people George Steinbrenner so admired; and George Vecsey, who wrote for the

Times and, more important, had collaborated with Loretta Lynn on her autobiography, *Coal Miner's Daughter*—all were Steinbrenner's guests at big games at Yankee Stadium. He confided in them, told them honestly what he thought of certain players, and he conned them. In Breslin's wonderful Watergate book, *How the Good Guys Finally Won,* George Steinbrenner emerged as an innocent bystander on the brink of sainthood. "My man," said Breslin of Steinbrenner, the ultimate approval. "The collecting of celebrities "was another step out of Cleveland," suggested Marty Appel, the former Yankee publicity man.

At least one celebrity Steinbrenner chose to cultivate eventually turned into an enemy: Fran Tarkenton, football hero, Atlanta businessman and television star. Steinbrenner met Tarkenton through a mutual friend and asked the then-quarterback of the Minnesota Vikings if he would make an appearance at Culver Military Academy. Tarkenton said he would, a coup for George and for his older son, Hank, then a Culver student. But when Tarkenton retired from pro football, Steinbrenner failed to respond to an invitation to attend a farewell dinner in Minneapolis. Not long afterward, when Joan Steinbrenner asked Tarkenton to attend a dinner in Tampa, the ex-quarterback declined, pleading a previous engagement. The excuse did not satisfy George Steinbrenner, who got even when Tarkenton brought his young son Matthew to New York for a holiday and took him to Yankee Stadium to see a baseball game. The mutual friend who had introduced Steinbrenner to Tarkenton arranged for the Yankee scoreboard to flash a message of welcome to Fran Tarkenton and his son Matthew. Steinbrenner vetoed the message, and Tarkenton, who knew the gesture would have delighted his son, was so bitter he became one of the few people, outside of Steinbrenner's employees, who would admit disliking him. "All power people use people," Tarkenton said, in one of his

kinder moments. "But George uses people worse than all the rest of us."

Besides gathering celebrities, Steinbrenner went to the places where celebrities gathered, to "21," Elaine's, P. J. Clarke's, Jimmy Weston's and, by 1981, George Martin's, a small, handsome restaurant owned by a man named George Martin and by Dave DeBusschere, the former New York Knicks basketball star, another midwesterner who, like Steinbrenner, had become a symbol of New York. George Martin's was frequented by Vitas Gerulaitis and John McEnroe, the tennis stars, and Dorothy Hamill, the figure skater who married Dean Martin's son, Dino. The special table at George Martin's was table ten, with its own television set, tuned usually to ESPN, the all-sports network. Table ten provided the regulars who sat there a degree of privacy. "George doesn't sit at table ten," George Martin said. "He sits in the middle of the room, and if people come over, he stands up, gives of his time, chats with them. He's very congenial. And the staff likes him. He takes good care of them."

Most often, Steinbrenner ordered a veal chop for dinner, with a vegetable and two bottles of Perrier mineral water, passing up potatoes and bread and wine, then squandering all the calories he saved on Häagen-Dazs ice cream. Some of his Yankee players also went to George Martin's, but most of them preferred Oren & Aretsky's, a nearby restaurant that Steinbrenner deliberately avoided ("I want the players to have one place where they know I'm not going to show up," he said). The one player who would dine at George Martin's frequently, whether Steinbrenner was there or not, was Reggie Jackson. They were two very different kinds of customers. "George won't allow me to buy him anything," George Martin said. "He insists on paying for everything. Reggie? Reggie would be shocked if he ever got a check."

Jackson spent much of the summer of 1977 in varying degrees of shock, which had nothing to do with paying bills. Only a few days after the Yankees returned from their trip to the West Coast, the trip that almost cost Martin his job, only a few days after George Steinbrenner returned from his trip to Havana, advance copies of *Sport* magazine carrying the article by Robert Ward, the article in which Jackson labeled himself "the straw that stirs the drink," began to circulate in the Yankee clubhouse. Thurman Munson, on the brink of a rapprochement with Jackson, looked at the article and was enraged, and almost all of his teammates took Munson's side. Yankees walked past Jackson's locker and kicked at his spiked shoes. When he took batting practice, his teammates looked away. No one spoke to him, and he was virtually ignored until the third time he came to bat against Bill Lee, the Boston pitcher, who said before the game that he had had a dream in which he was visited by the Ghost of Christmas Past. "It had Steinbrenner's face, and Billy Martin's body," said Lee, conjuring up the most distasteful vision he could imagine. Jackson attacked Lee with his bat, hammering a home run that tied up an important game at two runs each. As Jackson jogged around third base, his teammates, responding to his achievement, forgot their animosity and prepared to greet him with handshakes and pats on the back, the traditional reception for a home-run hitter. As Jackson crossed home plate, he pointedly ignored his waiting teammates and headed toward the far corner of the dugout, returning snub for snub.

The next day, in a meeting he requested with Martin, Jackson said, "Every player on this team hates and despises me." So did the manager, who wouldn't admit his feelings to Jackson, perhaps not even to himself. The closest Martin would come to articulating how much he hated Jackson was to say that he would play Hitler and

Mussolini in his lineup if he thought they could help the team. During this crisis, Steinbrenner managed to avoid saying anything publicly to antagonize Munson or Jackson or Martin. Even the owner, apparently, realized that constructive turmoil had its limits.

Eventually, the tension subsided. After a few tentative peacemaking overtures by Jackson were scorned, Munson relented and began shaking Jackson's hand again, permitting him back into the Yankees' fold. Jackson's batting average began to perk up. In early June, in fact, he hit safely in fourteen straight games, his longest hitting streak in three years. The streak ended on June 18, the day that any pretense of a decent relationship between Billy Martin and Reggie Jackson also came to an end. The Yankees were playing in Boston, with first place at stake, and in the sixth inning, with the Red Sox ahead by three runs, a pop fly fell in front of Jackson for a double. His speed in getting to the ball was not impressive—especially for a man who had run the one-hundred-yard dash in under ten seconds in high school—and his throw back to the infield was equally uninspired. Billy Martin decided right then, in the middle of an inning, to pull Jackson out of the game, to punish him for not demonstrating sufficient hustle. Martin ordered Paul Blair into right field. When Reggie saw Blair coming, coming through the infield, heading straight for him, he couldn't believe his eyes. "You coming after me?" Jackson said.

"Yeah," Blair said.

"Why?" Jackson said.

"You got to ask Billy that."

Jackson began running toward the dugout. NBC cameras, televising the national "Game of the Week," caught his expression, a mixture of anger and confusion, and tracked him right into the dugout, then zoomed in on his confrontation with Martin. Jackson spread his hands,

plaintively. "What did I do? What did I do?"

Martin snapped back, "What do you mean, what did you do? You know what you did."

"Why did you take me out?" Jackson demanded. "You had to be crazy to embarrass me in front of fifty million people."

Martin swore at Jackson, and Jackson swore back, and Elston Howard, the Yankee coach, moved between the two men. "You showed me up in front of fifty million people," Jackson said. "You're not a man. Don't you ever show me up again, you motherfucker!"

Martin, triggered by the ultimate epithet, charged, ready as always to prove his point with punches. Players and coaches reached out to restrain him. "You never did like me," Reggie shouted. "You never did want me on the ball club. I'm here to stay, so you better start liking me!"

Jackson was wrong on one count. Characteristically, he overstated his television appeal. There weren't fifty million people watching, not even half that number. But the one man who counted was watching. George Steinbrenner was livid. He had flown to Cleveland for a funeral, had tuned in the game on NBC and now, based on what he had seen, he was ready to bury Martin. He telephoned the press box in Boston and told Mickey Morabito, the publicity director, to tell Gabe Paul, who was at the game, to phone him immediately. Paul did, and Steinbrenner told him to fire Martin, who had disgraced himself and the Yankees and quite possibly the nation with his display on television. Paul cautioned the owner that precipitous action might make it seem as if Jackson were running the ball club, might make Reggie's relations with his teammates worse, if possible, than ever. Steinbrenner relented, at least until he could catch up with Paul and the Yankees the following day, in Detroit.

That was what happened, according to Bill Crowley, the Boston publicity man, who said he took Steinbrenner's call

and put Morabito on the phone; according to Morabito, who said he passed the message along to Paul; according to Paul, who said he phoned Steinbrenner; and according to Billy Martin, who said that Gabe Paul saved his job. Dissenting testimony, however, came from George Steinbrenner, who, a year later, told his version of the incident to *Sports Illustrated*'s Ron Fimrite. "There was only one point when Billy was out," Steinbrenner said, "and that was after the incident in Boston. I wasn't even there. I was in North Carolina. Gabe called and said we've got to do it— to fire Billy." The soft blue spotlight glowed once more, creating its own reality.

Immediately after the incident, Fran Healy, a second-string catcher and a first-rate diplomat, hurried to the locker room and persuaded Jackson to leave the ball park, to avoid a postgame confrontation with Martin. Jackson, his ego badly bruised, didn't want to leave. That the incident had occured on television, *national television,* kept gnawing at him; he was on national television all the time during the off-season, but as a commentator for ABC Sports, an articulate, commanding voice, not as someone to be abused by a manager who made Napoleon seem humble. Finally, Jackson took Healy's advice, and when the game ended, Martin alone held court in the locker room. "I ask only one thing of my players—hustle," Martin said. "It doesn't take any ability to hustle. When they don't hustle, I don't accept that. When a player shows the club up, I show him up."

Jackson held court later, in his hotel room, comforted by a sympathetic teammate (pitcher Mike Torrez, who joined the Yankees after the start of the season and who was represented by the same agent as Jackson), a bottle of Mouton Cadet, two reporters and a beautiful young woman. The woman was the last thing on Jackson's mind. He wore a gold cross and two medallions, and, occasionally, as he talked, he thumbed through the Bible. "It makes me

cry the way they treat me on this team," Jackson said, very close to tears. "The Yankee pinstripes are Ruth and Gehrig and DiMaggio and Mantle. I'm just a black man to them who doesn't know how to be subservient. I'm a big nigger with an IQ of 160 making seven hundred thousand dollars a year, and they treat me like dirt. They've never had anyone like me on their team before." Jackson rambled on, about his intellect, about his wealth, about his talent, about his blackness, about his Christianity. Job had it easy, Jackson implied; he never had to put up with Billy Martin.

But, like Job, Jackson was able to maintain his faith, including his faith in the principal owner of the New York Yankees. "I love that man," he said of Steinbrenner. "He treats me like I'm somebody. The rest of them treat me like dirt."

Jackson's faintly veiled charge of racism against Martin was reinforced a few years later by the man who first stepped between the manager and the slugger in the dugout in Boston, coach Elston Howard. "I'll tell you plain out what the whole thing between Billy and Reggie was all about," Howard said not long before his death in 1980. "Billy was jealous of him, hated the attention Reggie got, couldn't control him. That was part of it. The other part, the big part, was that Reggie's black. Billy hated him for that. I believe Billy is prejudiced against blacks, Jews, American Indians, Spanish, anything, if you don't bow down to him. He can get along with blacks if they don't challenge him. But Reggie challenged him in every way. Billy was always hostile to him. Did everything to make him unhappy. Went out of his way to see him fail. I think Billy wanted Reggie to fail more than he wanted the Yankees to win." Howard's assessment omitted one fact: Martin hated to be challenged by white men, too, even rich white men who owned controlling interests in baseball teams.

The morning after the confrontation in Boston, Gabe Paul, trying to be a peacemaker, almost became a matchmaker. He invited both men to breakfast in his suite. After they rode up silently in the same elevator, Martin, instead of offering to make up, offered to wage the fist fight he had been deprived of the previous day. Paul eventually effected an uneasy truce, and then the Yankees went out and lost their third game in a row to Boston.

During the next two days, in Detroit, the Yankees ran their losing streak to five games and slipped four and a half games behind first-place Boston. The slump was understandable. The Yankees were putting more time and energy into meetings than into playing ball. Fran Healy, trying to become the first baseball player to be nominated for the Nobel Peace Prize, met separately with Jackson, Martin, Steinbrenner and Paul, counseling calm and reason. Steinbrenner, meeting with Martin, counseled discipline and self-control, and Martin, in turn, counseled independence, a chance to manage free from interference.

A story began circulating that Martin would be fired within days and replaced by Yogi Berra, that the decision was already made. That story was broken by Milton Richman of United Press International, a reporter with an uncanny knack for *accurate* exclusive stories. Richman was believable, and his report stirred up a storm of pro-Martin, anti-Jackson, anti-Steinbrenner sentiment. Steinbrenner, in turn, decided to deliver a locker-room speech calling upon his players to stop showing prejudice toward any teammate or teammates. He decided to leak the information that Reggie Jackson was actually trying to save Martin's job, lobbying on his behalf. And he decided to spread the word that all decisions, including Martin's fate, were being made not by him, but by Gabe Paul.

Properly deputized, Gabe Paul went to the press box in Detroit and made an announcement. "There will be no change in our organization, regardless of what has been

said," Paul announced. "We don't feel there's a better manager than Billy Martin, and we want the Yankees to have the best."

"Who made the decision to keep Martin?" Paul was asked.

"This was my decision," Gabe Paul said.

The next day, George Steinbrenner held a news conference, and besides announcing that he had intimidated a "very subdued" Martin ("The next time you drive me to the wall," he said he had told his manager, "I'll throw you over it"), and besides revealing that his players had been absolutely inspired by his latest locker-room speech ("We want you around, watching things, pulling for us," he said his players had told him), Steinbrenner said unequivocally that the decision to keep Billy Martin "was my decision entirely."

If Steinbrenner had charged onto the field in the middle of a nationally televised game and yanked Gabe Paul out of his box seat, he could not have more blatantly humiliated the team president. Paul had had enough. He packed up and headed home to Tampa, his home, too, with Steinbrenner chasing after him, beseeching him to return, promising him that he would never again be treated so shabbily. Gabe Paul returned, for his final few months in Steinbrenner's employ.

The Yankees returned, too, to Yankee Stadium, and promptly won three straight games from the Red Sox. Within a week, they were back in first place, the perfect spot to celebrate George Steinbrenner's forty-seventh birthday. Considering the incredible chaos that had been created by the Yankees' three superegos, it was hard to believe that the 1977 baseball season was only half over.

The second half of the season was not appreciably different, a blend of intrigue and duplicity that moved the Washington *Post,* the newspaper that exposed Watergate, to label the baseball situation "Yankeegate." Martin,

Jackson and Steinbrenner continued to imitate the Flying Wallendas, with Martin most often the man alone out on the tight wire, and Steinbrenner down below insisting bravely that the act was much more dramatic without a net. Steinbrenner gave more pep talks and, before the break for the All-Star Game, gave each of his players three hundred dollars to go out and have a good time. Martin lost control of several of his players because he put so much of his effort into controlling one of them—Reggie Jackson. Munson and Lou Piniella, trusted veterans, both of whom liked to needle Steinbrenner (Piniella would tell the boss that they understood each other, that they were both "bullshitters"), went to Steinbrenner's hotel room late one night in July to talk about the impossible position Billy Martin was in, and Martin, passing by, heard their voices, knocked on the door and found them in an impossible position, going to the owner behind the manager's back. "What the hell's going on here?" Martin asked when Steinbrenner opened his door.

"Nothing's going on here," Steinbrenner said.

Martin pushed his way into the room, shoved open the door to the bathroom and discovered Piniella and Munson. Martin was less angry with them—they had been telling Steinbrenner either to fire Martin, if he was going to do it, or to stop driving him crazy—than he was with the owner. "He was lying to me at the door," Martin said later. "He doesn't know what truth is."

Still, Martin, Munson, Piniella and Steinbrenner talked through much of the night, and Martin, congenitally incapable of pulling his punches, when asked what was wrong with the team, told Steinbrenner, "You are. You're meddling in the club and making things bad."

Out of the meeting Martin scored one victory: Steinbrenner promised that Billy would receive his full salary even if he were fired for violating the small print in his contract, the clauses in which he swore to love, honor and, most

199

important, obey George Steinbrenner and his deputies.

Steinbrenner's meddling, as Martin called it, or his involved ownership, as George himself called it, did not cease. "I'm an involved guy," Steinbrenner later told *Sixty Minutes'* Harry Reasoner. "I never made any bones about it when I took over the Yankees. I said I'm going to be an involved owner." Actually, when Steinbrenner took over the Yankees, he had said that he was going to be an uninvolved owner, that he was going to concentrate on his family and on shipbuilding. But an accurate memory was never Steinbrenner's forte. "The reason baseball has its problems today," he said, "is because owners weren't involved twenty years ago. They treated baseball as a hobby, as a toy, and they left all the decisions in the hands of the general managers, who were baseball men. They weren't businessmen. They didn't know how to negotiate a labor contract or how to sign a big television deal. I'm an involved owner. I want my fans to know I'm involved because they mean a lot to me." By "my fans," Steinbrenner, of course, meant Yankee fans. "I mean when a guy driving a cab or working on a building in New York yells 'Attaboy!' or tells me to do this or do that, that's important to me, and I want them to know that I'm involved because I'm like they are. I die when we lose, just like they do." Or, as Steinbrenner phrased it on another occasion, "I'm like Archie Bunker. I get mad as hell when we blow one."

Steinbrenner's involvement drove Martin mad. Martin hated Steinbrenner's coming to him with stacks of statistics and telling him, based on the statistics, who should be in the lineup and who should be pitching. Martin wouldn't believe the numbers because he didn't believe Steinbrenner. He hated Steinbrenner's questioning every move he made that backfired, every pinch-hitter who failed, every relief pitcher who struggled. He hated Steinbrenner's acting as if he knew something about baseball or any other sport. Billy had played ball in schoolyards and in the minor

leagues, on bad fields and under bad lights, had felt ninety-mile-an-hour fastballs dig into his ribs and had ducked under pitches that were supposed to take off his head. What did Steinbrenner know about baseball, about strategy, about when to go with the percentages, and when to buck them? Martin scoffed at Steinbrenner's football training. He refused to believe that the overweight owner ever drew X's or O's or taught young men to block and tackle. Behind the owner's back, Martin ridiculed him. He said that, as a football coach, Steinbrenner's big job was to get tickets for the familes of the players. The manager said he'd love to see Steinbrenner in a dugout, under pressure; he would collapse, unable to make a decision. Martin hated Steinbrenner for loving Reggie Jackson some of the time, and for not loving Billy Martin all of the time. The manager denigrated the owner often, to friends and to reporters, and he bragged about his own appeal. He swelled up every time a crowd cheered him, and every time a crowd booed Steinbrenner. The fans knew, Billy said. They knew who was the hero, and who was the villain. If only George would go away, and perhaps take Reggie with him, then Billy would be able to win every game. He would outthink, outmotivate, outmaneuver everybody.

Martin got to the point where he hated to hear his phone ring, in his office or even in the dugout. Once, when the owner called the dugout immediately after a game, Billy tore the phone off the wall. But even Martin had to laugh about one call that came to the dugout in the middle of a game. Nettles answered. "It's George," he called to Martin.

"You gotta be kidding," Billy said.

"No," Nettles said. "It's really George."

Martin still didn't believe Nettles. The manager grabbed the phone. "Who is this?" he demanded.

"George," said the caller.

"Don't be calling me during the game, you asshole," Martin snapped and slammed the receiver down. Then he

turned to Nettles. "Imagine that," Billy said, "a guy trying to imitate George."

"That was George," said Nettles.

In the first printing of *Number 1,* Martin made a point of attacking Steinbrenner for violating his privacy. He claimed that the owner had a special telephone system installed in Yankee Stadium so that he could monitor anyone's calls, and that, using the tapped phone and other information, he was assembling a dossier on Martin's personal and financial life. The manager charged that, when his agent called on Steinbrenner, George pointed at his file cabinets and warned, "I have a file on Billy Martin. I have dates. I have names. I know everything about the man's private life, and let me assure you I won't hesitate to use it. I'll destroy this man if he pushes me too far."

That threat, and all other references to the file cabinets and the tapped telephone, disappeared from the second printing of *Number 1.* A statement from Eddie Sapir, Martin's attorney, explained the vanishing act. "Billy has been in George's office hundreds of times and now recalls that there are absolutely no file cabinets in the office," Sapir said, "and therefore George could not have pointed to any." As for Steinbrenner's listening to Martin's conversations, the Yankees furnished Judge Sapir with the installation manual for their phone system, and after studying the manual, the judge decreed, "The system in no way could allow for any kind of monitoring. I discussed this with Billy and Billy accepted it. Billy is sorry if the published reports have embarrassed or offended George or anyone else."

In July of 1977, as in March and April and June, and possibly May, Billy Martin once again was on the edge of being fired. He couldn't control his players; he couldn't control his tongue. "He seems to love being a martyr," Steinbrenner said. The rumors were persistent. Dick Howser, one of his coaches, was going to replace him.

Frank Robinson, baseball's first black manager, who had been fired by Cleveland, was going to replace him. Martin was gone, through, finished. Yet he survived. He survived to endure a new humiliation. He was handed, and so were the news media, George Steinbrenner's Seven Commandments, regulations posing as questions, establishing guidelines for Billy Martin to live by—and to be judged by:

1. Does he win?
2. Does he work hard enough?
3. Is he emotionally equipped to lead the men under him?
4. Is he organized?
5. Is he prepared?
6. Does he understand human nature?
7. Is he honorable?

Martin's reaction was simple: "Here was a felon setting himself up as judge and jury to decide whether I was good enough, moral enough . . . to manage his team." Martin kept that reaction to himself for three years, until the publication of *Number 1*. In 1977, he accepted the commandments without public comment.

Actually, the first six points were items that Gabe Paul had long considered whenever he attempted to select a manager. Steinbrenner had added the first point, and had turned Paul's rough guide into a rigid code. It took Moses years, after he got his set of Commandments, from his Boss, to reach the Promised Land. Martin made it in months. But not before he, too, had to cross some barren land.

During the first week of August, the Yankees lost four of six games on a West Coast road trip, including two in a row to lowly Seattle, prompting Steinbrenner to announce, "I'm embarrassed. I apologize to the City of New York." Reggie Jackson, who had told a reporter a few weeks earlier, "I don't want to play in New York, I don't want to be here anymore," revealed that he had an escape clause in his contract, a provision permitting him to leave the Yankees

after two seasons, prompting Gabe Paul to announce that Jackson's contract did not have "the so-called release provision." And Thurman Munson, who spent almost the whole season in a miserable mood, began growing a beard to show what he thought of his clean-shaven employer, prompting Paul to let Martin know that his job was being jeopardized by Munson's beard. Munson shaved to make life smoother for Martin.

And then the Yankees lost an exhibition game to their Syracuse farm team. The next day, an off day, August 9, 1977, the Yankees woke up in third place and fading, five games behind the Boston Red Sox. Then, suddenly, everything turned around. Martin admitted that he was responsible. First, he said, "I decided that Reggie was going to be my number-four hitter." Second, he persuaded Steinbrenner to allow him to bring in his old friend and drinking buddy, Art Fowler, to become pitching coach, and Fowler, according to Martin, revitalized the pitching staff, especially Ron Guidry.

The Yankees won twenty-three of their next twenty-six games, went from five games behind to four and a half games ahead and held first place the rest of the season. They had achieved a small miracle in overtaking the Red Sox, and a greater miracle in overcoming an owner who, according to the manager, was trying to keep the team from winning, and a manager who, according to the owner, was incapable of making a wise move on his own. Just before the start of the American League championship series, Steinbrenner told *Sports Illustrated*'s Ron Fimrite that the reason the Yankees had struggled until August was that Martin's ego drove him to compete with Jackson and Munson for attention, instead of working hard and providing leadership and discipline. As a result, the owner suggested, the players had not united behind Martin and had not played with pride. What transformed them into winners? Steinbrenner pointed modestly to his seven-point

code of managerial behavior, and to two strategic decisions: Moving Jackson into the cleanup spot and making Lou Piniella the designated hitter. Steinbrenner confessed he had been advocating both moves since spring training. "Every chance he got he was telling people how he had won it for New York," Martin charged, "and he downplayed the role Gabe and I played whenever he could."

Steinbrenner clearly felt he deserved credit not only for turning the Yankees around, but for turning Martin around. "Now Billy's really trying," the owner said. "He's better prepared. He's working longer and harder. He just had to learn that everyone has a boss, that everybody is accountable to someone. This is what Billy has needed all his life. In the past, nobody ever kept the heat on him the way we have. In all those other places, they'd let him get away with things, complain a lot and then fire him. I don't want to do that. I like Billy very much. I'm probably the best friend he's got. We'll make a better man out of him."

Still, Steinbrenner was not ready to guarantee that Martin would be managing the Yankees again in 1978. "Billy doesn't have to win it all this year to keep his job," Steinbrenner said. "He just has to meet Gabe's criteria— and remember, they're Gabe's criteria, not mine, as everyone seems to think." The owner had one final thought. "No," George Steinbrenner said, "I don't mind when he gets cheered at home plate."

In Steinbrenner's opinion, Steinbrenner had won the pennant; in Martin's opinion, Martin had. But each of them was willing to admit, if he had to, that he couldn't have done it without the players. Several of the Yankees were magnificent down the stretch, but two, in particular, stood out. One was Reggie Jackson, who, refreshingly, did not claim he had won the pennant, not in so many words. His bat spoke eloquently for him. From August 10 on, from the time he became the regular cleanup hitter, Jackson hit thirteen home runs and drove in forty-nine runs, a pace

that, if extended over the full season, would have made him the American League leader in both home runs and runs batted in. Jackson was awesome, to everyone except Billy Martin, who could still say, a year later, "He's never shown me he's a superstar. I look at him as one of twenty-five players. I never put him above Chris Chambliss or Thurman Munson or Willie Randolph or Mickey Rivers or Roy White."

Unappreciated by his manager, and by most of his teammates, Jackson felt depressed despite his brilliant finish. "I just might quit," Reggie said. "I can't stand the tension. I'm not enjoying anything about the game except playing it. The rest of it, the crowds, the fans, the press, the problems, I really don't want that anymore."

If Jackson took command in the stretch, so did Ron Guidry, a man so gentle and quiet that he seemed a misfit in the chaos of the Yankee clubhouse. Starting August 10, Guidry won eight games in a row, three of them shutouts, two consecutively. He became the dominant pitcher in the American League. Ironically, the two men who wanted the credit for masterminding the Yankees' surge—Martin and Steinbrenner—knew they had to split the credit for the performances by Jackson and Guidry. Steinbrenner, of course, merited full credit for Jackson; the owner had wooed him, had put up the money for him and had lobbied for him all season long, overcoming Martin's resistance. But if Steinbrenner was one of Jackson's strongest support- ers, he was one of Guidry's weakest. More than once, in spring training and during the regular season, Steinbren- ner had been tempted to send Guidry back to the minor leagues, or trade him, convinced that he was too frail to be a consistently successful major-league pitcher. But Gabe Paul and Billy Martin both sensed Guidry's possibilities, and both fought to protect him. They won, which meant that Steinbrenner, in this case, did not put up strenuous resistance.

Then came the playoffs, and for the second straight year, Kansas City represented the American League West, and for the second straight year, the Yankees and the Royals split the first four games, the series coming down to a decisive fifth game, this time in Kansas City. Jackson had fallen into a terrible slump at the worst possible time. In the first four games against Kansas City, he had gotten one hit in fourteen times at bat. Billy Martin decided to bench Jackson for the fifth game, to substitute Paul Blair, the same man who had replaced Jackson in Boston in June, setting off an explosion.

Martin said he was taking Jackson out of the lineup because Kansas City was using Paul Splittorff, a left-handed pitcher who, during the regular season, had held Jackson to two hits in fifteen times at bat; Martin had no objection to statistics as long as they confirmed his decisions. Martin did not say that he was benching Jackson because he wanted to prove, to Steinbrenner, to Jackson and perhaps even to himself, that he could win without Jackson. Martin didn't have to say that. His subconscious was showing.

The decision to use Blair instead of Jackson was both bold and defiant, certain to rankle Steinbrenner, likely to cost Martin his career if it backfired, if the Yankees lost and Blair, in even the smallest way, contributed to the defeat. Martin never hesitated. He sent Elston Howard, the coach, and Fran Healy, the diplomat, to inform Jackson of his decision. He informed Steinbrenner himself. As the manager was explaining the move to the owner, Catfish Hunter walked by. "Hey, Cat," Steinbrenner called, "can Reggie hit Splittorff?"

"Not with a paddle," Hunter said.

Steinbrenner turned back to Martin. "You can do it," the owner said, "but if it doesn't work, you're going to have to suffer the consequences."

"Fine," said Martin, "as long as if it works, I get the credit."

It worked. In the eighth inning, after a righthanded pitcher relieved Splittorff for Kansas City, Martin called upon Jackson as a pinch-hitter, and Jackson delivered, a single, driving in a run to cut Kansas City's lead to 3–2. Then, in the ninth, Paul Blair, Jackson's replacement, led off with a single that started a three-run rally that lifted the Yankees to victory and into the World Series for the second year in a row.

Steinbrenner applauded the victory, and, especially, Jackson's pinch-hit under pressure. "When he came in, he delivered a hit instead of sulking," Steinbrenner said. "That shows everyone in New York he's a team man."

Jackson was impressed, too, by his performance. "I can't explain it," he said, "because I don't understand the magnitude of Reggie Jackson and the magnitude of the event." Then, suddenly understanding everything, Jackson said, "I am the situation."

Martin had something to say, too. He sprayed champagne on Steinbrenner during the locker-room celebration and called out, "That's for trying to fire me."

The owner had the proper comeback. "What do you mean, 'try'?" Steinbrenner said. "If I want to, I'll fire you."

Then came the World Series, and while the official match-up was the Yankees against the Los Angeles Dodgers, the real match-up was Martin against Jackson, a war of words, all of them transmitted through intermediaries. First Martin told a circle of reporters that Jackson would be in the starting lineup during the World Series because, he said sarcastically, "Splittorff isn't pitching for them."

Stung by the needle, Jackson struck back. He told his own circle of reporters that Martin made a terrible mistake in the second game of the World Series starting Catfish Hunter, whose arm was painfully weak. Hunter gave up four home runs and didn't last three innings, allowing the

Dodgers to even the Series at one victory apiece. "Billy embarrassed him," Jackson said. "The man should never have been in there."

Advised of Jackson's criticism, Martin told his media audience, "He's got enough trouble playing right field without second-guessing the manager. He can kiss my dago ass."

Jackson did better than that. He saved Martin's Italian hide. Jackson batted in one run as the Yankees won the third game of the Series, hit a double and a home run as the Yankees won the fourth game, then wasted a home run in the fifth game, which the Dodgers won to stay alive.

The two teams did not play the next day, giving Martin, Jackson and Steinbrenner plenty of time to read *Time,* which carried a story revealing, among other things, that Jackson had told Steinbrenner he would not play another season under Billy Martin. Of course Jackson had made the statement—and had meant it, at the moment he said it—but now he flatly denied the remark, then confirmed it by implication. He said the source of the remark had to be "someone who never betrayed me before"—in other words, the man to whom he had made the remark.

George Steinbrenner used two hours of the day off to grant an interview to *The New York Times.* For the interview, conducted in his handsome office high in Yankee Stadium, Steinbrenner's blue tie, gold cufflinks and diamond ring all bore the "NY" or "NYY" symbol, and his hair was sprayed into perfect obedience. "It's lonely at the top," he said. "It's the loneliest place in the world." And he said much more.

The morning of the sixth game, the *Times* ran a front-page story headlined, "Steinbrenner Plans to Keep Jackson with Yankees in '78." Steinbrenner declined to say that he would also keep Billy Martin with the Yankees in '78. "It's Gabe's decision," the owner insisted. "He's a brilliant man on baseball, brilliant." The brilliant man arrived at his

decision very quickly. Only hours after the *Times* article appeared, Gabe Paul called a news conference to reveal that Reggie Jackson would be playing for his least favorite manager in '78. "We are pleased to announce," Paul said, "that Billy Martin will continue as Yankee manager and has been rewarded with a substantial bonus in recognition of the fine job he has done. We hope this will put to rest the unfounded rumors that a change was about to be made."

Martin's fifty-thousand-dollar bonus included a Lincoln Mark V, plus a four-hundred-dollar-a-month apartment in New Jersey rent-free. The news of this windfall was on the radio as Jackson drove to Yankee Stadium from his considerably more expensive Fifth Avenue apartment, which overlooked Central Park, in his silver-and-blue Rolls Royce, which was worth more than Martin's entire bonus.

After Jackson reached Yankee Stadium, he proceeded to put on the most spectacular batting show in World Series history. His first time up, he walked. His second time up, he swung at Burt Hooton's first pitch and drove a fastball into the right-field stands. His third time up, he swung at Elias Sosa's first pitch and drove another fastball into the right-field stand. His fourth time up, he swung at Charlie Hough's first pitch and drove a knuckleball deep into the center-field bleachers. Three pitches, three swings, three home runs, five runs batted in, seven World Series records tied, and one broken. The Yankees won the game and the world championship, and as joy and champagne splashed the Yankee clubhouse, George Steinbrenner posed with his arm around Billy Martin, and then Reggie Jackson, still floating on cheers, walked into Martin's office, and both of them were absolutely beaming. Jackson did not kiss Martin, not anywhere, but he did hug him. Martin hugged Jackson back, a warm embrace, as real as victory. Now the two men shared the same circle of reporters. "You did a helluva job, big guy," the manager said.

Jackson glowed. He was, for the moment and forever, Mr. October. "Billy Martin," he said. "I love the man. I love Billy Martin. The man did a helluva job this year. There's nobody else I'd rather play for."

No narcotic in the world magnifies and distorts feelings the way winning does. "Billy Martin and I are a lot alike," George Steinbrenner said, just before his team won the World Series. "If George Steinbrenner were a ballplayer," said Reggie Jackson, not long afterward, "he would be Reggie Jackson." Martin never went quite so far as to put Steinbrenner or Jackson on his level, but he did admit that he was very happy for both of them.

To Steinbrenner, 1977 had been an idyllic year, a year that had brought two million fans and a world championship to Yankee Stadium, a year that—like a good war—built character. ("World War Two, that was a great war," Steinbrenner once said, in explaining why he liked to read World War II books.) Now he felt the 1977 season had given his Yankee team "mental toughness," a quality Steinbrenner cherished. "Next year's Yankee team will have more stability," the owner said. "We won't have to go through this again."

Steinbrenner was right. The next year, 1978, was much more stable. In fact, if you discount the spending of almost three million dollars for one free-agent relief pitcher, Rich Gossage, who was worth every penny, and the spending of more than one million for another free-agent relief pitcher, Rawley Eastwick, who wasn't worth much more than a penny; if you discount the alienating of veteran relief pitcher Sparky Lyle, who, as Graig Nettles said, went from Cy Young to *sayonara,* shipped off to Texas, bitter enough to author a book called *The Bronx Zoo,* the ultimate in locker-room humor and locker-room language; if you discount the resignation of the team's president, and the forced resignation of the team's manager; and if you discount the stunning fact that the Yankees came from

fourth place, fourteen games out of first, more than half-way through the season, to win a one-game playoff for first place; if you discount all of that, it was almost an uneventful year.

5

When Gabe Paul departed at the beginning of 1978, five years after he had helped introduce a little-known Cleveland shipbuilder to New York, only three of George Steinbrenner's thirteen original "limited partners" were still limited partners. Of the nine top executives listed in the Yankee organizational chart at the start of the 1973 season—not including the co-managing partner, who had evolved into the principal owner—only one remained. And of the thirty-seven men who played for the Yankees in 1973, only five were around for the start of the 1978 season. Steinbrenner had reshaped the Yankees, had turned them into world champions, and he was, finally, and beyond question, a celebrity, his stature certified by a cover story—"That Damn Yankee"—in *The New York Times Magazine,* lifting him right up to the level of Giscard and Margaret Thatcher and Brezhnev and Deng Xiaoping and all the other people whose words and deeds shook the earth as perceived by *The New York Times.*

Steinbrenner loved being on the cover of the *Times Magazine,* and he very much liked the article, wonderfully researched and written by Tony Kornheiser, even though the article, never less than objective and occasionally harsh, was certainly not a puff piece. Steinbrenner, as much as any public figure, understands the value of publicity, and works hard to try to shape and influence coverage so that it turns out to be favorable. If, in the days of his Watergate problems, he used a sick child or a sick wife to try to stifle painful publicity, in later days he has favored more positive devices. For instance, when Kornheiser sought an interview, Steinbrenner reacted typically. "He said, 'I don't want to do this,'" Kornheiser recalled. "'I'm only doing it because I know you're truthful, I know you're fair. Don't hurt me.' He says the same thing to all the guys." Steinbrenner tried to impose two ground rules, that his family be kept out of the article, and that his Watergate conviction not be mentioned. Kornheiser agreed to stay away from the family. Kornheiser himself excluded from the article a story he had heard about a former Yankee secretary accusing Steinbrenner of improper advances. Kornheiser examined the charge and satisfied himself that the story had no substance.

Steinbrenner grew wise enough about the ways of the media not to waste his efforts on minor stories, to concentrate on the national magazines and network television. When Pete Axthelm wrote a major profile for *Newsweek,* George was at his most charming. "Several times during our lively talks," Axthelm reported, "Steinbrenner has lowered his voice and fixed me with a particularly sincere smile. Then he has confided intimate, sensitive details about his private charitable gestures or his delicate relations with Yankee players. Each time, I've been assured that I have received this information only because I was certain to handle it with utmost journalistic tact. My pride in becoming such a confidant has been dimmed only

slightly when I've read the same tidbits in the columns of other writers who have undoubtedly been similarly entrusted and flattered." Axthelm's story, like Kornheiser's, was fair and balanced and, still, pleasing enough to its subject so that a couple of years later, when Marie Brenner wrote of "Boss Steinbrenner: The Yankees' Biggest Superstar" for *New York* magazine, she spotted among George's memos one reminding him, "Make sure Pete Axthelm's daughter gets to meet Bucky Dent."

Kornheiser and Axthelm did not allow Steinbrenner's charm to alter their journalistic judgments. There is a persistent rumor, however, that one writer, who was working on a Steinbrenner article for a publication that did not normally cover sports subjects, was not quite so scrupulous. Steinbrenner promised the writer, directly or indirectly, that he would speak to his friend Bob Hope about having the writer collaborate on Hope's autobiography, a project that was certain to be very profitable, *if* the writer treated George favorably enough in his article. The writer responded with a story that made George seem like a cross between St. Francis of Assisi and Albert Schweitzer.

In a similarly flattering story about Steinbrenner in *Sport* magazine, a writer named Roger Kahn quoted Steinbrenner as saying, "Don't be a stranger. Is your hotel room okay? I really like your books. Don't forget to bring your kids to the Stadium. They'll be my guests. It will be great spending more time together." Kahn, who takes compliments very seriously, especially compliments about his books (he wrote the baseball book *The Boys of Summer* and the diet book *Calories Don't Count),* either did not know or thought it impolite to point out that praise for your work and concern for your welfare, coming from Steinbrenner, when you are about to write a story about him, is not quite the same as having John Updike praise your prose in *The New Yorker*. Kahn, after reciting

215

Steinbrenner's kind words, added, very earnestly, "The winter had been bitter cold, and my new novel was proceeding at a slow, strangely exhausting tempo. Now the world excited me anew."

Steinbrenner had a more numbing effect on Harry Reasoner when *Sixty Minutes* examined the Yankees' owner. Reasoner is an experienced and knowledgeable reporter, an admirable craftsman, capable of facing presidents and tyrants without being intimidated, without blunting his questions. But when Reasoner went one-on-one with Steinbrenner, he acted like a society reporter given his first hard-news story. He was practically fawning. Even interviewing Steinbrenner about Watergate, Reasoner could not bring himself to be professionally tough.

Reasoner: "George, every time a story on you comes out, there's a mention of the felony conviction."

Steinbrenner: "Yes."

Reasoner: "I don't even know really what it was about, but it's just a tag now that goes after your name."

Steinbrenner: "Yes."

Reasoner: "A felony conviction could be anything, rape or murder or anything else. I don't know what the real story was. What was it?"

It is almost impossible to imagine as good a reporter as Reasoner, backed up by producers and researchers, going into an interview with a national figure not really knowing what the subject's felony conviction was all about. It is conceivable that Reasoner was simply trying to play the innocent, attempting to draw out a good answer, but if he had been using that technique, Reasoner would have challenged Steinbrenner's response, which was riddled with inaccuracies and distortions.

"Well," said Steinbrenner, "it had to do with the violation of a fifty-nine-year-old law that most attorneys didn't even know about during the Nixon campaign. It had to do

216

with corporate donations to his campaign. Richard Nixon's campaign . . . What I did was I went to my boys and I said, 'Look, if you give a dollar, I'll give three to the campaign.'" That was precisely what *hadn't* happened; none of his "boys" put up, or were even asked to put up, a penny of their own, much less a dollar; his boys had put up twenty-five thousand dollars of the corporation's money, at his direction. "Many corporations in this country were guilty . . ." Steinbrenner continued. "I just feel a little differently than a lot of the others who let the number three and four man step in and take the blame. I firmly believe that if you are the boss, you step up and you take the blame . . . The captain of the ship has to take the blame, not put it on the first mate or the second mate, but you take it yourself and, I was convicted of a felony in, in regards to an illegal campaign contribution."

If anyone else had tried to slip such an evasive and self-serving answer past Reasoner, the chances are he would have picked the answer to shreds. Instead, Reasoner just said cheerfully, "Didn't lead you into a life of crime, though?"

"No, it didn't, thank goodness," said Steinbrenner, with a chuckle, delighted to be getting away with his answer. Then, with a straight face, Steinbrenner told Reasoner what great respect he had for the media because of the way the media covered "the whole incident of what happened," Steinbrenner's euphemism for his felony conviction. "Every time somebody wants to be critical of the media and the Fourth Estate," Steinbrenner said to Reasoner, "I stop and think where would we have been in this country without them. Because they, they're our conscience . . ."

Steinbrenner's tribute to the Fourth Estate, *and* the media, was not used on the air, but his "If you give a dollar, I'll give three" was—without challenge. Steinbrenner did not bribe Reasoner or Don Hewitt, the producer of the program, to treat him so gently. He couldn't have; he didn't

have to. He *charmed* them, or *conned* them. It's difficult sometimes to tell those words apart, they sound so much alike.

Steinbrenner's magic has worked even on so hardened a newsman as A. M. Rosenthal, executive editor of *The New York Times,* a Pulitzer Prize winner and a former foreign correspondent, a man who handles daily national and international crises with objectivity. Rosenthal, and his deputy managing editor, Arthur Gelb, occasionally enjoy pregame meals in the Great Moments Room and then watch games from Box 332, and while neither of them has ever ordered anyone on the *Times* to write a story favorable to Steinbrenner, both of them did seem genuinely upset when the Los Angeles Dodgers won the 1981 World Series. "It was awful the way we lost," said Rosenthal, who would never dream of being so partisan to a political candidate or a political issue.

Before the start of spring training, 1978, George Steinbrenner promoted Al Rosen from executive vice-president to president of the Yankees, the new buffer between the manager and the management. "It's not so easy for Billy to look Al Rosen in the face and say, 'What do you know about baseball?'" said Steinbrenner, who knew very well what Martin thought of his baseball expertise. But even with Rosen between them, the relationship between Martin and Steinbrenner deteriorated. Martin didn't like the trades Steinbrenner proposed, he hated the lineup changes Steinbrenner suggested and, most of all, he fumed because he believed Steinbrenner was feeding stories to the newspapers that were intended to make the manager look bad, to the public and to his players. The owner, of course, felt that he was doing no more than the things he had to do to make a better man out of Billy Martin.

Still, the season lasted almost two full months before the

two men had their first major confrontation, and by then the Yankees were in second place, trailing Boston by three games. At the end of May, with Thurman Munson nursing sore legs, Al Rosen promoted a young catcher from the minor leagues without informing Martin. Billy learned about his new player while watching a news show, and when Rosen finally did call, Billy hung up the phone on him—hard, and in front of reporters. A story appeared the next day recording Martin's reaction and using the phrase, "George's boys," a phrase Martin had employed during spring training to identify certain players. Martin said he had used the phrase only in jest, but George Steinbrenner did not laugh; the joke was not his own.

Martin came very close to being fired early in June. But he was spared. "Billy Martin is the manager of this ball club," Al Rosen said, "he has been the manager of this ball club, he will be the manager of this ball club."

Martin came very close to being fired late in June. Once again, interference triggered his anger. When a young pitcher named Jim Beattie started against the Boston Red Sox and was quickly knocked out, Steinbrenner, who was attending his first road game of the year, grumbled to reporters that Beattie looked "scared stiff" and ordered him shipped immediately to the minor leagues. Beattie, wounded to the point of tears, left the ball park before the game ended.

Steinbrenner later explained that he was simply trying to toughen Jim Beattie. "Beattie went to Dartmouth and I went to Williams," Steinbrenner said. "I know what it's like in an Ivy League setting. I knew that the kid had a great education in everything but street smarts. The next morning, I sent [pitching coach] Clyde King out to live with the kid, coach him and reclaim him. I know Jim resented me for it. But look what he did later." Later, in the same season, Beattie won three games in eleven days, the third victory lifting the Yankees into first place for the

first time all season, then won one game in the American League championship series and another in the World Series. The following year, he was sent first to the minors, then to the Seattle Mariners. Asked once about how George helped build his character, Beattie, an articulate young man, declined to comment. He didn't even say that Williams was not in the Ivy League.

The defeat in Boston dropped the Yankees eight full games behind the Red Sox, and once again rumors circulated that Martin's reign was over. "I won't put up with this much longer," Steinbrenner said. "I won't stand for what I see now." But, asked if Martin would soon go, Steinbrenner insisted, "It's Al Rosen's decision."

Martin, furious that Beattie had been demoted before he could even talk to the young pitcher, knew how Al Rosen would make the decision. "I'm sick and tired of hearing about being fired," Martin snapped. "I give George Steinbrenner one hundred percent loyalty, and I expect it in return. If he doesn't think I'm doing the job right, he should call Al Rosen and tell him to do something."

Al Rosen did not like being called a puppet. He also did not like being constantly reminded by George Steinbrenner that his job, too, was in jeopardy. "Billy, being a professional manager, knows what happens to managers who are supposed to win who don't win," said Rosen, after deciding, in consultation with Steinbrenner, that Martin had to be fired.

But once again Martin was spared, partly because no suitable replacement was available, partly because Steinbrenner sensed that the players and fans were on Martin's side and partly because Martin's agent, Doug Newton, presented a persuasive case for his client's retention. The principal owner himself announced that for "this year," Martin would remain the Yankees' manager. "This should end the speculation that has been developing of late concerning Billy's job," Steinbrenner said.

The owner was wrong on two counts. The speculation did not end—particularly after Bob Lemon, Rosen's friend and former teammate, became available, fired as manager by the Chicago White Sox—and Martin did not remain the manager for the rest of the year. If there was one man most responsible for Martin's departure—beyond Steinbrenner—it was, not surprisingly, Reggie Jackson. The love affair that had bloomed the previous October lasted only until March, until Jackson drove up to Yankee Stadium in Fort Lauderdale in his Rolls-Royce, late for the start of spring training. Steinbrenner had granted him permission to be late; Martin had not. "George understands me," Jackson said. "He's a businessman. I had business to take care of. Billy doesn't understand that. He's only a baseball manager."

Having demonstrated that he could still antagonize people instantly, Jackson then remained relatively free of controversy and out of the spotlight until the Yankees played their first home game of the season. A company called Standard Brands chose Opening Day at Yankee Stadium to introduce its newest candy, the Reggie bar, distributing thousands of the bars free to Reggie's fans. Reggie, unaware that the Baby Ruth bar was not named after Babe Ruth nor the O'Henry bar after Henry Aaron, had once said that if he played in New York they would name a candy bar after him. "Yes," said Catfish Hunter, "and when you unwrap one, it tells you how good it is." Now Reggie had his candy bar. That he had hit three home runs in the last game of the 1977 World Series hadn't hurt any. To make Opening Day even sweeter, Reggie delivered another home run, and, spontaneously, a large percentage of the 44,667 fans on hand decided to celebrate Reggie's feat by flooding the field with Reggie bars. Billy Martin sizzled. Candy never was his weakness, anyway.

For Jackson, the taste of the next few months was bitter. The Yankees slipped farther and farther behind the Boston

Red Sox, and if Ron Guidry had not won his first thirteen decisions—striking out eighteen California Angels in one of those victories—the Yankees might have been hopelessly out of contention by the Fourth of July. As it was, their hopes were slimmer even than Guidry. In the outfield, Jackson was a model of insecurity—an insecurity Martin nourished at every opportunity, with ridicule—and, at the plate, a model of inconsistency. Martin may have been losing the battle for the pennant, but he was winning the war for Jackson's mind. Martin turned Jackson from a starting outfielder into, first, a designated hitter, then a part-time designated hitter. In the locker room, Reggie once again was a fulltime pariah. His teammates and his manager resented the fact that he was the only player who attended Steinbrenner's birthday party and that he was the only player whose face appeared on T-shirts given away to fans at Yankee Stadium one day (Standard Brands paid for the T-shirts, and the company probably suspected that Sparky Lyle's face would not help sell Reggie bars.)

Right after the All-Star break, on July 13, Steinbrenner met with Martin and suggested several lineup changes, which Martin accepted. Steinbrenner said it was the best meeting he had ever had with his manager. Then Steinbrenner met with his players and delivered his first clubhouse speech of the year. "I'm not going to lie down and die like a dog," he said, "and neither are you. I expect you to accept whatever role you're given without griping and do it the best you can. You're among the best-paid athletes in the world, and I expect something in return since I sign the paychecks. We're going to do it the way I want to do it and the way Billy has agreed is the proper way to do it. If you don't like it, I'll try to accommodate you elsewhere."

Jackson sensed, reasonably, that several of Steinbrenner's remarks were aimed directly at him. He also sensed that Steinbrenner and Martin were getting closer, that he

was becoming the odd man in the triangle. The day after the clubhouse meeting, Steinbrenner and Martin filmed a commercial in which they argued over the merits of a certain beer. Steinbrenner settled the dispute by saying, "Billy, you're fired."

"Oh, no," Martin said. "Not again."

It was a very funny idea, at the time.

Two days later, Jackson, half afraid that the Yankees would trade him and half afraid that they wouldn't, attended the Yankees' Sunday morning chapel, then talked to Tom Skinner, a man who had preached at the meeting. "I've had enough," Jackson said, after explaining his situation.

"Don't give up," Skinner said. "Stick to it. God's preparing you for something. You can't do anything till you hear from God."

The next day, Jackson sat down and talked to Steinbrenner. "I'm afraid I'm losing control," Jackson said, looking for help. Steinbrenner said later he tried to be supportive. He said he told Jackson he participated in the decision to make Reggie the designated hitter, but added, "You should also be batting cleanup. I want you to bust your ass, and I want you to turn it on in the second half and make a pennant race of it, give the fans something to cheer about." The owner's words did not noticeably cheer Jackson. Martin said that Reggie emerged from the meeting in a miserable mood, scowling, mad at the world.

That night, against Kansas City, Billy Martin, heeding Steinbrenner's suggestion, had Jackson batting cleanup. Reggie went hitless his first four times at bat. He came up again in the tenth inning, the score tied, a man on first, none out. Martin flashed the bunt signal, asking Jackson to give himself up, to advance the runner. Not once all season had Martin asked Jackson to bunt. Only a handful of times in his career had Jackson been asked to bunt. Martin's request was an insult, which could be justified

strategically, but only barely. Martin seemed more interested in beating down Jackson than in beating Kansas City.

Jackson accepted the command. He turned to bunt the first pitch, then took it, high and inside, a ball. Martin noticed the Kansas City infielders moving in, crowding Jackson. He decided that winning the game was paramount, and took off the bunt sign. He signaled that Jackson should hit away. To make certain Jackson understood, Dick Howser, the third-base coach, called time out and approached the batter. "He wants you hitting away," Howser said.

"I'm going to bunt," Jackson said.

Jackson bunted, and missed the ball. He bunted again, and fouled off the ball. He bunted a third time and fouled off the ball once again, an automatic third strike. Martin, enraged, pulled Jackson out of the game for defying his orders. Martin was even more enraged when the Yankees lost the game the following inning. The manager stormed into the clubhouse, threw a clock radio on the floor, heaved an empty beer bottle against a wall and, visibly shaking, screamed, "No interviews, no fucking interviews."

Across the room, Jackson, of course, was conducting an interview, explaining that he had tried to do the best he could, considering that he was only a part-time player.

Cedric Tallis, the Yankees' vice-president, disappeared into Martin's office. The door closed. The two men talked. Then they talked by telephone to Al Rosen, then to George Steinbrenner, who was in Tampa. Then Billy Martin opened his door and made an announcement. "As of this moment," Martin said, "Reggie Jackson is suspended without pay, effective immediately, for deliberately disregarding the manager's instructions during his time at bat in the tenth inning. There isn't going to be anybody who defies the manager or management in any way. Nobody's bigger than the team. If he comes back again, he does

exactly what I say. Period. I don't get paid three million dollars. I don't disobey my boss' orders. He tells me to do something, I do it."

Martin said Jackson would be suspended for at least a week, but Rosen announced the next day that the suspension would last only five days. Jackson flew off to visit his home in California, and his agent in Arizona, and Martin and the rest of the Yankees flew off to Minneapolis, to start a one-week road trip that would end, in high drama, in Kansas City.

Martin was remarkably cheerful for the manager of a team that was fourteen games out of first place with seventy-three games to play. His health seemed to have improved, too. For much of the season, Martin had not seemed well physically. Steinbrenner confided to more than one reporter that the manager was having liver problems. Martin confided that he was having Steinbrenner problems, that the owner's harassment was making him sick.

The first day of Jackson's suspension, the Yankees didn't play. The next four days, the Yankees played, and won. Then Jackson came back, rejoined the team in Chicago, returned to a locker brightened by a dozen roses from an admirer and to a locker room overcrowded with reporters, all of them swarming around him. The whole scene disgusted Martin, who was in a bad mood, anyway. He had learned the night before that a few weeks earlier, Steinbrenner and Rosen had tried to trade him to the White Sox for Bob Lemon. Jackson repeated over and over, for each wave of questioners, that given the same situation, he would do the same thing, he would bunt. "I don't think what I did was wrong," he said. "I didn't regard it as an act of defiance."

Finally, he was asked what he had thought about most often during the five days he was suspended. Jackson considered the question, allowed a suitable amount of

silence and then said, "The magnitude of me."

Clearly, the suspension had not humbled him. Martin did not use Jackson that afternoon, against the Chicago White Sox, and the Yankees won their fifth straight, cutting Boston's lead to ten games. Afterwards, Martin did two things he would have been better off not doing. First, he asked a few reporters what Jackson had said and he found out that Jackson still felt he had done no wrong. Second, he drank several scotch and sodas. On the chartered bus taking the Yankees away from the ball park, Martin turned to Murray Chass of *The New York Times* and said, "When we get to the airport, can I see you for a few minutes?"

Chass said sure, and at the airport, Martin walked up to him, steaming. "I'm saying shut up, Reggie Jackson," Martin said. "We don't need none of your stuff. We're winning without you. We don't need you coming in and making all those comments. If he doesn't shut his mouth, he won't play and I don't care what George says. He can replace me right now if he doesn't like it."

The reporter listened carefully and checked to make certain Martin was talking on the record, for publication. Martin was. Chass promptly telephoned a story to the *Times,* then joined another reporter, Henry Hecht of the *Post,* waiting for the plane to Kansas City. Martin approached the two newspapermen.

"Did you get all that in the paper?" he asked Chass.

Chass said he had. Martin was delighted and, still in a talkative mood, told Chass and Hecht that Jackson, along with all his other faults, was a liar. "He's a born liar," Martin said. "They deserve each other. One's a born liar, the other's convicted."

When the Yankees reached Kansas City, Chass and Hecht both called George Steinbrenner, to get his reaction to Martin's harsh words. The owner was, understandably, shaken. "I . . . I just don't know what to say," he managed

to say. "I've got to believe that no boss in his right mind would take that."

By the next morning, after checking to make certain Bob Lemon was available, Al Rosen was on his way to Kansas City, to fire Martin, and Martin, to avoid being fired, was on his way to resign.

The two men's paths crossed in the Crown Center Hotel in Kansas City. "Tell George I didn't say those things," Martin told Rosen. Then, wearing dark glasses and a pair of World Series rings, Martin faced a group of newsmen. "There will be no questions and answers with anyone after the statement is made," Martin said. "That means now and forever, because I am a Yankee, and Yankees do not talk or throw rocks."

Then Martin turned to his notes and, fighting back tears, began to read. "I don't want to hurt this team's chances for the pennant with this undue publicity," Martin said. "The team has a shot at the pennant, and I hope they win it. I owe it to my health and my mental well-being to resign. At this time, I'm also sorry about those things that were written about George Steinbrenner. He does not deserve them, nor did I say them. I've had my differences with George, but we've been able to resolve them. I would like to thank the Yankee management, the press, the news media, my coaches, my players and, most of all, the fans." By the end of his statement, Martin was sobbing, and a friend led him away.

Martin's feelings were genuine, even if his words were not completely honest. In time, he would throw rocks, and he would admit that he had said those things about George Steinbrenner. But for the moment, he was a shattered man, stripped of the job he had always wanted, and his exit evoked a great amount of sympathy, though not from Reggie Jackson. Jackson was relieved. Mike Lupica, the columnist for the *Daily News,* was ecstatic. "Martin made the Yankee clubhouse the most unpleasant place in sport,"

Lupica wrote. "He was positively brilliant in creating an atmosphere of fear and hate . . . He deserves what he got . . . The Yankees are better off without him."

But Lupica's was a minority opinion, and as fan support for Martin swelled, Steinbrenner agonized, calculated, manipulated, then made the most flamboyant, the most dramatic move of his career. Three years earlier, on Old Timers' Day, 1975, Martin had been introduced as manager of the Yankees. Now, on Old Timers' Day, 1978, Bob Lemon, already in his fifth day on the job, was introduced—and instantly promoted. Bob Sheppard, the Yankees' announcer, informed the crowd over the public address system that, in two years, Lemon would move up from manager to general manager of the Yankees. "Managing the Yankees in the 1980 season," Sheppard said, "and hopefully for many seasons after that will be Number One . . ."

The crowd went crazy. There were 46,711 people in the stands, and perhaps 46,000 of them understood the moment they heard his uniform number mentioned that their hero was coming back, that Billy Martin was once again going to be the manager of the Yankees. Martin ran onto the field, and the crowd cheered for seven solid minutes. A reconciliation had been effected. Doug Newton, Martin's agent, had done a fine job of negotiating, and, more important, Billy Martin had said the three little words that mean so much to George Steinbrenner: I am sorry. "What he said to me," Steinbrenner said, "showed me that he was a man who realized he had made a small mistake, and it was small in the total picture."

Machiavelli himself would have envied Steinbrenner's maneuver. With one spectacular gesture, George accomplished much. He pacified the fans. He eliminated Martin as a critic. He made himself seem compassionate, forgiving, magnanimous. He salvaged the beer commercial in which he pretended to fire Martin—the advertising agency

228

was on the brink of scrapping it—and he won newspaper headlines from coast to coast, and network television coverage. Never on Broadway, not even with *Applause,* had Steinbrenner demonstrated such a flair for the theatrical. Even he had trouble maintaining a straight face. "There was a little bit of show biz in that," he confessed.

The move had only one disturbing side effect. Reggie Jackson was hurt. "I am bewildered," he said. He felt betrayed. He had, in his way, been very loyal to George. When he received his award as the Most Valuable Player in the 1977 World Series, he presented it to Steinbrenner, inscribed, "To George, No. 1, from Reggie, No. 44," a jab at Martin, as well as a bow to the boss. When a reporter asked Jackson during spring training, 1978, to summarize his attitude toward Steinbrenner, Reggie said, "I don't call anybody, 'Boss.' I call him, 'Boss.'" But now the Boss had turned on him, had promised publicly to bring back his enemy during the last two years of Reggie's five-year contract. Jackson might have been more upset if he, along with many other people, had not soon realized that the fact that Steinbrenner said Martin was coming back in 1980 did not necessarily mean that Martin was coming back in 1980. For one thing, Steinbrenner did not always do what he said he was going to do—sometimes for reasons beyond his control—and for another, Billy Martin had a year and a half in which his talent for self-destruction could ruin his career. The realization that Martin might never return consoled Jackson; so did the gentle treatment he received from Bob Lemon, who praised Reggie's skills and placated his ego.

Jackson and the Yankees both responded magnificently to Lemon's presence. The team won forty-eight of its last sixty-eight games under a manager whose trademark was enormous patience, not an enormous ego. The Yankees peaked between September 2 and September 16, when they shot from six and a half games behind Boston to three and

a half games in front, a remarkable surge. They won thirteen of fifteen games in those fifteen days, including six in a row from the Red Sox. Jackson again sizzled in September, hitting eight home runs and driving in twenty-six runs, his most productive month of the season.

The Yankees and Boston finished in a tie for first place, and in a one-game playoff in Boston, the Yankees permitted the Red Sox a 2–0 lead, then moved in front on Bucky Dent's three-run home run in the seventh inning and won the game, 5–4, the winning run scoring on Reggie Jackson's twenty-seventh and final home run of the regular season. Ron Guidry was the winning pitcher, lifting his record to 25–3, giving him the highest winning percentage in baseball history for any man who won twenty or more games. Guidry's earned run average, 1.74, was the lowest in baseball, and the lowest for a lefthanded pitcher in the American League in sixty-four years, and his nine shutouts tied the American League record for a lefthander, which had been set sixty-two years earlier by Babe Ruth. Guidry's pennant-winning victory was preserved by Rich Gossage, who got credit for his tenth save, plus two victories, in his last fifteen appearances. Guidry clinched the Cy Young Award, Gossage the Relief Man of the Year Award.

In the American League championship series, with the Yankees eliminating Kansas City for the third straight year, this time in four games, Jackson was sensational. He batted .462, with two home runs and six runs batted in. In the World Series, with the Yankees losing the first two games to the Los Angeles Dodgers and then winning the next four in a row, Mr. October was almost as good. He batted .391, with two home runs and eight runs batted in. Still, he was overshadowed in the Series, by Graig Nettles, whose incredible fielding at third base saved the third game and destroyed the Dodgers' spirit, and by Bucky Dent, who batted .417, with seven runs batted in, four of

them in the last two games. Guidry won once, Beattie won once, and in the decisive game, the winner, with relief help from Gossage, was Catfish Hunter, whose ailing arm had sprung back to life under Lemon.

Steinbrenner, who had sought, at different times, to send both Guidry and Beattie to the minor leagues, was especially pleased by Hunter's victory. "Catfish was the cornerstone of the Yankees," George said a few years later. "He came to us and taught us how to win. He was a wonderful guy, and one of the all-time best competitors." Steinbrenner relished the memory of Hunter's World Series victory. "Now he was coming down to the end of his career," the owner said. "He retired after the next season. I went to the training room where he was gettin his arm rubbed down. I was thinking about this movie I once saw, called *Angels in the Outfield,* with Paul Douglas. A great old film about an old pitcher who gets a last chance and wins the big game. Great film. So I walked into the training room, and Catfish is there, and so is the trainer, Gene Monahan. I said, 'Cat, I want to tell you—you're gonna do it tonight. I know it. There's this film—' And I started telling him about it. He's got his arm back and Monahan has stopped rubbing and they're both staring at me like I'm crazy. I didn't care. I said, 'You're gonna do it.' And, damn it, he beat the Dodgers and we won the championship."

At the end of the 1978 season, George Steinbrenner had every reason to be immensely proud of what he had accomplished with the New York Yankees. After three building years, he had won three straight pennants and two straight world championships, he had the best pitcher in baseball in Ron Guidry and the best relief pitcher in Rich Gossage, he had the most charismatic and controversial of superstars in Reggie Jackson and his batting order included a present or former All-Star at every position. Behind his major-league roster he had a flourishing minor-

league system, a system he had overhauled and expanded at great expense, adding coaches and instructors, upgrading uniforms and equipment, even providing the same luggage as the Yankees used. Steinbrenner said he wanted everything to be first class, to generate pride and success. In 1977, two of the four Yankee farm teams had finished first in their leagues; in 1978, three of the four; by 1979, five out of five would finish first; and in 1980, six out of seven. (Curiously, despite the impressive success of the minor-league system, it produced only one significant member of the 1981 Yankees, Ron Guidry, and he had joined the Yankee organization two years before Steinbrenner bought the team.) George had spent a fortune assembling his major-league team, and his minor-league network, but the investment had paid off, on the field and at the box office. The Yankees' attendance in 1978 was their largest in thirty years.

That attendance would climb even higher in 1979, but in every other way, Steinbrenner's budding dynasty would crumble. The Yankees slipped into fourth place by the end of April, never again rose higher than third, never were in contention after the end of June and had to end the season with eight straight victories in order to finish fourth, thirteen and a half games behind Baltimore.

The Yankees' troubles ran from the beginning of the season to the end. In April, the team lost its relief ace, Rich Gossage, out for twelve weeks with a torn ligament in his right thumb, the result of a semi-playful locker room tussle with Cliff Johnson, at six-foot-four and 225 pounds a very dangerous plaything. In early June, the team lost its cleanup hitter, Reggie Jackson, out for four weeks with a partial muscle tear in his left thigh, incurred without violence, simply while he was trotting off the field. In mid-June, the team lost its manager, Bob Lemon, who was fired and replaced by his predecessor, Billy Martin. In July, the team lost its president, Al Rosen, who, no longer able to

cope with Steinbrenner's demands, opted for a calmer life, as vice-president of a gambling casino in Atlantic City. And in August, tragically, the team lost its captain, Thurman Munson, killed when his new Cessna Citation crashed as he was practicing a landing.

Munson's death brought home, if only fleetingly, the relative unimportance of games won and games lost. It was a lesson Bob Lemon had learned ten days after the 1978 World Series, when his son died in a car crash. The great victory paled next to the far greater loss, and Bob Lemon's drive to win was affected. "It's not that I didn't want to win," Lemon explained later, "but when I lost it didn't bother me as much."

Billy Martin remained Billy Martin. Less than a month after the Yankees won the 1978 Series, Martin was accused of punching a sportswriter. To Martin's way of thinking, it was practically self-defense; after all, the sportswriter had asked him a question first. The incident took place in Reno, Nevada, where Martin was being paid to help promote the Reno Big Horns' opening game in the Western Basketball League. The sportswriter, Ray Hagar, sought to interview Martin in the bar of the Centennial Coliseum, and as a result, he claimed, he suffered a black eye, three chipped teeth and a variety of bruises. Hagar filed both criminal and civil charges against Martin, who, according to George Steinbrenner, was supposed to be on his best behavior if he wanted to manage the Yankees once more.

The day Martin had his altercation, the Yankees consummated a ten-player trade with the Texas Rangers. Only one of the players was prominent, Sparky Lyle, discarded exactly a year and two weeks after he won the Cy Young Award, and only a few months after Steinbrenner told him, when the Yankees were lagging far behind the Boston Red Sox, "I want you to know that just as much as you were responsible for getting us into the playoffs last

year, you're just as responsible for us having to struggle so much this year. If you had pitched halfway the way you can, we would have run away with it." If Lyle was the player in the trade with the brightest past, the one with the brightest future was Dave Righetti, a young lefthander who, in two minor-league seasons, had averaged better than a strikeout an inning. Righetti would be an important Yankee by 1981.

But Righetti's contributions were still in the future, and a few days after the ten-man trade, the Yankees gave their pitching staff an immediate boost by signing a pair of expensive free agents, two proven veterans: Luis Tiant, an ageless Cuban with a bizarre motion and immense courage, a star of the Red Sox staff for several seasons, and Tommy John, a good-natured midwesterner with a surgically reconstructed arm who had become a big winner with the Dodgers and had, in fact, defeated the Yankees in the opening game of the 1978 World Series. Still, the beefed-up world champions managed to lose ten of their first eleven games in spring training, a fair harbinger of the 1979 season.

Steinbrenner complained about a lack of discipline in the training camp, but since Steinbrenner always seemed to complain during the exhibition season, and since the Yankees always seemed to play poorly in Florida, neither the players nor their fans were terribly concerned. Then, two weeks into the season, Johnson sidelined Gossage. Dick Tidrow moved in as the main relief pitcher and did so poorly Steinbrenner banished him to Chicago, and RON Guidry, the most selfless player in pinstripes, volunteered to work as a relief pitcher while the Yankees regrouped. The Yankees did not regroup. Billy Martin did.

Martin scrubbed his image. He apologized to Ray Hagar, the sportswriter in Reno, and Hagar dropped both the criminal and civil charges. "I'm very sorry I hit Ray," Martin said. "We're good friends now."

"I wanted an apology from Martin—and I got it," Hagar said. "I feel better about him now than I did." The Reno Big Horns gave Hagar $7,500, which made him feel even better. "I wish Billy the best of luck in his dealings with George Steinbrenner," Hagar said.

Martin's dealings with George Steinbrenner resumed a few weeks later, in mid-June. The two met in Columbus, and Steinbrenner offered Martin a chance to manage the Yankees again, with a new contract, one hundred twenty thousand dollars a year, plus expenses and minus the restrictive clauses that had bothered Billy so much during his previous incarnation as Yankee manager. Two days later, Lemon was fired, and Martin popped out of the Yankee dugout and trotted toward home plate to present a lineup card to the umpires for the first time in eleven months. The organist played "Billy Boy," the scoreboard beamed "WELCOME BACK, BILLY" and, for one hundred and thirty seconds, the fans cheered Billy's return.

Columnist Lupica did not cheer. He greeted the reunion of Martin and Steinbrenner with the unkindest line: "They really deserve each other."

"I think if it can be turned around," Steinbrenner said, "Billy is the guy to do it. Last year I needed someone one hundred and eighty degrees from what Billy was. This year I needed someone one hundred and eighty degrees from what Bob Lemon was. Billy is the right guy for the moment." Steinbrenner sounded as if the eleven-month layoff he had inflicted on Martin had, as planned, made a better man of Billy. "I don't want him to change out on the field," Steinbrenner said. "I want him to change in his public behavior, and I think he has."

Martin couldn't resist a response. "Maybe he sees something in me that I don't see," Martin said. "I'm the same Billy Martin."

The same Billy Martin made one quick conciliatory gesture toward Reggie Jackson. "Reggie is a very impor-

235

tant part of our club," Martin said, in his best perfunctory manner. "We need him to win the pennant."

A few months earlier, at the opening of a Manhattan store called Billy Martin's Western Wear, someone had asked Billy if he had any cowboy boots for Reggie Jackson. "Yeah," he said. "Snakeskin." (Not coincidentally, Reggie appeared the following year in a newspaper ad for a store called Blacksmith, situated only a few blocks from Billy Martin's Western Wear. The ad showed Reggie surrounded by boots, and the copy read: "Reggie Jackson never settles for second best. That's why he buys all his western boots at Blacksmith.")

Even before Martin displaced Lemon, when rumors began to circulate that Billy *might* return in mid-1979, Jackson was so upset he placed a telephone call to George Steinbrenner. "Is it true you're planning to bring Billy back?" Reggie asked.

"It's none of your goddamn business," Steinbrenner snapped. "This is my club. You're only a goddamn player here. I'll do what I want."

"I won't play for him," Jackson said.

"You've got a contract," Steinbrenner said.

Jackson never called Steinbrenner "Boss" again, not with affection.

"I'm just gritting my teeth," Reggie said, when Martin's return became official. "I'm afraid to say anything." He did, however, indicate publicly that he was willing to be traded, and privately, in a meeting with Steinbrenner, that he wished to be. The Yankees did not trade him, and while Jackson managed to maintain a cool peace with Martin, his relationship with Steinbrenner suffered. When Al Rosen resigned, Jackson spoke up. "Al was a good man who tried to be a good president of the club," Jackson said. "He just couldn't take being subservient to the man. He had pride. He had done things in this game. What George has done to him is terrible. George just thinks he can buy

everybody. Some guys have pride. You can't buy them."

"What'll happen after George reads this?" Jackson was asked.

"Nothing can happen to me because I can hit the ball over the wall," Reggie said. "When I can't hit the ball over the wall, they'll get me, too. I know that. George will get me someday."

As the relationship between Steinbrenner and Jackson worsened, the relationship between Steinbrenner and Martin seemed to improve. One day not long after Martin came back, Steinbrenner was sitting in the manager's office, in Martin's chair, demonstrating his baseball expertise to a group of reporters a few hours before a game against Boston. Steinbrenner had a set of statistics in his hand. "Look at this," Steinbrenner said. "These are the stats that really count—batting average with men in scoring position, number of men left on base in scoring position, number of men left on third base with less than two out."

A few minutes later, Billy Martin entered and saw the owner sitting in his chair. "George just took over as manager," a reporter said. "You're out again, Billy. Sorry about that."

Martin smiled. "Good," he said. "I'll trade with him any day."

"Look at these figures, Billy," Steinbrenner said. "Randolph is killing us. He's way off the plate. You've got to get him up close. They're getting him out on outside pitches."

"Willie says those pitches are balls," Martin said.

"You want to film him to show him?" Steinbrenner said.

"I got a camera on all of 'em," Martin said.

"I may not know much about baseball," Steinbrenner said, "but he's too far off the plate."

Then the owner suggested that on an open date, during an upcoming trip to Seattle, it would be a good idea for the Yankees to take batting practice. "All right, Billy?"

"Good idea," Martin said. "Let's do that."

After Steinbrenner left the manager's office, Martin settled behind his desk and said, "He's been super. And you know why? Because it's him and me one-on-one now, nobody in between."

Under Martin, the Yankees continued to lose, and Jackson continued to hit. Reggie had an explanation for his own success. "I was probably helped by Billy's return," he said. "I didn't want any more fuss. I wanted to do well. I concentrated harder, so there would be no excuses for not playing me. It helped make me a better hitter. I owe Billy that."

The first week in August, Munson died in the fiery crash of his plane, and for most of the Yankees the season ended then. Steinbrenner arranged for a chartered plane to take the entire team to Munson's funeral in Canton, Ohio. Billy Martin cried. Reggie Jackson sat quietly, respectfully. Bobby Murcer delivered a moving eulogy, then, the same night, delivered a game-winning home run. George Steinbrenner reminisced about his special relationship with Munson. The two men warred, over contract and beards, but they understood each other. Munson never looked for love, either. "I remember how he used to come up to my office," Steinbrenner said, warmly, "and put his feet up on my desk and we'd talk." Actually, Munson had told friends he used to put his feet up on Steinbrenner's desk because he knew it infuriated the owner.

The last seven weeks of the season were uneventful, except that the fans turned on Reggie Jackson, booing him when he fell chasing a fly ball on a wet field. He responded with an obscene gesture and Billy Martin, of all people, sprang to his defense. "I like Reggie, I really do," Martin said. "He's been super." Jackson talked about wanting to leave New York, and Martin talked about wanting him to stay. "Sure I want him to stay," the manager said. "Hell, yes."

Reggie stayed, but Martin didn't. Only a few weeks after

the season ended, with the Yankees in fourth place, their worst finish since Steinbrenner's rookie year, Billy Martin got into another public brawl. He threw a punch that hit a marshmallow salesman named Joseph W. Cooper, who had been needling the Yankee manager in a bar in a Minnesota hotel. Cooper hit the floor so hard he wound up in the hospital nursing a badly cut lip, and George Steinbrenner hit the ceiling. The Yankee image, he decided, had been tarnished once too often. "How much can we take and still command any respect?" Steinbrenner said. "How can the Yankees, as an organization, keep putting their heads in the sand? The public, at some point, thinks we are part and party to it. Then there are the players, especially the younger ones. How can I stand up and talk to them about the Yankee tradition?"

Five days after Martin's fist fell on Joseph Cooper, George Steinbrenner fired him—for his own good, the owner explained. "I did it to save his life," said Steinbrenner. "The next time he hits somebody, the guy might pull a knife." Then Steinbrenner considered the alternative. "What if Billy had killed the guy? How would it look— Billy Martin, manager of the Yankees, indicted for murder?"

Steinbrenner's comments brought a quick response from Martin's agent. "It is clear to me," Doug Newton said, "that George Steinbrenner does not want Billy Martin in baseball in the next year and would prefer him out of the spotlight."

"My only thought," said Steinbrenner, "was that Billy's own personal life would best be served by getting him out of the baseball limelight where he is constantly finding it difficult to stay out of fights."

"I do not want or need any more of George Steinbrenner's so-called help," said Martin.

The same day Martin was fired, Dick Howser became either the fifth or sixth Yankee manager to serve under

Steinbrenner, depending on whether Billy Martin counted as one or two. Actually, Howser himself had managed the Yankees previously, but only for one day, the day between Billy Martin's first departure and the arrival of Bob Lemon, and no one counted that one game as an official managerial tour. At the end of the 1978 season, Howser had resigned from the Yankee coaching staff and had taken a much more peaceful job, baseball coach at Florida State University, which Howser had attended, along with his childhood friend, Burt Reynolds. When Steinbrenner decided Martin had to go, he thought of Howser immediately. He remembered an encounter with Howser back in 1973, George's first season. During spring training, when he mistakenly thought Howser had made a coaching error, the new owner yelled, "Wake up down there at third base!" Howser turned toward the owner's box seat and said "Go to hell," possibly in stronger words.

"He had the balls to stand up to me," Steinbrenner recalled. "I filed that away. I'm hard on people, I know that, but those are the kind of things I remember."

The new Yankee manager was young, only forty-two, but he was experienced, a major-league player for eight years, with Kansas City, Cleveland and the Yankees, and then a Yankee coach for ten years. Reggie Jackson, despite Billy Martin's late burst of affection, was delighted by the change. He liked Howser, and Howser liked him.

When Howser became manager, Gene Michael became general manager, and in the following few weeks, Steinbrenner, with his staff's advice and consent, once again reshaped his Yankees. He persuaded Toronto to trade him Rick Cerone, a promising young catcher, and Seattle to give up Ruppert Jones, a promising young outfielder, and he turned a pair of free agents, first baseman Bob Watson and pitcher Rudy May, into Yankees by giving them multiyear contracts worth more than a million dollars apiece, which lifted his total investment in free agents to more than fifteen million dollars in five years. Mickey

Rivers (traded), Chris Chambliss (traded), Sparky Lyle (traded), Roy White (playing in Japan), Catfish Hunter (retired) and the late Thurman Munson were gone from Steinbrenner's first world championship team, but he had found suitable replacements. He also bid for the most expensive free agent on the market, pitcher Nolan Ryan, but lost him to the Houston Astros, who were being run, ironically, by John J. McMullen, one of Steinbrenner's disenchanted former limited partners. "There's nothing as limited as being a limited partner of George's," said McMullen, after he departed.

Steinbrenner, clearly, did not intend to finish fourth again. At the end of the 1979 season, he had received a consolation gift from an acquaintance, a cigarette box with a poem inscribed on it:

> I am wounded
> But I am not slain.
> I shall lay me down and bleed awhile
> Then I shall rise and fight again.
>
> —Anonymous

The Yankees' owner appreciated the sentiments so much he had a copy of the poem sent to potential season-ticket buyers. *The New York Times* reprinted the poem, inspiring a reader to note that the author of the verse was not unknown, that the lines came, with minor word modifications, from "Johnnie Armstrong's Last Goodnight," written by John Dryden, the British poet. Steinbrenner, of course, would have been more comfortable with an American poet.

By Steinbrenner's standards, the first seven months of 1980 were incredibly tranquil. He did fine Reggie Jackson one thousand dollars for arriving two days late for spring training—Jackson's fellow businessman had become less understanding than he was in 1978—but after that mild disturbance, Dick Howser settled into his new job relatively free from controversy and from interference, yet

fully aware of his responsibility to the owner. "If we win," Howser said, "I expect to get along with him."

When Howser's Yankees started slowly, losing six of their first nine games, the owner remained surprisingly calm, and his patience was soon rewarded. By the middle of May, the Yankees were in first place, the position they would occupy for the rest of the season. A month later, the Yankees ran off nine victories in a row, sailing along so smoothly Steinbrenner-watchers were worried that the master of turmoil had lost his touch. Even the arrival at Yankee Stadium of the Oakland A's, with their brand-new manager, Billy Martin, resurrected once again, did not produce fireworks.

In fact, Martin and Steinbrenner sat down together, in a handsome restaurant, and Martin promptly began complaining about his travel schedule, his eating habits and his team. "It's enough to give a guy an upset stomach," Martin said. Just then, a waiter, passing by, handed Martin a bottle of Pepto-Bismol. Billy lifted the bottle to his lips and gulped the liquid down.

"Use a spoon, Billy!" Steinbrenner snapped.

"Oh, no!" said Martin. "He's still trying to tell me what to do."

The two men, obviously, were filming a commercial, and George's fee, he informed the press, was going to charity. "When we did that beer commercial," Steinbrenner said, "I turned over my share of the profits to the Mission Society in the Bronx. It came to twenty-five thousand dollars. Six hundred South Bronx youngsters had a better summer than they would have had." The Pepto-Bismol fee, George said, was going to the National Association for the Society to Prevent Blindness. "It's for a good cause," Steinbrenner said, justifying his willingness to do the commercial. "Billy and I would do a commercial with a gorilla or Hitler if it helped kids." Then George admitted once again that he really liked Billy Martin. "But," he said, "there are things

that happen in a relationship—in sports, in business, in marriage—when it's just not right for two people to continue a relationship."

The next day was George and Billy's anniversary, Old Timers' Day at Yankee Stadium, and Martin received his usual thunderous ovation when he was introduced—as an old Yankee, and as the new manager of the Oakland A's. The cheers lasted for more than a minute, and when they seemed to be subsiding, Billy waved his cap to the crowd and beamed. The cheers revived for another minute.

"I felt like applauding, too," said Dick Howser, who had no problem with his ego. He also had no problem with his employer, not yet. "He's demanding, he's active, he's competitive," Howser said. "But to be honest, I haven't had that much contact with him. He phoned me a couple of times when we were out west to find out about the guys who were hurt. And three or four times we've had a meeting in his office before a game. That's about it."

Steinbrenner offered a self-deprecating explanation for his new manner. "I've learned I ain't the smartest guy in the world," he said. "I'll make a suggestion in a good-natured way, and if Dick doesn't want to go with it, that's fine. It really is. I've mellowed some."

To match the owner's new mood, the Yankees introduced a new theme song, music to mark the end of each game, "New York, New York," the Frank Sinatra rendition, permission cheerfully granted by the singer, and the recording provided by Le Club, a Manhattan discotheque whose manager, Patrick Shields, supplied all the tapes played at Yankee Stadium ("George is an empire builder," Shields once said. "The only trouble is that he was born a little too late. Most of the world has already been parceled out.") Steinbrenner's musical tastes had evolved since his Williams Glee Club days. He loved a disco beat, and, understandably, the man who had made it in New York loved the lyrics of "New York, New York." "I noticed Mr.

Steinbrenner was always dancing to the song," said Ricardo Irvin, the disk jockey at Le Club.

The king of the hill, top of the heap, among the Yankee players in 1980 was, beyond question, Reggie Jackson. "At Last, Jackson Is 'The Straw That Stirs the Drink,'" *The New York Times* said in a headline, and Jackson had the statistics to back up the metaphor. He was on his way to his first .300 batting average, to a season of 111 runs batted in and forty-one home runs, including the four-hundredth of his career, the kind of numbers that would have made him Most Valuable Player in the American League in almost any other year. But George Brett chose 1980 in which to bat .390, and so Jackson finished second in the MVP balloting.

"I'm more at peace with myself than at any other time in my career," Jackson said at mid-season. "The manager has been very helpful to me. He makes me feel like I'm better than I really am." Jackson was not only hitting; he was almost being humble.

By the middle of July, the Yankees had a nine-and-a-half-game lead and remarkable harmony. Five weeks later, their lead had dwindled to half a game, and their harmony had been shattered. The Yankees had played eight games in eleven days against second-place Baltimore, and with Graig Nettles sidelined by hepatitis, and Bucky Dent and Willie Randolph hurting, they had lost six of the eight games. The sudden slump brought out the absolute worst in George Steinbrenner. He assailed his players and the umpires, and he publicly second-guessed Dick Howser's judgment. "He knows his job rests on the bottom line, which is winning," Steinbrenner warned. The boss saved his harshest words for his finest player. Once before, when their relationship first began to fall apart, Steinbrenner had hurt Jackson with a remark: "You better get your head screwed on straight, boy." But now the owner was crueler. "Reggie hit .120 in the Baltimore

series," Steinbrenner said. "If that isn't tanking, I've never seen tanking."

Conceivably, Steinbrenner didn't realize precisely what he was saying. "Tanking," going nto the tank, in sports parlance, means losing deliberately, throwing a game. It is the most vicious possible accusation. Steinbrenner may have slipped on his syntax. Perhaps he meant merely to accuse Jackson of "choking," folding under pressure, a crime one degree less heinous. Yet Steinbrenner never retracted the "tanking" line, never apologized.

Howser reacted mildly to the owner's outburst. "This is just his way of stirring people up," the manager said. "But that's his way of doing things, not mine. That's his philosophy, not mine."

The Baltimore Orioles were delighted by Steinbrenner's philosophy. "I expect to go home from this road trip in first place," said Sammy Stewart, a Baltimore pitcher. "The Yankees have George Steinbrenner getting on them now, and I think maybe they're looking over their shoulders a little bit."

Eventually, Steinbrenner's panic subsided, assuaged by a Yankee surge that produced eighteen victories in twenty games. Their lead swelled to six games. Steinbrenner puffed up, too. "If the players hadn't gotten their asses roasted," he said, "do you think we would have won?"

Steinbrenner did not roast only his players. During the winning streak, while he was traveling with the team and staying at the Boston Sheraton, he tried to make a telephone call from the hotel bar. For some reason, the operator refused to charge the call to George's room. He had her fired within a day. He did not offer to send her on vacation or her son, if she had one, to summer camp.

When the Yankees finally clinched first place, only the day before the regular season ended, Jackson, fittingly, hit the home run that decided the game and the pennant race. Then Jackson shared his glory with Dick Howser. "He's

been very fair to me and a friend," Jackson said. "And I have appreciated playing for him as much as I have for my favorite managers—Earl Weaver, Al Dark, Dick Williams. But this guy is the best person I've ever played for." It was no accident that Jackson mentioned every manager for whom he'd played a full season during the previous decade, except one.

On the final day of the season, the Yankees needed to draw 29,000 fans to a meaningless game in order to break the American League attendance record for a season. They drew 35,879, lifting the attendance for the year to 2,627,417, and rewarded the record-setting crowd with their one hundred and third victory of the season, the team's highest total in seventeen years. Then, for the fourth time in five years, the Yankees faced the Kansas City Royals in the American League championship series. But for once, the Yankees did not win, not even one game of the series.

The first game was one-sided, 7–2, with Reggie Jackson going hitless in four times at bat and leaving five runners on base, with Ron Guidry lasting only three innings and giving up four runs, with Bucky Dent losing a fly ball in the sun and with George Steinbrenner carping. "Reggie didn't come through four times," the owner complained, "and Guidry didn't execute. You can't pitch for your pitcher and hit for your cleanup hitter." As for the fly ball that Dent couldn't see, Steinbrenner said, "He should have had it."

"The game always looks easier from up in the stands," said Dent.

The next day, Reggie showed up at the ball park with a trace of a beard, an excuse for the owner to send a command to the manager. "I had to give orders for Reggie to get rid of the beard," Steinbrenner said later. "I have nothing against beards. My son, Hank, has one sometimes. But once you have rules, you have to enforce them."

Reggie shaved, but, still, Kansas City won again, 3–2, and this time Steinbrenner did not blame the players. In fact, he specifically exonerated them. "My players didn't lose this one," he said. His third-base coach lost this one, Steinbrenner charged.

In the eighth inning, with the score 3–2, and Willie Randolph on first base, Bob Watson delivered a double into the left-field corner, and Mike Ferraro, coaching at third, elected to send Randolph home. Even though Randolph had stumbled momentarily between first base and second, the decision seemed a wise one. Willie Wilson, playing left field, picked up the ball and threw it toward the shortstop, U. L. Washington, who had come out to short left field and was supposed to relay the ball to the plate. Wilson's throw sailed over Washington's head, and Randolph seemed certain to score. But George Brett, backing up Washington, took the throw, spun and fired a perfect strike to home plate, in time to cut down Randolph for the final out.

"Randolph stumbled," Steinbrenner grumbled. "That's what the third-base coach doesn't see. He hasn't seen it all year."

As Randolph was called out at home, an ABC camera focused in on Steinbrenner in the stands. Even an amateur lip-reader could tell that the owner was mouthing an obscenity. Even an illiterate could tell that he was furious. He swore, then stormed away from his seat. "My mother was watching the game on television," Steinbrenner said months later, "and when I spoke to her—I always call my parents to tell them why I did what I've done—she said, 'Dear, did you say what I thought you said?' You have to know my mother. She's a Christian Scientist, a very gentle person. And I said, 'I didn't know the camera was on me, mother, but I said it. Because that's the way I felt.'"

"Steinbrenner's action," Ira Berkow wrote in *The New York Times,* "seemed the essence of an arrogant, petulant, boorish poor sport."

"You have to understand how I feel," Steinbrenner responded. "There are five million Yankee fans just like me sitting in front of TV sets with beer and hollering the same thing when Ferraro sends Randolph home and he's out. I want this team to win. I'm obsessed with winning, with discipline, with achieving. That's what this country's all about, that's what New York's all about—fighting for everything, a cab in the rain, a table in a restaurant at lunchtime—and that's what the Yankees are all about."

The third game of the championship series was almost predictable. The Yankees led, 2–1, until in the seventh inning Rich Gossage, who had run third in the voting for Most Valuable Player in the league, faced George Brett, and Brett demonstrated why he was *the* Most Valuable. He hit a three-run home run that won the game, won the series and made it imperative for most of the Yankees' executive staff to come back to Yankee Stadium very early the next morning, a Saturday morning, for a four-and-a-half-hour meeting in George Steinbrenner's office. "I was never so disappointed," said Steinbrenner of Kansas City's three-game sweep. "It's embarrassing as hell to me. It's even more embarrassing than Cincinnati." Steinbrenner did not say whether his roasting of the players' asses after the first game had anything to do with their failures in the second and third.

The meeting in Steinbrenner's office focused largely on prospects within the Yankee organization. Significantly, Dick Howser, the manager, was not invited to the session. Contacted by reporters, asked about his plans for the next season, Howser said, candidly, "This is where I want to be—right here in New York." Did he have any thoughts of resigning? "I'm certainly not going to walk away from this ball club," Howser said.

During the following week, without consulting Howser, Steinbrenner attempted to hire Don Zimmer, the deposed manager of the Boston Red Sox, to replace Mike Ferraro as

the third-base coach for the Yankees. "I certainly should be given the courtesy of approving or disapproving of the coaches that are added to the ball club," said Howser, gently.

"I don't appreciate Dick Howser popping off like that," George Steinbrenner responded.

Howser's star was obviously not in the ascendant. The fact that he had won 103 games, and that he had conducted himself with dignity, was no more important to Steinbrenner than the fact that Howser had two years remaining on his contract. "I'm very upset, very disappointed in him," the owner said, then confided to favored members of the press that Howser, besides making some very unwise strategic decisions, had not enforced proper discipline and had grown egotistical over his 103 victories. For more than a month after the championship series ended, Steinbrenner orchestrated the perils of Dick Howser, a will-he-or-won't-he-return cliffhanger, good for almost daily headlines for the owner and frequent anguish for the manager.

Finally, on November 21, 1980, George Steinbrenner put Dick Howser out of his misery. The boss displayed the same sort of mercy he would display if one of his racehorses broke a leg.

Steinbrenner summoned fourteen reporters to his office to witness what Dave Anderson, in the *Times,* called "the execution of Dick Howser." The witnesses—by invitation only, a manipulation of the press that even the *Daily News'* Dick Young, a Steinbrenner fan, found an insult to his profession—were offered roast beef, turkey and ham sandwiches. None of them ate.

The principal owner settled into a large tan vinyl chair behind his round desk, freshly polished. He wore a soft blue shirt, and a navy-blue-and-green-striped tie. A gold number "1" decorated his desk, and so did a small sign that said, "Lead, Follow or Get the Hell Out of the Way." There was also a brass ship's throttle, set, for the occasion, on

"Standby." Usually, the throttle read, "Full Speed Ahead." Dick Howser sat to the right of the owner, perhaps ten feet away, his left index finger frequently pressed against his left cheek, obstructing his view of Steinbrenner, and Steinbrenner's view of him.

"Dick has decided," the boss said, "that he will not be returning to the Yankees next year. I should say, not returning to the Yankees as manager."

Dick has decided. Of course—and just a few weeks earlier, Jimmy Carter had decided not to serve a second term as President of the United States. The American electorate had no more to do with Jimmy Carter's decision than George Steinbrenner had to do with Dick Howser's. Howser, Steinbrenner explained, was being lured away from him by an incredible opportunity to develop real estate in Florida, an offer Howser could not turn down. The reason the decision regarding Howser's fate had been dragged out for so long, Steinbrenner added, was that Dick was trying to make up his mind whether or not to accept the real-estate opportunity. Steinbrenner himself had had nothing to do with the delay.

"Could Dick still be the manager if he wanted to be?" someone asked.

"Yes," Steinbrenner said.

"If you had won the World Series, instead of being eliminated in the playoffs," Howser was asked, "would you have taken this real-estate opportunity?"

"That's hard to say."

"Were you fired, Dick?"

"I'm not going to comment on that," Howser said.

"I didn't fire the man," insisted Steinbrenner.

Even though he didn't fire the man, and even though Howser was stepping into an unbelievable real-estate opportunity, Steinbrenner was still going to pay him, for occasional scouting chores, his managerial salary of roughly one hundred thousand dollars a year, for each of

the two years remaining on his contract. "I feel morally and contractually obligated to Dick and his wife Nancy," said Steinbrenner, who, of course, had no contractual obligation if Howser really were quitting. "I took him out of Florida State, where he could have stayed for life. If it hasn't worked out, maybe it's my fault."

The new manager of the Yankees, Steinbrenner announced, would be Gene Michael, the only man in the office who was tasting the sandwiches. "What advice would you give Gene Michael?" Howser was asked.

"To have a strong stomach," Howser said, "and a nice contract."

"Will I be a puppet?" Michael said a few days later. "My answer is, 'No.' George doesn't want people giving him the answers they think he wants. George wants your opinion."

"Gene is loyal," said Steinbrenner. "That's his greatest asset."

Nine months later, George Steinbrenner would fire Gene Michael, for disloyalty, and Dick Howser, no longer in real estate, would be managing the Kansas City Royals.

6

In 1981, major league baseball survived its most bizarre season. The middle third of the schedule was lost to the sport's first prolonged strike, and as a result, the season's statistics, so vital a part of the mystique of the game, became meaningless. In the American League, for instance, no pitcher won even fifteen games, no batter hit more than twenty-two home runs and the abbreviated race for the batting championship created so little interest that, on the final day of the season, when the commissioner of baseball, Bowie Kuhn, was asked who won that race, he confessed he did not know. For the record, the batting champion was Carney Lansford of the Boston Red Sox, memorable mostly as the first righthanded hitter to win the title in a decade, and the Most Valuable Player, another honor little noted nor long remembered, was Rollie Fingers of the Milwaukee Brewers, the first relief pitcher to be MVP in the American League. The man who dominated the league in 1981, appropriately, was neither a

hitter nor a pitcher. The year belonged to George M. Steinbrenner III.

In the National League, a few individuals stood out despite the shortened season. Fernando Valenzuela of the Los Angeles Dodgers, a rookie, started off brilliantly, with eight straight victories including five shutouts, and opposing batters were eager to go on strike just to escape him. Two older pitchers also excelled, Tom Seaver of Cincinnati, with the best won-lost record of his distinguished career, and Nolan Ryan of Houston, with the fifth no-hitter of his, an unprecedented feat. Pete Rose, at the age of forty, hit and hustled as if he were twenty and became the league's all-time leader in base hits. His Philadelphia teammate, Mike Schmidt, Most Valuable Player for the second straight year, led the league in both home runs and runs batted in for the second straight year. But in a year when turmoil, not achievement, was the essence of baseball, the National Leaguers, too, were overshadowed by Steinbrenner. He was, beyond question, the straw that stirred the drink.

In 1981, Steinbrenner usurped another of Reggie Jackson's titles. The owner became Mr. October. Like a true champion, he peaked during the dramatic final three weeks of competition. In the middle of the first intradivisional playoffs in baseball history, he produced his most stunning clubhouse speech, a postgame attack upon his players so stinging that one of them said, to his face, "Fuck you, George!" A week later, at the victory party following the American League championship series, two of his prize players got into a fistfight, a brawl that infuriated Steinbrenner. And a week after that, during the World Series, Steinbrenner himself got into a fight, in an elevator, with two Dodger fans and no witnesses, a brawl that provoked skepticism and derision.

If Steinbrenner's season ended, symbolically, with a clenched fist, it began with an open hand, extended toward

Dave Winfield, a gifted athlete who looked like central casting's idea of a superstar. Six-foot-six and 220 pounds, a basketball star at the University of Minnesota, intimidating enough physically to be drafted into the National Football League even though he never played college football, Dave Winfield chose baseball for a career and spent eight seasons with the San Diego Padres. He had two magnificent seasons, in 1978 and 1979; the Padres had none. When Winfield then opted for free agency, he became, by far, the greatest prize in the 1980 re-entry draft. George Steinbrenner paid him the ultimate compliment. Steinbrenner did not hustle Dave Winfield the way he'd hustle a broad. Better than that. He hustled Winfield the way he'd hustled Reggie Jackson four years earlier. And once again, against sturdy competition, Steinbrenner won.

The price of playing the free-agent game had gone up considerably. Steinbrenner ended up giving Winfield the richest contract in baseball history, a complicated pact, including a one-million-dollar bonus for signing and a series of built-in cost-of-living increases, that could pay Winfield as much as twenty-three million dollars for ten years. In other words, Steinbrenner was promising to pay Winfield more than he had spent on Catfish and Reggie and Gullett and Gossage and all his other previous free agents combined. In fact, Steinbrenner was promising to pay Winfield, over ten years, more than twice as much as he and his partners had paid for the entire Yankee organization eight years earlier. At the news conference announcing the signing, Winfield wore a banker's suit and a broad smile. Reggie Jackson came to the news conference, to observe, to expound and to dream of the magnitude of the contract he would sign sometime within the next twelve months.

Only a few weeks after Steinbrenner jumped at the chance to pay Winfield more than two million dollars a

season, he had to be forced to pay Rick Cerone four hundred forty thousand dollars for the 1981 season. In 1980, Winfield, playing for San Diego, had batted .276, with twenty home runs and eighty-seven runs batted in. Ironically, Cerone, playing for the Yankees, had achieved remarkably similar results: He had batted .277, with fourteen home runs and eighty-five runs batted in.

The difference was that Winfield had gone into the free-agent market, an arena Steinbrenner respected, while Cerone had gone to binding arbitration, the final step in resolving contract disputes between players and management. Steinbrenner, after paying Cerone one hundred twenty thousand dollars in 1980, had offered him three hundred fifty thousand for 1981, a very impressive increase. But Cerone had demanded four hundred forty thousand, and the arbitrator had ruled in the catcher's favor. Steinbrenner considered himself betrayed by an ingrate. He called Cerone "Brutus." He called Winfield "a fine young man."

The amount of money baseball players were earning by the 1980s was, to use one of Steinbrenner's favorite words, "unreal." No one had contributed more to the sense of unreality than George himself, the man who had dipped most deeply and, in the long run, most wisely into the free-agent field. The average salary in baseball exceeded one hundred fifty thousand dollars a year; the average salary on the Yankees was close to two hundred thousand a year. The figures had soared swiftly. In the early 1970s, Bobby Murcer had become only the third Yankee to earn one hundred thousand dollars in a season; by the early 1980s, a hundred thousand a season had become an insult. Murcer himself was getting far more than that to be a part-time Yankee. The numbers, swollen beyond comprehension, had become chiefly a means of keeping score, a matter of self-esteem, and no player in baseball had more self-esteem than Reggie Jackson.

With his five-year contract running out, Jackson realized he might have to spend most of 1981 sparring with Steinbrenner over a new agreement. The battle began in March. Denied permission to report late to spring training, Jackson showed up two days late anyway. Steinbrenner announced that the price of tardiness had gone up, to twenty-five hundred dollars a day, a five-thousand dollar total for Reggie. Jackson spent that each month on Simoniz for his fleet of cars, but Steinbrenner's words cut more deeply than the fine. "I'm very hurt that a man looking for a new big contract would pull something like this," said Steinbrenner. "You kind of hope that a guy known as Mr. October who wasn't Mr. October in 1980, who didn't drive in a single run in the playoffs, would want to come back with the same dedication as the other guys."

Steinbrenner implied that if Jackson had reported on time, the new contract might have been quickly settled. But now Jackson had to be disciplined for his disobedience. The contract talks were put off. Convinced that Steinbrenner was avoiding him, Jackson, a master of labels, described himself as "a walking keg of dynamite." Steinbrenner boldly lit a match. "Dave Winfield has looked so good in the exhibitions," the owner said, "and Reggie has been struggling. That's what's bothering Reggie." When he heard that Winfield was looking good to Steinbrenner, Reggie countered, "Gene Autry and Fred Wilpon are looking better to me every day." Autry, of course, owned the Angels, and Wilpon was the president of the Mets, and the Mets and the Angels were among the teams likely to bid for Jackson if he did not sign again with the Yankees. Reggie mentioned Autry because he knew the former movie cowboy was one of the few baseball owners who could afford to outspend Steinbrenner, and Wilpon's name because he knew that any mention of the Mets would touch the same raw nerve in Steinbrenner as, say, any mention of Watergate.

Steinbrenner's antagonism toward the Mets went back to the mid-1970s, when he felt the itinerant Yankees were treated shabbily by the permanent residents of Shea Stadium. The antagonism flared up again during spring training, 1981, when Frank Cashen, the Mets' general manager, was reported to have suggested that the movie *Fort Apache, the Bronx,* the story of a neighborhood shattered by violent crime, be retitled, *Fort Apache, Yankee Stadium.* Steinbrenner, with reason, considered that remark a slur on his stadium and its environs, a suggestion that anyone who attended a Yankee game was risking, if not his life, at least slashed tires on his automobile. Cashen denied originating the remark; he said he was simply repeating it.

One of the most predictable occurrences of spring training was that, whenever the Yankees lost an exhibition game to the Mets, especially a game televised back in New York, George Steinbrenner would explode. When the Yankees lost, 9–6, in Fort Lauderdale in 1981, the owner's reaction was inevitable. Steinbrenner said Cerone looked terrible, which was one of the nicest things he would say about Cerone all year (at least until Cerone snapped, "Fuck you, George!" and earned the owner's respect). Steinbrenner also attacked a young pitcher named Mike Griffin in much the same way he had previously assailed other young pitchers, most notably Jim Beattie. "We found out about Mike Griffin today," the owner said. "You say you can't tell from one outing? The hell you can't. This spells it for Mike Griffin. He's got to go down to the minors and prove himself again."

Steinbrenner even had mild criticism for his new favorite, Dave Winfield. Winfield's spring training batting average dipped to .156, and Steinbrenner said, gently, "You can't be pleased by that performance." The owner did have a few kind words for Jackson—"Reggie was our star

today; he didn't pack it in; he did a good job"—the result of a conciliatory meeting between the two men, a meeting that materialized when they accidentally encountered each other in Michael's office. Ominously, Steinbrenner called the meeting with Jackson "one of the best I've had in baseball," which was approximately what he said about his meeting with Billy Martin less than two weeks before he replaced Martin for the first time.

During spring training, Jackson made two very interesting remarks about his negotiations for a new contract. The first was one he wanted to believe: "I love New York and I love playing for the Yankees, but I don't need them." In fact, Jackson's love was not constant, and his need, from a commercial standpoint, was greater than he was willing to admit. But his second remark was both honest and perceptive: "I don't know if I'm mature enough or secure enough not to make as much as Dave Winfield."

Significantly, despite George Steinbrenner's best efforts, no real rivalry ever split Jackson and Winfield. Not that they were especially close, but there was no enmity, and not even much envy, perhaps because they were such different types, one impetuous, the other restrained. And even though they were so different, they were linked by a bond Steinbrenner could not threaten, the bond of race.

Late in spring training, as usual, the Yankees stopped in Tampa and checked in at the Bay Harbor Inn, a resort hotel owned by George M. Steinbrenner III. At Bay Harbor, Steinbrenner's temper was legendary. When he spied messy trays of food sitting outside rooms, his voice sometimes thundered through the corridors, warning of imminent firings. Once he startled fellow diners in the hotel's restaurant when he found chunks of ice in his ice cream. It was as if Popeye had found chunks of sand in his spinach. George complained, loudly. "There was no excuse for those ice chunks in the ice cream," Steinbrenner said a

few years later. "I demanded to know who was in charge of the food quality." No one was fired, George said, not for the first offense.

Reggie Jackson felt that he could identify with the staff of the Bay Harbor Inn. "I hit forty home runs and he gets all over me," Jackson said to the manager of the hotel. "If he's grilling me, you guys must be getting murdered."

The following day, the Yankees made another traditional stop on their exhibition tour, at Chapel Hill, North Carolina, to play the University of North Carolina Tar Heels. The game did not do a lot to sharpen the Yankees' competitive skills, but it did give the owner an opportunity to visit with his older daughter, Jennifer, a senior at UNC. An attractive blond, she was a member of Delta Delta Delta sorority and, before matriculating at Chapel Hill, captain of the cheerleaders at Culver. Jennifer, an excellent student majoring in business administration, was a Morehouse Scholar, a prestigious honor that meant she had a full scholarship plus a summer internship. She spent her internship working with the Consumer Protection Agency in the North Carolina attorney general's office. Her proud father told *New York* magazine's Marie Brenner that Jennifer was Phi Beta Kappa at North Carolina; actually, she wasn't, but she missed by only a very narrow margin.

Steinbrenner clearly was attached to his children. His schedule did not permit him to spend a great deal of time with them, and, as a result, he may not have been perfectly attuned to their feelings, but he did care about their achievements and interests. His happiest moments at spring training seemed to be when he was standing in the outfield, during batting practice, having a catch with his younger son, Harold. Of course he wanted both his boys to be interested in sports, though neither seemed an exceptional athlete. The best athlete among the Steinbrenner children may be the younger daughter, Jessie, who plays on a strong basketball team at Culver Girls Academy. In

the mid-1970s, George sent the older boy, Hank, then in his late teens, on a trip to the Rose Bowl with the Ohio State football team, the Big Ten champions. His host and guide was a defensive back for Ohio State, Craig Cassady, Hopalong's son, who later played for the New Orleans Saints. Hank got to meet Craig's teammates, including the two-time winner of the Heisman Trophy, Archie Griffin. "He was a good kid," said Cassady of Hank Steinbrenner.

Steinbrenner and Jackson occasionally alluded to their contract negotiations as the season approached, but no real progress was made. Nor was there progress on a parallel front, negotiations with John Schneider, a lawyer from Louisiana who represented Ron Guidry. Like Jackson, Guidry was eligible to become a free agent after the 1981 season. Guidry had won twenty-five, eighteen and seventeen games in the three previous seasons, an average of exactly twenty victories a season, for an average salary of less than two hundred thousand dollars, slave labor by the standards of a Winfield, a Jackson or even a Rick Ceron. Schneider and Guidry were seeking a multiyear package worth roughly one million dollars a year, and the important thing in the negotiations, Schneider kept reminding himself, was "not to let George intimidate you." The trouble with that theory is that, as soon as you concede the importance of not being intimidated by Steinbrenner, you have, in effect, been intimidated by Steinbrenner.

At the end of spring training, neither Guidry nor Jackson had a new contract, nor one in sight, and Jackson, Winfield and Steinbrenner each had a problem. Jackson had a torn tendon in his right calf, which would keep him from playing during the first week of the season; Winfield had a batting average in exhibition games of .212, which did not endear him to New Yorkers who earned less than two million dollars a year; and Steinbrenner had his own cause for frustration. His attempt to acquire Jason Thompson, a quality first baseman with a lefthanded swing ideal

for Yankee Stadium, had failed. First, the deal had been held up when Bowie Kuhn pointed out that the amount of money involved, eight hundred fifty thousand of George's dollars, exceeded the limit the commissioner had set for cash transactions. Then, the deal had collapsed when the Yankees and the Pittsburgh Pirates, who had secured Thompson from California with the intention of passing him on, were unable to renegotiate a mutually satisfactory trade involving less cash. Steinbrenner, naturally, did not take the setback casually. He publicly attacked the integrity of a Pittsburgh executive and the competence of one of Commissioner Kuhn's aides.

Steinbrenner consoled himself with the acquisition of Jerry Mumphrey, a fine center fielder from San Diego, but once the season began, he found a fresh reason to be displeased. The 1981 Yankee yearbook went on sale with a picture of the principal owner on page three, and in the picture his lips were so red he seemed to be wearing lipstick. The trouble was that the Yankees had decided to put a little red apple on each page of the yearbook, a symbol of New York, and the apple had created a coloring problem which turned the owner's lips red. The yearbook was on sale for half a dozen games before Steinbrenner, his masculinity mocked by the photograph, ordered all remaining copies pulled off the stands. Newspaper reports said that fifty thousand copies were removed, but Larry Wahl, the Yankees' first publicity director of the season, said, "The whole thing was overplayed. It was only five or six hundred copies."

On the field, the Yankees quickly lost Rick Cerone, with a broken thumb, regained Reggie Jackson and got off to a slow start. The Oakland A's got off to the swiftest start in American League history, eleven straight victories, prompting Steinbrenner to wire congratulations to his former manager Billy Martin, his former pitching coach Art Fowler and his former publicity director Mickey Morabito,

all reunited on the A's. To no one's surprise, Martin was even more cocky than usual. The first time the Yankees and the A's met, in Oakland, Martin, a superb needler, took aim at Winfield. "He couldn't make our outfield," Martin boasted. Then he ridiculed Winfield's power. Winfield proved he could protect himself. He said that Martin should stop picking on him because, "I'm not a marshmallow salesman." (A week later, when Martin's team came into New York, Steinbrenner missed the festivities because he was in Tampa, celebrating his twenty-fifth wedding anniversary at a party organized by his children.)

By the time the season was a month old, Winfield was batting well over .300, justifying Steinbrenner's investment, but Jackson was batting under .200, damaging his negotiating position, and the Yankees were in third place, upsetting the owner. He fired his first salvo long-distance, ordering Larry Wahl to inform the press that the owner was unhappy with his team from the manager down, except for a few members of the pitching staff.

By the final week in May, Steinbrenner was even more unhappy. After a game in which Cleveland beat the Yankees, 12–5, Steinbrenner spoke up. First, he played his two expensive outfielders against each other. "Dave Winfield has done all I could ask of him," he said. "Reggie has killed us." Then, turning to the rest of the team, he said, "I've got the facts to back me up, stats about guys not producing in critical situations. I'm embarrassed, and if some of them were more embarrassed, it would be better. I'm just not getting dedication." The Yankees were about to play three games against the Orioles. "If they embarrass New York in Baltimore," the owner said, "there's going to be hell to pay."

There was hell to pay. After the Orioles won the first game, and Ron Guidry complained that his pitching had been hampered by a sore foot, Steinbrenner snapped, "Don't give me any stuff about a sore foot. He's been lousy

all this year except for one game against Detroit. He's not pitching like a million-dollar pitcher."

After the Orioles won the second game, Steinbrenner phoned the press box from Tampa to dictate a statement condemning the umpiring, particularly a decision made by umpire Terry Cooney in the fourth inning, calling a Baltimore runner safe at second base. "It was one of the worst calls of any season," said Steinbrenner, who had watched the game on television and who had a habit of sending TV tapes to the American League office. "The replay clearly showed that the man was out. This turned the momentum of the ball game." Steinbrenner said the umpiring "had been so bad that not even Gehrig, Ruth and Lazzeri could have overcome it." Sarcastically, he accused the president of the American League, his former general manager, Lee MacPhail, of—"in all his wisdom"—putting an incompetent in charge of the umpires, and he praised Earl Weaver, the manager of the Orioles, as "a master intimidator of umpires."

When he wasn't insulting his pitching star and the umpires, Steinbrenner was examining the possibility of hiring Gene Mauch to replace Gene Michael. Mauch had a reputation as a brilliant manager, but his image was flawed by the fact that, in twenty years of managing big-league teams, he had never won a pennant. The plan to fire Michael fell through when Gene Autry signed Mauch to replace Jim Fregosi as manager of the Angels. Deprived of any choice, Steinbrenner decided to stick with Michael, even though, in the owner's opinion, "He's been having a tough time making the right decision."

Steinbrenner summoned Michael to Tampa for a meeting, made a decision for him to replace pitching coach Stan Williams with Clyde King, then announced, "Stick will remain as manager." Michael, for his part, said, "I'm not going to let this get me down." And one observant newspaperman noted that twenty-six major-league teams had

not fired their managers that day, but the Yankees were the only ones who got headlines for not doing it.

Properly chastened, the Yankees then responded as they often, but not always, did to the owner's outbursts. They won nine out of ten games and, by June 11, when the season screeched to a halt, they were in first place.

That night, as time ran out on negotiations between the Major League Baseball Players' Association and the major-league owners, Steinbrenner, the most visible and vocal of owners, appeared on ABC's *Nightline*. Asked about the financial difficulties of major-league baseball, he offered a lament for the poor fan. "There's going to come a day soon, and it's the day I dread," said Steinbrenner. "And that day will be when the fan who brings his family to the ball game is going to get hit with an increase in ticket prices. And that's really the person I'm concerned about, when it hurts them. And it's going to inevitably happen. And I don't want to see the fan suffer when that does happen." Steinbrenner's nerve was unbelievable. He was talking as if Yankee ticket prices had never risen before. As a matter of fact, since 1976, when the team moved back into Yankee Stadium, ticket prices had gone up every year except one.

A few minutes later, Steinbrenner offered another example of his special rhetoric. "I may get struck down by some of my peers for saying this," he said, "but you know, with all the problems we have in this country today, and when we have people on unemployment in some of the mid-western cities, and many of our big industries are under such pressure, and interest rates are so high, you know, I've come to the point where I say if we're so silly as players and owners that we would take this away from the fans, then we don't deserve anything. Because on my priority list in this country, this strike is down about tenth." It isn't easy to figure out precisely what Steinbrenner meant by those two sentences, but he seemed to be saying that he

was against going out on strike. Of course he was against going out on strike. The owners weren't threatening to strike; the players were. And on the players' priority list, the strike probably ranked higher than tenth.

"I can tell you the New York Yankees and George Steinbrenner want nothing to do with the strike," Steinbrenner informed his late-night audience. Then he said he was optimistic that a strike could be avoided. "At the zero hour, something always seems to happen," he said. At the zero hour, something happened. Marvin Miller, the executive director of the Players' Association, announced, "The strike is on."

Steinbrenner was among a small group of owners who pressed, unsuccessfully, for an early settlement. They included the owner of the Baltimore Orioles, Edward Bennett Williams, who, a few years earlier, during the Watergate days, had been Steinbrenner's attorney. "I like George," said Williams of his former client, "but if I had to describe him in one quick sentence, it would be: 'If something is wrong, it has to be someone else's fault.'"

The strike was not Steinbrenner's fault. The issue—the degree of compensation a team losing a free agent should be entitled to—was not a major issue in his mind. The players wanted no compensation; the owners, as a group, wanted ample compensation. Steinbrenner, who specialized in gaining free agents, not losing them, wanted the season to resume. He wanted to be able to second-guess Gene Michael again, to call Rick Cerone names, to harass Reggie Jackson. Publicly, he picked on Marvin Miller, the players' chief negotiator, and privately, he urged the owners to replace Ray Grebey, their chief negotiator, but his attacks didn't have the same enthusiasm he reserved for his own employees. Steinbrenner spoke often of his own vast experience in negotiating with labor unions, and in the first week of the strike, he predicted its early end.

The strike ended after fifty days, and when the season

resumed, George Steinbrenner needed less than a month to dispose of Gene Michael and replace him with Bob Lemon. In the final weeks of the season, with the Yankees assured a spot in the playoffs, their reward for being in first place the day the strike began, Steinbrenner concentrated on shaking up his players, toughening them for postseason play, and postseason abuse.

Steinbrenner told his players they had to "put up or shut up," and told the press that he had already devised two plans to improve the Yankees in 1982. "Plan A is if they win the world championship," he said, "and Plan B is if they lose." The implication was that Plan A meant a few changes in the Yankee roster, Plan B a complete overhaul.

Of course Steinbrenner had other things to worry about besides baseball during the final week of September. He told his shipyard workers in Ohio to put up or shut up, too. He threatened to move thirty-six million dollars in ship repair work from Lorain to Tampa unless workers who had been laid off would agree to a wage reduction. The choice came down to work for less or don't work. The men agreed to the cut in pay, and one thousand of them were called back to the job.

Steinbrenner talked tough on the docks and on the diamond. His toughest words were still aimed at Rick Cerone, who came down to the end of his four-hundred-forty-thousand-dollar season with a batting average of .244, only two home runs and only twenty-one runs batted in. "He's gotten the big head definitely," Steinbrenner charged. "Suddenly, he's Mister New York. He's the Italian Stallion. He's going to disco joints. I have a way of bringing guys down to size."

Dave Winfield's batting average had slipped in the second half of the season, down to .294, still respectable, and Reggie Jackson's had gone up, to .239, still disappointing. A week before the end of the season, however, Jackson

stirred up his teammates, and the owner. Knocked down by a pitch thrown by John Denny of the Cleveland Indians, Jackson got up and headed toward the mound, setting off a free-for-all that emptied the Yankees' bench. Jackson and Denny both survived the scuffle, and the next time Reggie came up, he drove one of Denny's pitches into the right-field stands. When he finished his home-run trot, Jackson and Denny charged each other again, and a fresh battle erupted. Teammates had to pull Reggie away, and as they did, he clapped his hands. He was having great fun, for one of the few times all season. Steinbrenner, from his Tampa base, joined in the fun. He threatened legal action against pitchers who knocked down his players. "I will not tolerate our hitters being assaulted with a deadly weapon," Steinbrenner said. "The Yankees are knee-deep in lawyers, and we will use them to protect our players."

The Yankees wound up the second part of the split season under .500, buried in sixth place in the Eastern Division, a dismal performance. The Milwaukee Brewers came in first and hosted the first two games of the divisional playoffs. The Yankees won both games, impressively, and then the series moved to New York, and at this point, the season ended for the purists, the people who thought the heart of baseball was the diamond. At this point, George took command, turning the playing field into nothing more than a backdrop for the most dazzling show ever staged by an owner in any sport. For three weeks, he transcended the players, transcended the competition, transcended the game. Baseball became The George Company.

He put all the different Georges on display. He was the patriot and the bully, the host and the hypocrite. He was compassionate and petty, charming and cruel, incredibly efficient and unbelievably childish. He had trouble with his temper, and trouble with his credibility. But Patton would have been proud of him. He charged straight on, his path traced in screaming newspaper headlines, more head-

lines in three weeks than most of his fellow owners earned in a lifetime:

> Steinbrenner Erupts
> Mistakes Have Steinbrenner Seething
> Yanks, Not Steinbrenner, Deserve All the Glory
> George's Gall Vs. Billyball
> George, Billy Rap the Umpires
> Steinbrenner Blasts MacPhail
> Steinbrenner on Reggie: "Had It Up to Here With Him"
> The Boss Should Bite His Tongue
> Give 'Em Hell, George
> George Cheerful Despite Wounds
> Steinbrenner's Panic Infected Lemon, Yanks
> George Promises Immediate Changes

The three-week blitzkrieg began on a high note, with a demonstration of Steinbrenner's patriotism—and persistence. Before the third game of the playoffs against Milwaukee, in ceremonies held at home plate, the widow of Corporal Will James accepted the Distinguished Service Cross her husband had earned for his heroism thirty-seven years earlier in the Battle of the Bulge. His face shattered by machine-gun fire, Corporal James fought on, one of a platoon of eighteen American soldiers who, in a memorable stand, destroyed five hundred German soldiers and turned back thousands more. Then the platoon was overrun, the Americans captured by the enemy. Because of his imprisonment, and subsequent bureaucratic confusion, Corporal James was never decorated for his bravery—not until George Steinbrenner read an article about him and started a campaign to have his heroism recognized. James' widow and his four sons attended the ceremonies at Yankee Stadium as George's guests.

To throw out the first ball for the first postseason game played at Yankee Stadium, Steinbrenner called upon two-year-old Travis John, the son of pitcher Tommy John. Less than two months earlier, Travis John had fallen from a third-floor window of his home and had been rushed to the hospital, close to death. Tommy John left the team and hurried home to wait with his wife as doctors fought to save the child's life. Millions of New Yorkers shared the Johns' vigil, and rejoiced when Travis recovered, and were touched when the child threw out the first ball at Yankee Stadium. It was theatrical, of course, but it was a perfect gesture, Steinbrenner at his best.

The bad parts of the evening came later, first when a fan who, according to police, had been drinking heavily ran onto the field and tried to assault the third-base umpire, and then when Milwaukee rallied in the closing innings to win the game and prolong the series.

The next day, Milwaukee won again, 2–1, evening the series. But it wasn't only the fact that the Yankees lost that triggered Steinbrenner's temper; it was the way they lost. Trailing in the sixth inning, 2–0, they had the tying runs on second and third, none out, Reggie Jackson up, Mr. October. He had hit the fifteenth postseason home run of his career in the second game of the series, but this time he struck out. When the next batter, Lou Piniella, grounded to shortstop, Dave Winfield tried to go to third and was thrown out. The Yankees' only run scored on the play, but the chance for a big inning was gone.

In the seventh inning, the Yankees had another chance. With one out and Larry Milbourne on first, Rick Cerone drove a single into left field. Milbourne went to third; so did the left fielder's throw. Cerone, unwisely, took a wide turn around first, ignoring the counsel of the first-base coach, Mike Ferraro, banished from third base after Steinbrenner condemned him in 1980. Milwaukee's

third base man alertly threw to first, trapping Cerone off the base. Then, as the Brewers closed in on Cerone, Milbourne strayed off third, and a quick throw cut him down. Cerone retreated to first, and once again the Yankees' hopes dimmed.

They had one more opportunity in the ninth inning, the potential tying run on third, the potential winning run on second, two men out. The batter, with any kind of a base hit, could have been a hero, could have wiped out a year of frustration and disappointment. Instead, Rick Cerone struck out.

"Stupid, stupid baserunning." The words seemed to foam from George Steinbrenner's lips as he stormed toward the losers' clubhouse. "It was that way the whole damn ball game." He marched in, the door closed behind him, and he dressed down his troops. "I'm embarrassed to look Bud Selig in the eye," said Steinbrenner, referring to the owner of the Milwaukee Brewers. Then he attacked his players in general, and their baserunning in particular. He struck familiar notes. The players were lacking in dedication. They weren't earning their huge salaries. They were letting down the people of New York. They were a disgrace to their pinstriped uniforms. The players, already angry with themselves, turned their anger toward the boss. The tension was so great Reggie Jackson anticipated a fistfight.

"Fuck you, George," said Rick Cerone. "We don't need to hear this."

"I pay the bills around here," Steinbrenner shouted. "I'll say whatever I want. And we'll see where you're playing next year."

"Fuck you," Cerone said again.

The dialogue ended, Steinbrenner swept out of the locker room, and reporters moved in, eager to find out what they had missed. "I'll tell you what I got out of the meeting," Reggie Jackson said. "If we don't win tomorrow, I ain't gonna be here next year." Then Jackson had another thought. "Cerone showed me a lot of guts today."

Cerone himself was subdued. "I don't want to say anything I'll regret tomorrow," he said, with curious timing.

Even Steinbrenner, his fury spent, was no longer combative. Of Cerone's outburst, the owner said, "As far as I'm concerned, it's meaningless." Of the team's failure, he said, "I'll take the blame for it. I drew up this team. I went out and got these players and I was the one who thought they could win." But of his own decision to go into the locker room and lecture the players, Steinbrenner was fiercely defensive. "If anyone doesn't like the idea of me going down and having my say with my players, that's tough. I have the right."

Columnist Mike Lupica did not deny Steinbrenner's right, but said he was wrong. "The fat man," Lupica wrote, "has tried to inspire them with his frenzied threats, but has only made them angry and bitter instead, made them wonder if they want to win for him."

The next day, before the fifth and decisive game of the series, Jackson called Cerone at home and offered the young catcher encouragement, then called upon George Steinbrenner in the owner's office. Reggie delivered his own speech. "I'm not really a fan of what you did last night," Jackson said, "but I realize you're the boss, and you pay the bills, and you're entitled to get mad. I get mad if somebody leaves the lights on all over the house, and I have to pay the bill. I've learned a lot about you in the five years I've been here. But I don't think you know your ballplayers. They're playing like sonsabitches. They are busting ass out there. I just want you to know your catcher is one helluva pressure kid, and one helluva catcher."

Steinbrenner listened, then opened his desk and pulled out a letter he had written. The owner asked Jackson to deliver the letter to Rick Cerone. Jackson said he would, and as he headed toward the locker room, Steinbrenner

couldn't resist a needle. "And when are you going to start hitting?" he said.

Jackson delivered the note, and Cerone read, "Your strikeout to end the game with a man on third carries little weight with me. Stupid mental errors like rounding first too far does. Your vulgarities to me in the clubhouse afterward is water off a duck's back. It was said out of frustration, just as my answer to you was said out of anger. It has no bearing at all, and I want you to know that."

"Are you going to apologize to George?" someone asked Cerone.

"I won't apologize to him," Cerone said, "and he doesn't have to apologize to me. If I say things, it's because I don't like to lose."

Cerone, was a center of attention before the game. So was Jackson. "I'm interested in finding out how much of this Reggie Jackson crap is true," Reggie said. "Everybody is always saying I come through in the big games. Well, if I'm ever gonna do anything, it'll be tonight."

Ron Guidry started for the Yankees, with three days' rest, knowing he would pitch only the first four innings, and when he finished his tour, Milwaukee had a 2–0 lead. Then, in the bottom of the fourth, with one out and one man on, Reggie Jackson came through. He drove a fastball into the upper deck in right field, and as the ball flew off his bat, he broke into a huge smile. The home run counted for two runs, tying the score, but meant much more. The pitcher, Moose Haas, was understandably shaken, and the next batter, Oscar Gamble, like Bobby Murcer a born-again Yankee, returned to the fold, delivered a home run that put the Yankees in front. In the bottom of the eighth inning, with the score 5–3, Milwaukee still in contention, Rick Cerone came up and hit a two-run home run that clinched the game and the Eastern championship.

"That's the one that did it," said George Steinbrenner. "That was the big hit."

"For one second, when I got to home plate," Cerone said, "I thought of tipping my hat to George. But that would have shown him up. I don't show up my pitchers, my teammates or my boss."

Reggie Jackson, too, was delighted with his performance, a pair of singles to go with his home run. "I've been privileged to wear this Yankee uniform for the last five years," Jackson said, "and if I'm not here next year, I wanted to go out the best I could. I wanted the fans to remember me as someone who came through for them once in a while."

The good feeling was contagious. Steinbrenner did not say that the team could not have won without his speech. In his private suite, George greeted a long line of well-wishers and said the game was the third-most-satisfying of his Yankee ownership, behind only the game in which Chris Chambliss' ninth-inning home run gave the Yankees their first pennant in twelve years and the game in which Reggie Jackson hit three home runs and gave birth to a candy bar. "It was electric," Steinbrenner said, of his latest triumph. "Cerone was magnificent, Reggie was magnificent, they all were magnificent. They respond to pressure just like New Yorkers respond to pressure."

Then Bud Selig, the Milwaukee owner, came into George's suite, and George looked him straight in the eye. Selig was close to tears. Steinbrenner hugged him. "Your team showed incredible heart," the Yankee owner said. "There'll be another year."

The following day, the champions of the Western Division arrived in New York for the start of the American League championship series. The champions of the West were the Oakland A's, Billy Martin's Oakland A's, with an ex-Yankee for a pitching coach, an ex-Yankee for a publicity man and six ex-Yankees in uniform, each eager

to beat George, each with his own memories of his Yankee days. Mickey Morabito vividly recalled the long hours he had put in for Steinbrenner. He remembered the time he had worked until three thirty in the morning after a World Series game, and then had shown up five minutes late the next morning for an early meeting in George's office. Steinbrenner had bawled him out, would hear no excuse. "He wants you when he wants you," Morabito recalled. "If only he'd pat you on the back once in a while, it would make it easier when he jumps all over you." Still, Morabito was grateful for the opportunity George had given him, making him the team's publicity director when he was only twenty-four, when Gabe Paul wanted someone older. "It was an invaluable experience," he said.

But Morabito and Art Fowler and all the A's who had played for the Yankees, Cliff Johnson and Fred Stanley and Mickey Klutts and Tom Underwood and Mike Heath and Jim Spencer, were only incidental to the central confrontation: Billy Martin returning from exile to face his former tormentor, George Steinbrenner. It was like Lancelot rising up against King Arthur, except that Lancelot and Arthur really loved each other. And if there was no Guinevere to complicate the Martin-Steinbrenner relationship, there was at least Reggie Jackson to complete the triangle. Only the three principals tried to pretend that their personal conflicts were less exciting than the American League championship series.

"This is the Oakland A's versus the New York Yankees, not Billy versus George," Steinbrenner insisted.

"Reggie-Billy antagonistic comments, remarks and negatives are degrading to me," said Jackson in more elegant language.

Billy Martin was right; they were both liars. So was he. "I have no vendetta in me against Steinbrenner," he said.

That was the party line, though each of the three men had sniped at the other two many times, Jackson often in

anguish, Steinbrenner in whispered rumors, Martin in anger and even in a book. Martin had said terrible things about George in *Number 1*, but now on the eve of the championship series, Steinbrenner said of Martin, "Like him? I love the guy."

The words were an echo from the locker room after the final game of the 1977 World Series. "Billy Martin. I love the man," Reggie Jackson had said. Jackson could be forgiven. He was high on home runs.

Now only Martin, of the three, came close to being honest. Reminded that Reggie Jackson rose to great heights in October, the Oakland manager was not impressed. "We'll go right at him," Martin said. "We're not afraid of him. Mr. October, hey, check my record. I was a better October hitter than him. When he hit that third home run against the Dodgers in 1977, he broke my Series record for total bases. I was Mr. October before him. What's his World Series average? Mine's .333. I have five World Series homers."

No one bothered to tell Martin that Reggie's average was .360, with nine home runs.

"I know about October," Martin continued. "You got pumpkins in October and witches. October's when you got the pot boiling and all that stuff."

Martin did not completely disguise his feelings about Steinbrenner, either. He said he thought the world of George—"heck of a guy"—but he didn't think that the owner's clubhouse speech during the Milwaukee series had benefited the Yankees. "When I was managing here and he did that," Martin said, "it took me two weeks to unwind them."

Then Martin went a step further. "I saw Rick Cerone's comment," he said, "and he was right."

There was another small breach in the feigned peace, a heated dispute over illegal pitches. Billy Martin's four starting pitchers had all been accused, at some time in

their pitching lives, of throwing spitters, violating the rules. Steinbrenner decided to strike a blow for law and order. The day the A's arrived in New York, he had a meeting with Lee MacPhail and suggested that the president of the American League order his umpires to strictly enforce the rule against illegal pitches. "This is a championship that has to be decided within the rules," Steinbrenner insisted. He said he wouldn't want to win a championship by bending the rules, and he was certain Billy Martin wouldn't want to, either.

Martin did not like Steinbrenner's going to Lee MacPhail. He also did not like the fact that, the last time the A's played in New York, before the strike, the Yankees had shot tapes of the Oakland pitchers, so that their styles could be studied, and had complained so much that the umpires had harassed Billy's pitchers. "I guarantee I won't let that happen again," Martin said. "I guarantee all the money in the world. My pitchers will walk to home plate, hand over the ball and lift their arms and let the umpires check for spitballs or guns or whatever else they want."

Martin and Steinbrenner were too polite to talk about the spitter to each other. They talked about it to the press. Then they went up to Steinbrenner's office together and posed for pictures, toasting each other, their faces split by smiles so sincere they might have been filming a beer commercial. Steinbrenner had the best of two worlds. His picture appeared on both the front page and the back page of the New York *Daily News*. On the front page, he was smiling, greeting Billy Martin, and on the back page, he was stern, attacking Martin's pitchers. Smaller photographs of some of the New York and Oakland players appeared inside the newspaper.

Inevitably, with the Yankees facing the A's, and with Billy Martin managing the team Reggie Jackson himself had once symbolized, someone asked Reggie to compare George Steinbrenner and Charles Finley. Jacksons answer

277

did not disappoint. "George Steinbrenner plots and plans, he's got his guns loaded," said the Babe Ruth of metaphor. "He's saying, 'Here are my pearl-handled revolvers.' But when you test him, George'll say, 'Just kidding.' Charley Finley had a derringer. Just one. But when it came time to draw, he did."

In the first game of the American League championship series, Jackson and Rick Cerone both went hitless, and the Yankees won the game, 3–1. They won on Graig Nettles' three-run double in the first inning, and on the strong pitching of Tommy John, with help from Ron Davis and Rich Gossage. The game succeeded in bringing George Steinbrenner and Billy Martin even closer together. At the end, they both questioned the competence of the umpires. The details of their displeasure were not nearly so significant as the fact that, in *The New York Times'* coverage of the game, neither Nettles, John, Davis nor Gossage got headlines, while Steinbrenner and Martin did. Steinbrenner also got attention for ordering the security police to confiscate a sign that said: "George, Get Out of Town, Billy Is Back." The security forces descended upon the man waving the sign. He was an attorney, and he threatened to sue. The security forces backed down.

In the second game, Jackson and Cerone again went hitless, and again the Yankees won, 13–3. Nettles was once more the batting star, with four hits, including a home run, and Steinbrenner afterward was strangely silent. He said he was too busy to talk. He had to get his team to Oakland for the third game of the series.

The Yankee party, ninety strong, including players' wives as well as Mrs. Steinbrenner, left Yankee Stadium in a three-bus caravan. George and Joan Steinbrenner sat up front in the lead bus, George barking commands to the driver: "Take a left. Now a right. Right again." A man from Cleveland with a home in Tampa was telling a New York City bus driver how to get from the Bronx to Newark

Airport. The trip took considerably longer than usual, but still, when the Yankees reached their chartered DC-8, comfortably in time for their assigned takeoff, the pilot announced that Oakland's charter was still waiting for the A's. During the flight to Oakland, the Yankees were served a dinner of rubbery fried chicken, followed half an hour later by dessert, Chipwiches, ice cream tucked between huge chocolate chip cookies. When the plane landed, Steinbrenner got off first. Then, as the rest of the party deplaned, he handed out room keys to the Oakland Hyatt. He had arranged for the party to be preregistered, which was not uncommon, and for the keys to be delivered to the airport, which they were. He didn't want his players to be slowed up in the hotel lobby. He wanted them to rest. When each member of the Yankee entourage entered his room, he found a tray of food waiting, a club sandwich, potato salad, chilled beer and cold Cokes. George didn't want his players waiting for room service or wandering about looking for an open restaurant if they wanted a midnight snack. His attention to detail was awesome.

The next morning, Steinbrenner sat in the lobby of the Hyatt, complaining loudly to a representative of United Airlines. "No more of that bullshit food," the owner announced. He wanted steaks served on the flight home, first-class service for everyone, salt and pepper shakers, and above all, no more Chipwiches. It was not Steinbrenner's nature to take a stand against any form of ice cream, but he had a strong aversion to Chipwiches. He had heard that John McMullen, the owner of the Houston Astros and a former investor in the Yankees, was remotely involved with Chipwiches, and Steinbrenner and McMullen had had a bitter falling-out. "You're never going to see Chipwiches again on our plane," Steinbrenner thundered. He didn't care how much the players and the reporters liked them. On the next flight, steak and Popsicles would replace chicken and Chipwiches.

The championship series ended in three games, again with no help from Jackson, who sat out the game, nursing an injured leg, or from Cerone, who was inconspicuous. The score was 4–0, Dave Righetti the pitching star, the last three runs coming in the ninth inning, on Nettles' double with the bases loaded. In the three games, Nettles had nine runs batted in, a .500 batting average. He was, overwhelmingly, the Most Valuable Player in the series. "You're going to have to be Mr. November this year," he kidded Reggie Jackson, "because I've got October." Nettles was in the perfect mood to go to George Steinbrenner's victory party at an Oakland restaurant called Vince's. He took his wife, Ginger, and their four children, and his mother and father and brother. The party, Steinbrenner said, was strictly for family, the Yankee family and relatives.

Reggie Jackson went to the party, too. He had five guests, but only one of them was a relative, a niece. The other four were friends, two men, two women. They sat down at a table that had been occupied by Ginger Nettles and her children. She came back with her three-year-old son, Jeffrey, asleep in her arms. She started to sit down, and one of Jackson's guests told her the table was taken. Ginger Nettles protested. Upset, she decided to leave the party with her children. Her decision upset her husband.

Graig Nettles went to look for Reggie Jackson to complain about Reggie's friends. Nettles and Jackson had never been close; Graig was friendly with Thurman Munson and never forgave Jackson for his remarks about Thurman. Besides, Nettles made no secret of his distaste for Reggie's attitude, his scorn for Reggie's style of play. When he found Reggie, and explained the problem, the two men stepped outside the dining room, into a corridor. Nettles had a bottle of beer in his hand. Jackson remembered a fight among the Oakland A's in which a player got cut by a beer bottle. "I was thinking about that," Jackson

said later, when he reached out and slapped the bottle out of Nettles' hand. Nettles reacted promptly and violently. He threw a punch that hit Jackson and knocked him to the floor. Jackson got up, a few lesser punches were exchanged, walls rattled, and the fight was over. Steinbrenner moved into the middle, screaming. "We're disgracing the Yankees," he yelled, "in front of all these people."

Jackson screamed back at the owner. "I don't have to take no shit from anybody!" Jackson said. "I don't have to take nothing. I'm thirty-five, and I don't have to take no more of this. I don't have a contract, and I don't have to be here." Jackson offered a parting shot. "You'll pay for this," he told the owner.

"I've had it up to here with him," said Steinbrenner later. "He's got to be the boss of everything. He has to be the big shot and run everything. Well, he's not going to get away with it any more. This is it." He referred to Jackson as "the former number forty-four."

Soon, tempers subsided. Nettles was embarrassed; he wouldn't even admit he had dropped Jackson with one punch. "Let's just say we shoved each other," he suggested.

"We're both sorry it happened," Jackson said. "It was a misunderstanding."

Steinbrenner, too, calmed down. "It was a shoving match as far as I'm concerned," he said. "It's an in-house thing, and I don't regard it as very important." He said Jackson's future with the Yankees would not be affected. He still had not offered Reggie a new contract.

Then, a little later, Steinbrenner altered his stance once more. "If Reggie wants to come back as a Yankee," George said, "he's got to understand that it will be as a team man, not as an individual who does as he pleases, when he pleases." George did not sound like a man who was going to offer Reggie Jackson a new contract.

Aboard their chartered DC-10 flying back from Oakland, the Yankees were served a movie to go with their steak

and ice cream. The movie was *Zorro, The Gay Blade*. It made fun of heroes and villains, and of grown men dueling.

When the plane touched down at Newark Airport, on a remote runway, far from the mob waiting to cheer and maul the American League champions, more than a dozen limousines were poised to take the players and their families directly to their homes. There was also a bus for players who wanted to go to Yankee Stadium to pick up cars or gear. George thought of everything, and everything, as usual, was first class.

The next day, while the Yankees waited to find out whether Los Angeles or Montreal would represent the National League in the World Series, the team worked out. Afterward, Reggie Jackson and George Steinbrenner met. They had the kind of conversation the owner always enjoyed. "We had a pretty nice talk," he said. "Reggie apologized to me—which Nettles had already done—which means a lot to me. He said he was awfully sorry and that he felt very bad about it." Steinbrenner said that he felt bad, too. He didn't exactly apologize, but he did say, "I guess I was too strong."

Steinbrenner moved right on to his next cause. He announced that he wanted Jimmy Cagney, the veteran actor, the Yankee Doodle Dandy of films, to throw out the first ball for the opening game of the World Series. But, Steinbrenner said, Commissioner Bowie Kuhn had vetoed Cagney, citing a rule prohibiting actors and politicians and, presumably, other undesirables from making ceremonial pitches at baseball games. Steinbrenner was outraged by the ruling. Soon, the public was outraged, too. Cagney was a monument, a national institution. The headlines delighted George: Cagney and Steinbrenner against Kuhn. The commissioner was overmatched; he would have had a better chance against apple pie and Mom. By the time someone finally solicited Kuhn's opinion, and found out that he did not have any objection to

Cagney's throwing out the first ball, Steinbrenner had generated all the emotional coverage he wanted. Kuhn's defense got very little coverage. Joe DiMaggio threw out the ball for the first game—no one had accused Joe of being an actor, based on his commercials—and Cagney, wearing a Yankee cap, took over for the second. There was an extra touch: Three members of the Golden Knights, the U.S. Army's spectacular parachute team, dropped through the Bronx air into Yankee Stadium unfurling an American flag.

"The Star-Spangled Banner" boomed, and Steinbrenner beamed. He was in his glory. DiMaggio paraded through his suite, and Cagney, and Cary Grant, and Lee Iacocca, and Martina Navratilova, the tennis champion, and Shelley Hack, the ex-Angel, all of George's good friends. The Washington *Post* sent a team of five reporters to interview him in his office; neither Woodward nor Bernstein was among them. Lesser newspapers dispatched smaller delegations. Howard Cosell had launched a new magazine-format show, and he wanted George, not a ballplayer, not a manager, to be his guest. Steinbrenner loved appearing with Cosell, showman against showman, ego against ego, a fair match. George had his part of the act down perfectly. He employed the same technique he used on favored writers. He pretended that he was revealing to Cosell facts and feelings he would never dream of telling anyone else. Sugar Ray Leonard himself could not have avoided Cosell's journalistic jabs any more adroitly than George Steinbrenner did.

The Los Angeles Dodgers won the National League championship. They won it, finally, in chilly Montreal the day before the World Series was to start. They won on the pitching of Fernando Valenzuela, who was still only twenty, and the hitting of Rick Monday, who was thirty-six. The Dodgers were drained, emotionally and physically. They had won their divisional playoff with three straight

victories after trailing Houston, two games to none. They had won the National League pennant with two straight victories after trailing Montreal, two games to one. They didn't get even one day off before the start of the eleventh Dodger-Yankee World Series confrontation.

Rested and confident, the Yankees pounced on the Dodgers, won the first game, 5–3, and the second, 3–0. The starting pitchers, Ron Guidry and Tommy John, were credited with the victories, and Rich Gossage came on to save both games. Graig Nettles contributed a fielding play in the first game that defied belief, a lunging catch of a line drive, and Bob Watson, who had so disappointed Steinbrenner during the regular season, contributed a three-run home run in the first game and two more hits in the second. Bob Lemon, in the dugout, pushed all the right buttons and relaxed. He didn't mind giving up the spotlight to Steinbrenner. "He owns the boat," the manager said. "I'm only riding on it."

The only disturbing note was that Reggie Jackson, hampered by a strained muscle in his left calf, and by the fact that the Series was being played under National League rules, eliminating the designated hitter, had to sit out the first two games. Steinbrenner did not seem especially disturbed by the possibility that the Yankees might win the World Series without Jackson's help. The possibility that the Yankees might lose the Series did not seem to occur, at this point, to Steinbrenner or to anyone else. In fact, George Martin, the proprietor of the Manhattan restaurant Steinbrenner frequented, went to the Yankee owner and asked if it would be all right if he and two other prominent restaurateurs—Oren Stevens, of Oren & Aretzky's, the players' hangout, and Jim McMullen, of McMullen's—organized a victory party for the Yankees at Xenon, a fashionable disco. Steinbrenner gave the party his blessing. The only question seemed to be how soon to schedule the celebration. Sunday, the day after the fourth

game was to be played, would be a bit presumptuous. The party was scheduled for Tuesday, and if by any chance the Series should last long enough for the Dodgers to come back to New York, then the Dodgers would be invited, too.

The Yankees took off for the West Coast without their owner. He flew, instead, to Nashville, for a news conference concerning the Nashville Sounds, a farm team for the Yankees. At the conference, Steinbrenner was asked if Bob Lemon would be back managing the Yankees in 1982. "He's real family," Steinbrenner said. "A loyal, loyal guy. It's his choice."

Steinbrenner had gone more than a whole week without once criticizing his manager or his players for anything that they had done on the field. The team had won six straight games since he and Cerone exchanged pleasantries. Only two more, and the whole world would realize how effective George Steinbrenner was as a locker-room orator.

From Nashville, Steinbrenner flew on to Los Angeles, and soon after he arrived, the world shook twice—first at ten thirty in the morning, and again at noon, a pair of minor-league quakes, no more than .5 on the Richter scale. Steinbrenner had been known to register higher than that all by himself. When the earthquake struck, a palm plant in Steinbrenner's hotel suite began to sway back and forth, and his wife called to him, "Get me out of here!" George remained calm. "You know, I never did like California," Joan Steinbrenner told a reporter. "In Tampa, all we have is hurricanes."

The Yankees were shaken further by the news that Graig Nettles, who had been hitting and fielding brilliantly, had jammed his left thumb, diving for a ground ball, and the pain was so severe he would not be able to play. Nettles was, however, still able to talk. He knew that Aurelio Rodriguez would replace him at third base and would face the Dodgers' rookie pitcher, Fernando Val-

enzuela, Mexican against Mexican. "There's gonna be a lot of Chevvies in the parking lot," said Nettles, the master of clubhouse humor.

Jackson said he was ready to return to the lineup, but Bob Lemon decided to leave Lou Piniella in right field, to face Valenzuela. "With the lefthander pitching and Lou going so good," said Jackson, mildly, "I can't really argue with it. I'll play tomorrow, I guess. One more day won't hurt."

Someone remarked that Jackson's calm acceptance of Lemon's decision seemed out of character. "Why create anything now?" Reggie said. "I'm too close to freedom. It's not as though I've never been in a World Series."

Without Nettles, without Jackson, the Yankees squandered an early 4–3 lead. Valenzuela, far from his best form, surrendered nine hits and seven walks, but under pressure, he was magnificent. After the third inning, he didn't give up a run. The Yankees, trailing 5–4, came very close to tying the score in the eighth inning. They had runners on first and second, none out. Bob Lemon sent Bobby Murcer up to pinch-hit. Lemon told Murcer to bunt, not to sacrifice, not to give himself up, but to try to bunt for a base hit, a far more demanding assignment. Murcer tried, but he bunted too hard. He popped the ball up. Larry Milbourne, the runner on first, thought the ball was going to fall. He broke for second. But Ron Cey, the Dodgers' third baseman, dove for the bunt, caught the ball just on the foul side of the third-base line, then fired to first for a double play. "I didn't have a chance to get back," said Milbourne, who, replacing injured Bucky Dent, was doing an admirable job at everything except baserunning. "I got too greedy," said Lemon. To compound the crime, when Willie Randolph then hit a ground ball to third, the runner on second, Aurelio Rodriguez, did not wait to see if Cey would throw out Randolph, a difficult play. Instead, Rodriguez raced for third. Cey simply waited for him and tagged him out.

As soon as the game ended, George Steinbrenner hurried to the Yankee locker room. He went inside, and reporters waited outside, wondering what sort of speech he was delivering, to what sort of reaction. When the locker room was opened to the press, the owner was sitting quietly in Lemon's office. "I didn't say anything," Steinbrenner said. "They did all the talking—on the field. They made mental errors. They made foolish mistakes."

Steinbrenner managed to put part of the blame for the Yankees' defeat on Bowie Kuhn, because the commissioner presided over a divided empire. In the American League, the designated hitter was accepted. In the National League, the designated hitter was unknown. For the World Series, Kuhn had taken Solomon's example and had ruled that the baby be cut in half. The designated hitter would be permitted in even years, would not be permitted in odd years. In the first three games of the 1981 Series, the Yankees' pitchers, unaccustomed to wielding a bat, had not gotten a hit. "It's about time Bowie Kuhn either made the designated hitter a permanent thing in the World Series or got rid of it," Steinbrenner said. "Either have it or don't have it. This every-other-year crap is ridiculous."

The Yankee owner had one more complaint. "We're not getting any production out of two and three," he said, referring to Jerry Mumphrey and Dave Winfield, the second and third hitters in the batting order. Mumphrey was hitless in seven times at bat in the last two games, Winfield hitless in ten times at bat in the World Series. Winfield's slump went back into the championship series, two hits for his last twenty-eight times at bat. He had made a truly remarkable leaping catch against Oakland, but he wasn't getting two million dollars a year for his glove.

The next day, no earthquake shook the Yankees, only their owner. He had Lemon bench Mumphrey. He had Winfield switched to center field, Piniella to left and

Jackson returned to right field. For three innings, Steinbrenner looked like a genius. With their revised lineup, the Yankees built a 4–0 lead. Then Steinbrenner's image faded.

When Jay Johnstone, a former Yankee, hit a two-run home run in the sixth inning, the Dodgers drew to within one run, 6–5. Then Davy Lopes lofted a fly ball into short right field. Jackson lost the ball in the sun. He zigzagged back and forth, trying to pick up its flight, but he did not know where it was until it hit his shoulder and bounced away, a two-base error. One base hit later, the score was tied. The Dodgers added two more runs in the seventh inning, helped by some uncertain fielding by Bobby Brown in center field, usually Mumphrey's turf. Even though Jackson hit his tenth lifetime World Series home run in the ninth inning, his third hit of the game, the Yankees wound up one run short, 8–7. The Series was even. The defeat was a team effort, bad pitching, bad fielding, bad baserunning and bad managing, but Steinbrenner, for once, chose to look on the positive side. "We changed the lineup to produce more offense," he said, "and it worked. We scored seven runs. Any time you score more than four runs, you should win."

Steinbrenner had, in effect, taken over managing his team, prompting Dave Anderson, *The New York Times'* Pulitzer Prize-winning columnist, to take note of the contrast between the Yankees' owner and the Dodgers' owner. "Peter O'Malley has never visited the clubhouse except to console his players after World Series losses in 1974, 1977 and 1978," Anderson wrote.

"I don't think it's necessary for me to make an appearance in the clubhouse," O'Malley told Anderson. "Tommy [Lasorda, the Dodgers' manager] knows what I want. There's nothing that I can add."

In the ten years since O'Malley had become president of the Dodgers, the team had won four pennants and had

never finished worse than third, and he could remember firing only one person. "We try to hire people we won't have to fire," said Peter O'Malley, mildly. Without turmoil, screaming, second-guessing or even investing heavily in the free-agent market, O'Malley's Dodgers had, from 1977 through 1980, drawn an average of three million fans a year, better than half a million fans a year more than George Steinbrenner's Yankees.

Before the fifth game, George Steinbrenner went to the Yankee clubhouse once again to deliver a small pep talk. He didn't rant. He didn't rave. He tried reason. He told his players that their job was simple, to win two out of three games. He reminded them that two of those three games would be played in Yankee Stadium, where they had beaten the Dodgers six straight times, going back to 1977. "If I had written a script," said Steinbrenner, assessing the situation, "I wouldn't have written it any other way."

Then the Yankees went out to play, and if Tommy Lasorda had written the script, he wouldn't have written it any other way. Jerry Reuss pitched for the Dodgers, Ron Guidry for the Yankees, a fine match-up between gifted lefthanders. In the second inning, Reggie Jackson led off with a double, giving him four for four since the manager, Lemon/Steinbrenner, had decided he could return to the lineup. Then Bob Watson grounded to Davy Lopes at second, and when Lopes bobbled the ball, the Yankees had men on first and third, none out. Lou Piniella singled, putting the Yankees ahead, bringing Rick Cerone to bat with another chance to be a hero, another chance to justify the arbitrator's decision. Cerone hit into a double play. The rally fizzled.

Two innings later, the Yankees threatened again, runners on second and third, none out, Cerone once again the batter. This time he grounded weakly to shortstop. The runners held, and two outs later Reuss was out of the inning, still trailing by only 1–0.

Reggie Jackson also had two chances to win the game—in the third inning, with two on and two out, and in the fifth, with one on and one out. In the third, Reggie struck out, and in the fifth, he hit into a double play.

Still, the Yankees led until the bottom of the seventh inning. Then, with one out, Pedro Guerrero, playing his first full season in center field, and Steve Yeager, a catcher used only sporadically all season, hit back-to-back home runs. The Dodgers had a 2–1 lead, which Reuss protected the rest of the way.

Suddenly the Dodgers had three victories in a row and needed only one more to win the World Series. They were happy. They were loose. They were even kidding about the opposing owner. "Find out how much he charges for a pep talk," Tom Lasorda called out. "We may want him to give one to the Dodgers." Lasorda was laughing. Steinbrenner was not.

The banner headline on the front page of the sports section of *The New York Times* read: "Steinbrenner Is Critical of Strategy in 5th-Game Loss." The sub-headline added: "Also Cites Cerone." (Not once on the whole page was the score of the game mentioned; in the sports section of the *Times,* George had become bigger than the game.)

Steinbrenner felt that Bob Lemon's error was an obvious one, and to back up his view, George hauled out the sort of statistics that used to infuriate Billy Martin. "Ron Guidry pitched a great game," Steinbrenner said, "but I went over some numbers with Lem, and Guidry's earned run average over the last three innings is ten-plus. We had a strategy not to let him go more than six—and Lem didn't choose to go with it. Sometimes when you have a strategy and don't go with it, it gets you."

Lemon's decision to leave Guidry in was understandable to anyone less prescient than Steinbrenner. In the first six innings, Guidry had permitted the Dodgers only two harmless hits. He had struck out eight. He struck out the

first man up in the seventh inning. He had had four full days' rest. He looked strong. "I was trying to get seven innings out of him," Lemon said. "I mean, look at the way he was pitching. I didn't see any reason he couldn't do it."

Guidry shared the manager's opinion. "I didn't see any reason why I should come out," he said.

In Steinbrenner's postgame opinion, there were two reasons: Guerrero's home run—and Yeager's.

Turning to Cerone, Steinbrenner said, "Their catcher had the game-winning hit, and my catcher took us out of two game-winning rallies. We told him not to be over-anxious, but he swung at the first pitch in the fourth and the first pitch in the ninth."

Steinbrenner also was not pleased by Dave Winfield's performance, or his sense of humor. In the fifth inning, after sixteen failures, Winfield got his first hit of the World Series, a soft single to left. Winfield stopped the game and asked for the ball, a souvenir of his first World Series hit. He said later he wasn't being serious; it was his kind of joke. But not Steinbrenner's. "I'm not going to talk about that," the owner said.

The *Times* ran a total of five pictures accompanying its written coverage of the game. Three of the five photos captured baseball action, one showing Ron Cey sinking to the ground after being beaned by a Rich Gossage fastball. (Cey was taken to the hospital, not seriously injured.) A fourth photo showed the Dodgers celebrating their victory, and the fifth showed George Steinbrenner after the game eating an ice-cream cone.

Steinbrenner was not prepared to give up ice cream just because he was trailing in the World Series. He was, however, ready to give up locker-room speeches. "I'm through," he said. "I've said all I'm going to say. The players understand what they have to do. I don't think they want to be an embarrassment to New York. That's why I'm cocky and sure we're going to win."

When Steinbrenner left the ball park, he had no idea that, several hours later, shortly before midnight, Bill Kane, the traveling secretary, would be rounding up reporters and bringing them to the owner's hotel room to hear him tell the following story:

At eight o'clock that night, he left his suite on the eleventh floor of the Hyatt Wilshire Hotel and went to meet his wife and a couple of Yankee officials for dinner. He got onto an empty elevator and pressed the button for the lobby. The elevator stopped before it reached the lobby, and two young men got on. They looked as if they were in their twenties and in their cups. One was wearing a Dodger cap and holding a beer bottle.

"Steinbrenner—right?" one of the young men said.

"Yes," said Steinbrenner.

"You're going back to the fucking animals in New York, and you're taking your choke-ass ballplayers with you," the man said.

"Go fuck yourself," said Steinbrenner.

Then one of the young men swung at Steinbrenner with a beer bottle, and the fifty-one-year-old owner responded with three punches, two rights and a left. Both men went down. Then they fled. They vanished before Steinbrenner could report them.

As the story unfolded, one of the reporters who had been invited to Steinbrenner's suite, Dick Young of the *Daily News,* got up, walked to the phone and began dialing.

"What are you doing?" Steinbrenner called out.

"I'm calling my paper," Young said.

"I'm not sure I want this in the papers," said Steinbrenner, who had just summoned the reporters to his room.

Young kept dialing. When he reached his office, he began dictating: "George Steinbrenner, the president of the New York. . ."

"I'm not the president," Steinbrenner interrupted. "I'm the principal owner!"

Flustered, Young started over: "George Steinbrenner, the principal owner of the Los Angeles Dodg—"

"The Yankees!" shouted the man who wasn't sure he wanted the story in the papers. "Principal owner of the Yankees! Not the Dodgers."

Young finished his story. Steinbrenner finished his. "I clocked them," he said, of his two foes. "There are two guys in this town looking for their teeth."

Why had he exploded? To defend his team—and his town. "It's okay for me to criticize my ballplayers because I pay the checks and we're in this together," Steinbrenner said. "But when other people call them chokers, I've heard enough. And I just get sick and tired of people being critical of New York."

Steinbrenner displayed his bruises, the knuckles on his right hand cut, the left hand throbbing, probably a broken bone. The Los Angeles *Herald Examiner* ran a medical diagram, explaining possible metacarpal damage.

The New York *Post* gave Steinbrenner the whole front page; a cartoon showing him in the ring, wearing boxing gloves and a fighter's robe, his hands raised in triumph over his head; a black box filled with a quotation from George ("I may have a broken hand, but one of them isn't smiling too well"), and a huge headline, all in capital letters—GIVE 'EM HELL, GEORGE!

The *Post* also produced an eyewitness to the fight, a fifty-four-year-old Yankee fan from Long Island, a former fighter himself. The eyewitness said he happened to be walking down the hallway of the Hyatt Wilshire when he saw the two young men enter the elevator and overheard their exchange with Steinbrenner. Then he said he saw the fight. "George connected with a one-two combination, real

professional," said the eyewitness. "Reminded me of my own boxing days." The *Post* did not reveal the name of the eyewitness to protect him, from his wife, who did not know that he had gone to Los Angeles to see the World Series.

The same issue of the New York *Post* also said that Steinbrenner was a boxer in college, a revelation to Williams College and to George's classmates.

There was no World Series game scheduled for Monday, and rain postponed the game scheduled for Tuesday, so for two full days, stories of George Steinbrenner's battle dominated the news of the World Series. Baseball purists may have been appalled, but Rick Cerone and Dave Winfield were grateful.

Ironically, the alleged incident could not have been perpetrated if the Yankees had left Los Angeles immediately after the end of the game, standard procedure during the regular season. But this was the World Series, and Steinbrenner, looking for any conceivable edge, had checked with doctors to determine whether it would be wiser, mentally and metabolically, for the Yankees to fly right out of Los Angeles and go to bed at three or four in the morning in New York, or to stay overnight in Los Angeles and fly to New York in the morning. The best medical advice was that the Yankees should get a good night's sleep in Los Angeles and then fly home. Steinbrenner elected to follow his doctors' suggestion, which turned out to be unhealthy, but only for him.

The next morning, as the Yankees prepared to leave Los Angeles, George got all the attention. His left hand bandaged, the cuts visible on his right hand, his lip swollen, Steinbrenner found himself surrounded by cameras and reporters, all eager to record his impressions of the fight. "You'd think this guy was the President," another hotel guest was overheard to say.

He wasn't the president. He was the principal owner.

"All I have to say is the fight had nothing to do with Los Angeles," Steinbrenner told his audience. "We've been treated beautifully here. This is just one of those things that happens."

On the chartered flight home, Steinbrenner turned to Graig Nettles, a fellow puncher, and asked, "Where were you when I needed you?"

"You told us to go to bed early," Nettles responded.

"There are other ways to get guys loose, and this is the last time I'm doing it this way," Steinbrenner said.

Reggie Jackson prowled the plane, doing his Howard Cosell imitation into an imaginary microphone. "You say you're invulnerable to a left, George," Jackson mimicked. "Tell us what happened, straight from the hip."

Everybody had a comment, including, of course, Billy Martin. "I understand exactly how you must have felt in that elevator," Martin wired Steinbrenner. "I only hope you don't have a good-behavior clause in your contract. By the way, the marshmallow man I hit was saying bad things about New York and the Yankees. Seriously, hope you are O.K. and good luck the next two games."

Another telegram to George—"Just heard the bad news; you're fired"—was also signed "Billy Martin," but this one really was a joke, sent by an impostor.

Many people were skeptical about the fight. Some doubted that it took place at all; others doubted that it took place the way Steinbrenner said it did. Cynics suspected that if Steinbrenner punched anything, he punched the wall of the elevator. Bud Furillo of KABC radio in Los Angeles received a phone call from a listener who identified himself as "John M," and said he was one of the two Dodger fans in the elevator. John said that he and a friend named Paul encountered Steinbrenner and traded obscenities. Then, John said, Steinbrenner punched the elevator door, Paul punched Steinbrenner and the battle

was quickly over. Except as a voice on the telephone, John never materialized. Nor did Paul. Nor did the New York *Post*'s eyewitness.

A Dodger official who asked to be unnamed—even though his wife did know he went to the World Series— said, "How could all this happen in a busy hotel without anyone seeing it?" Edward Bennett Williams, Steinbrenner's fellow owner and former attorney, expressed the same theory. "I've heard of phantom punches, but never phantom victims," Williams said with a smile. "If the fight really took place the way George says it did, this is the first time a millionaire has ever hit someone and not been sued."

Behind all the jokes, there was a serious undertone, a questioning of Steinbrenner's values, his judgments, his professed concern for the Yankee image. Dave Anderson of the *Times* captured the feeling well. "George Steinbrenner always talks about 'the Yankee tradition,' meaning class and dignity," Anderson wrote. "But every so often, the Yankees betray that tradition, as Billy Martin did, as Reggie Jackson and Graig Nettles did in an Oakland restaurant less than two weeks ago, and as George Steinbrenner did Sunday night in the Hyatt Wilshire Hotel."

Clearly, the rest of the World Series was going to be anticlimactic, but it had to be played. Most important, Steinbrenner was fit enough to watch the sixth game. Secondarily, Graig Nettles and Ron Cey were fit enough to play in it. Jerry Mumphrey was restored to the Yankee lineup. The rain subsided.

As the sixth game approached, Bob Lemon, who had not managed brilliantly throughout the Series, was asked how he was able, in the eye of so many storms, to remain calm. "I don't have a dog," Lemon said. "Maybe that's why." But Lemon was affected by the pressure; he just didn't show it until the bottom of the fourth inning of the sixth game. The

score was tied, 1–1. The Yankees had two runners on base, two men out and Tommy John coming to bat. John started to move toward home plate, and, suddenly, Bob Lemon called him back. Lemon was sending Bobby Murcer up to pinch-hit. He was pulling John out of the game. John couldn't believe the decision. He marched up and down the dugout, his disbelief and dismay transparent, caught vividly by the TV cameras. Many of the viewers shared John's shock.

Lemon was managing boldly, against the percentages, against the conventional, against the knowledge that no matter what he did, if it didn't turn out exactly right, the owner would let him and the rest of the world know about it. Lemon wanted a run so badly he managed against his own instincts. Still, all Murcer had to do was deliver a hit, preferably a home run, and Lemon, at least temporarily, would look like a genius.

When Bobby Murcer lined out, the third out of the inning, Bob Lemon did not look too smart. A few minutes after he sent George Frazier in to relieve John, Lemon looked downright dumb. The Dodgers scored three runs off Frazier in the fifth inning, got four more runs in the sixth and, for all practical purposes, the game, the World Series and the strangest of seasons were over. The Dodgers were the champions of the world. The final score was 9–2, and some of the final statistics were equally embarrassing. Reggie Jackson, Rick Cerone and Dave Winfield among them—a three-million-dollar-a-year trio—went zero-for-twelve in the sixth game. Cerone finished the Series with a batting average of .190, which was more than four times higher than Winfield's average. Winfield had one marginal hit in twenty-two times at bat. George Frazier had become the first pitcher in sixty-two years to lose three games in one World Series.

George Steinbrenner did not come to the Yankee clubhouse immediately after the game. He stayed up in his

suite for perhaps fifteen minutes, drafting a statement. Then he went to the locker room, shook the hands of as many players as he could find, including Jackson's, then left. Copies of his statement arrived a few minutes later. "I want to sincerely apologize to the people of New York and to the fans of the New York Yankees everywhere for the performance of the Yankee team in the World Series. I also want to assure you that we will be at work immediately to prepare for 1982."

Reggie Jackson read the statement. "I got nothing to apologize for," he said. And then Reggie said goodbye, to the city and to the stadium, to the fans and to the reporters, to his arena and to his audience. "I gave you everything I could," he said.

Dave Winfield said goodbye, too, but only for a few months. He left the locker room and he went upstairs to George Steinbrenner's office. "I just wanted to apologize to you," Winfield said. "I know I let you down and embarrassed you and I feel very badly about it. I just wanted you to know it will not happen again."

Early the next morning, of course, George Steinbrenner was at his desk, working, plotting changes. "The fellows coming back will work harder than any Yankee team I've had," he promised. "I'll tell them if they're not willing to give me that dedication they won't be back. It takes total dedication these days. For the money these guys are making, they should be totally dedicated."

In the weeks that followed, George Steinbrenner went out and bought more dedication. He acquired two gifted Cincinnati Reds, Ken Griffey and Dave Collins, and he negotiated a new contract with the most loyal of Yankees, Ron Guidry. He lifted Guidry and Griffey close to the million-dollar-a-year level; he made certain that Collins would not starve. He gave a handsome three-year contract to thirty-eight-year-old Lou Piniella, a reward based as much on sentiment as sense. With Griffey, Mumphrey and

Winfield, he had a marvelous outfield; with Piniella, Collins, Watson, and several other batters, he had an imposing flock of designated hitters. He made no attempt to re-sign Reggie Jackson, did not even make him an offer. Jackson said he would be a team man, said he was willing to be strictly a designated hitter, said he'd learn how to handle a first baseman's glove so that he could be more versatile, more valuable. The owner said nothing. Jackson talked to the California Angels, the Baltimore Orioles, the Atlanta Braves, trying to salvage his career, and his dignity.

Strangely, Jackson still wanted to play for Steinbrenner. Bob Lemon still wanted to manage for him.

Five weeks after the World Series ended, the Yankees announced that their manager in 1982 would be Bob Lemon.

The following day, the Yankees announced that their manager in 1983, and 1984, and 1985, would be Gene Michael.

George Steinbrenner's world had come full cycle. Only three months had passed between the day he fired Gene Michael and the day he rehired him, three months of incredible turmoil and endless headlines. "I'm smarter now," Michael said. "I think I've learned a few things."

Gene Michael was back in the camp. He was loyal. He was going to be a good soldier.

George Steinbrenner was happy, for a moment.

7

George Steinbrenner walked to the window of the conference room in the Bay Harbor Inn and looked out toward
Tampa Bay. In the middle of winter, the temperature
outside was eighty degrees, and the Florida sun danced on
the clear blue water. "There's been only One Guy who
could walk on that," Steinbrenner said. "Of course I have
dents in my armor."

He had invited me to Tampa, finally, to discuss this book.
He would have preferred that I simply send him the
manuscript, permit him to make whatever additions and
deletions he considered necessary, then publish the book
precisely as he wanted it. But he never really expected
that. I would have liked him to tell me his innermost
feelings, to reveal to me dramatic incidents and conversations not previously reported, to strip bare his life and
his psyche. But I never really expected that. We both had
to compromise.

I gave him a chance to present his viewpoint, his version

of events. He gave me a chance to question him, to observe him. Within the framework of our relationship—a friendly adversary relationship—I think we both tried to be fair. He was charming, as usual, and he was candid, within limits. He did not pretend to be someone he wasn't, though his perception of himself was a very generous one. He did exert pressure on me, not heavy, but not subtle, either; he tossed around the name of Elton Rule, the president of ABC, the company for which I work, as easily as if he were lobbing a football back and forth with his younger son. He told me of meetings with Rule and with Howard Cosell, and hinted that he and ABC would soon be embarking on a joint commercial venture.

We spent more than nine hours together, starting at the Bay Harbor Inn, his hotel, then visiting Tampa Bay Downs, his race track, then eating dinner at The Club at Malio's, his favorite restaurant in Tampa. (We both groped for the check, and both lost; the owner of the restaurant treated us.) Finally, George drove me to Tampa Airport, which is not his, not yet. The day passed quickly. Whatever his faults, Steinbrenner is good company. He is not boring. He is also not above self-serving remarks.

We talked, first, about power. "The only good thing about having power," he said, "is that you can use it to help other people." He mentioned, for instance, an acquaintance in Tampa who had called him the day before and had said that his daughter had been in New York for several weeks, searching unsuccessfully for a job. "I made a call this morning," George said, "and I got her a job." That's what power is for, he suggested, to dispense favors and kindnesses and generosity. He said he really doesn't want to get credit for all the good things he does, but he admitted he is hurt when people write about him and fail to give him credit. I told him I thought he often got credit. I could hardly remember a major article written about him in

which the story wasn't told about the little girl whose life he had helped to save.

In some articles, he tells the story himself. "One day I read in the papers that a seven-year-old girl had a piece of a board pierced through her head," George told Ira Berkow, "and she had one operation which she owed six thousand dollars on, and she needs another operation to save her life, and her family doesn't have the six thousand dollars the second operation costs. She's going to die otherwise. I called up her home. They couldn't believe it was me. I said, 'Come to my office, I'll send a check to pay for the two operations.' Her parents later sent me a letter thanking me for saving their little girl's life."

In other articles, the author tells the story. George showed Marie Brenner the "thank-you from the child who's still alive because Daddy Warbucks stopped [his limousine] on the Long Island Expressway and made a phone call offering to pay for her operation after reading about her case in the *Post*."

Steinbrenner was worried that not enough people knew he did things like that. I assured him that many of his kind and charitable acts were chronicled in this book. Still, he said, he worried about the book. He worried, particularly, about the impact it might have on the health of his wife. A year earlier, he had told Marie Brenner that he worried about the impact of her article on the health of his wife, and almost a decade earlier, he had told Roy Meyers that he worried about the impact of Meyers' series of articles on the health of his wife. "I know you wouldn't want to have that on your conscience," George told me. He said that he was working on trying to strengthen his marriage, and he suggested that I mention some of the positive things about his wife. "She was queen of the military ball at Ohio State," he said. "She was an A student."

We talked about Watergate, and he repeated what he

had told Harry Reasoner about encouraging his employees to make political contributions by offering to put up three dollars of his money for every dollar they put up. "But the money they put up wasn't their own money," I said. "They got bonuses from the company to pass on as contributions." Steinbrenner didn't break stride. "Oh, yes," he said, a couple of them did have that kind of bonus, but the others had legitimate bonuses, or were giving their own money, or something like that, and he moved off the subject quickly and on to different areas.

Early in the afternoon, we left the Bay Harbor Inn. George generously tipped the young man who brought him his blue Chrysler Imperial—he is loyal to Lee Iacocca's company, which is also one of the Yankees' sponsors—and he drove us to Tampa Bay Downs, a small and friendly track, a comfortable place to spend an afternoon, not even a bad place to lose money. We arrived as the third race was ending, and a few of George's racing friends were buzzing because Trackman, the anonymous handicapper in the track program, had pickd the first four finishers in the third race in exact order. Steinbrenner beamed. Trackman is, in reality, George's twenty-three-year-old son, Hank Steinbrenner. George was delighted because Hank's interest in the track, and in the Kinsman Farm, was growing. "Hank's going to build the stable back up," Steinbrenner said, proudly. Hank was listed in the program as assistant treasurer of Tampa Bay Downs Inc. Joan Z. Steinbrenner was listed as vice-chairman of the track. George was not mentioned. "I've got it all out of my name," he said, "because Bowie asked me to."

Hank Steinbrenner greeted his father not warmly, but politely, respectfully. The son is taller than the father, much more slender and more informal. George was wearing a brown suede jacket, brown slacks, a yellow shirt and a striped tie. Hank was wearing an open sports shirt. Unlike his father, he is not at all intimidating. Hank

struck up a conversation about chess. He is a Bobby Fisher fan, and he had heard rumors that Fisher, no longer committed to the religious sect that had dominated his life for several years, might be willing to make a comeback, an attempt to regain the world championship he won and quickly abdicated almost a decade ago. "Fisher is a genius," Hank Steinbrenner said. "I've been trying to talk my father into promoting Bobby's comeback, putting up enough prize money to get Karpov [the Russian world champion] to play him."

George Steinbrenner moved around the track easily, trading greetings and small talk with friends and strangers. "Gonna sign Reggie?" someone called. "Doesn't look good," said Steinbrenner, who had already made up his mind not to attempt to sign Jackson. "I really wish Reggie well," George said to me. "He did so much for us. He really carried us for a couple of years. I think he's got one really good year left. Maybe two. I hope so, for his sake." George said a few more things about Reggie, and the words were, for the most part, laudatory, but the message was not. The message was: Reggie who? He had been Steinbrenner's greatest bargain, $600,000 a year for millions of dollars worth of charisma and publicity, but now he was used up, ready to be discarded. Regrets? Sadness? If George had any regret, it was that Reggie would never be in a position where he would be grateful to work for George again, as a conditioning coach or a scout, like Hopalong Cassady, or as team president, like Al Rosen or Lou Saban. Once, Reggie had been truly grateful to Steinbrenner, but he never would be again, and from George's point of view, that was what seemed to be sad.

The next day, Reggie Jackson agreed to terms with the California Angels. At a news conference celebrating a four-year contract, worth close to $1 million a year, Gene Autry posed with his arm around Jackson, and Reggie turned aside all questions about his relationship with George

Steinbrenner. "That doesn't matter now," Reggie said.

A man who seriously needed a shave came up to Steinbrenner at Tampa Bay Downs and pointed toward the bar in the grandstand. "They never buy one for the regulars," the man said. At first, Steinbrenner didn't understand. "The regulars," the man said. "The regular customers. The house ought to buy us a drink once in a while."

"They don't?" Steinbrenner said.

"Never," the man said.

Steinbrenner hailed one of his aides and handed him a five-dollar bill. "Here," he said, "buy this gentleman a couple of drinks." The regular smiled, shook George's hand and moved off toward the bar. "He'll tell a hundred people about that," Steinbrenner said.

The next stop was the ice-cream stand. George ordered vanilla, soft ice cream, in a sugar cone, plucked from a special stack. "You've got to taste the vanilla," he said. "It's really good. It's smooth, not too grainy. It used to be too grainy, but I told them I wanted it just like the ice cream at the jai-alai. Really smooth. And they've got it now. Taste it. See, smooth." He could not have been more earnest. "The chocolate's not that smooth," he said. I could tell he was telling the truth; I didn't try the chocolate.

George sat in a box overlooking the finish line, right behind a pair of trainers, Bob Guciardo and Jud Van Worp, with whom he traded horse talk. Guciardo's horse won the fourth race, Van Worp's the fifth. Steinbrenner teased them because the leading trainer at Tampa Bay Downs, after three weeks of racing, was a woman. George's own trainer, Bill LaRue, a sixty-seven-year-old veteran of the sport, came by and joined him. Steinbrenner had two fillies running, Ever Wonder in the eighth race, Vita Peach in the ninth. Ever Wonder was the favorite in her race. "She's ready," La Rue said. But when Steinbrenner left the box for a few minutes, LaRue said he was going back to the

paddock. "I don't want to be around here if that filly don't win," the trainer said, half-kidding.

I had been betting, modestly, following George's lead, and I was far enough ahead to do what he was going to do in the eighth race—wheel Ever Wonder in the trifecta, which meant a seventy-two-dollar bet on a ten-horse field, actually seventy-two one-dollar bets on Ever Wonder finishing first and every other possible combination finishing second and third. As long as Ever Wonder came in first, we would get back something. If long shots finished second and third, we could make a handsome profit. Ever Wonder, the favorite, won easily, but unfortunately, from our point of view, the second choice came in second, and the third choice third. The trifecta paid only $17.90, which is about as little as a trifecta can pay. In other words, we lost $54.10 on the seventy-two-dollar bet. It certainly made the setup—Steinbrenner's own horses running at his own track—seem very honest.

George drowned his defeat in the second half of his lunch, his second soft vanilla ice cream of the afternoon. He had everyone around him eating the vanilla, too, and complimenting its texture.

Steinbrenner did not expect his filly, Vita Peach, to win the ninth race, but he did expect her to put up a good show. She was one of the reasons he had gone to Chicago the previous summer; she was running at Arlington Park while Gene Michael was daring Steinbrenner to fire him.

The conversation, naturally, turned to Michael. "You know, when he asked to see me a couple of months ago, and we met at the bar at the Carlyle," George said, "he told me that he finally realized what he had done was wrong. He still thought that he was right in the way he felt, but wrong in the way he acted. That was all I wanted to hear. I didn't want any big apology from him. I just wanted him to realize you can't take on the boss like that, even if the boss

is wrong. He realizes that now. I love Stick. I love him like a son. He'll be our manager in '83, and I hope for a long time after that.

"But he won't be our manager this year. No. Bob Lemon's going to be our manager all year. You can bet on it. I don't care if we come in last. I swear on my heart he'll be the manager all season. That's all he wants, one full season, and then he wants to go back to Southern California, and I owe him that much. He's been a good man. He's been loyal. When he lost twenty pounds after the World Series, he showed me he was really trying. And he switched to white wine. He knew I was worried about his drinking. He showed me he cared, and I owe him a full year."

The talk of managers led to Billy Martin, and George said, "The second time I fired Billy . . ." Billy gets upset when people say he was fired twice by the Yankees. He points out that the first time he resigned. Steinbrenner knows that, technically, Martin resigned. He also knows that Billy was about to be fired. "The second time I fired Billy," Steinbrenner said, "it wasn't because he hit that marshmallow guy. No. All he had to do was tell the truth, that the fellow was harassing him, and I would have backed him up. In fact, right after it happened, Mickey Morabito called me, and I told him, 'Mickey, you just tell Billy to tell the truth, and I'll back him up. But don't let him put me in a corner. Don't let him lie.' The next thing I see is a big headline in which Billy is denying he ever hit the guy, and by then, I know he did hit the guy, and I know there are witnesses, and Billy's got me in a corner, and I have to fire him."

The ninth race was about to start, and someone handed George a pair of binoculars so that he could watch Vita Peach challenge the favorite, Secret Kingdom, a filly with far more impressive credentials. Vita Peach faded early, but George kept cheering, loudly, right down to the finish

line. He was cheering for the wrong horse, for number seven, Amber's Sting, instead of number five, Vita Peach. George had been looking at the wrong horse from the moment they came out of the gate. His mistake was understandable. Amber's Sting was wearing light blue and beige, Vita Peach blue and brown. Amber's Sting came home second; Vita Peach finished far back. "Give that filly a rest for a few weeks," George Steinbrenner told his son.

During the ride from the track to The Club at Malio's, we covered a variety of subjects, including George's reading interests and his musical background. He had been reading a Time-Life series of books on the early history of the American west, and he was up to the Indian chiefs. "Did you know that Sitting Bull wasn't even at the Battle of Little Big Horn?" Steinbrenner said. "He was up in the hills praying. Chief Crazy Horse was leading the battle against Custer, and Sitting Bull was up in the hills. I'm naming all my yearlings this year after Indian Chiefs. I've got a Crazy Horse and a Quanah already." George said he loved to read about battles, and he liked to reread Thoreau, to dip into *Walden* occasionally. He talked about playing twin pianos at Williams, and he reminisced about the glee club. He didn't have a very good voice, he conceded, but he enjoyed the singing. He still remembered Stephen Sondheim vividly from the glee club.

We talked of baseball, and the Yankees, and he mentioned that Roy White, the former Yankee, had been in touch with him. White was getting ready for his third and final season of baseball in Japan, and then, Steinbrenner said, he would rejoin the Yankees, in the front office. "He'll be our general manager someday," Steinbrenner said, and the thought of having the first black general manager clearly excited him.

He reviewed, with delight, his contract negotiations with Lou Piniella, who had come into his office at the age of thirty-eight seeking, but not anticipating, a two-year

contract. "I said to him," George said, "'Here's my offer, take it or leave it: 1982—three hundred and fifty thousand dollars.'" Steinbrenner paused for several seconds. "Then I said, 'And 1983—three hundred and seventy-five thousand dollars.'" Another deliberate pause. "'And 1984—four hundred thousand dollars. Now get the hell out of here before I change my mind.'" Steinbrenner laughed. "You know," he said, "Lou's wife called me to thank me." He swelled up, proud of the way he had rewarded Piniella, long one of his favorites. Piniella was the Yankees' first major acquisition after Steinbrenner purchased the team. Besides, he came from Tampa, and he frequently spent afternoons during the off-season at Tampa Bay Downs. "He was out the other day," George said. "Looked like he hadn't shaved in a few days. I gave him money for a razor."

We talked of pampered ballplayers. "They're so damned sheltered," he said. "They're not ready for real life when they finish playing. They don't understand that life can be tough out there. I've been on Piniella about that for years. I think I'm getting through to him."

"Obviously, you make most of your own baseball decisions now," I said. "How'd you learn? Who'd you listen to?"

"Everybody," Steinbrenner said. "I used to talk to Al Lopez down here, hours at a time. I learned from him. And from Birdie Tebbetts. Gabe taught me a lot. So did Ralph Houk. And, of course, Billy." His thoughts touched upon the love/hate relationships he developed with Billy Martin, with Gabe Paul, to a lesser degree with Ralph Houk. "I know I'm not easy to work for," he said.

"But you never had to work for anyone like you," I said.

"Yes, I did," he said. "My father."

When we reached the restaurant, a private club, which offered excellent Italian food and a busy disco, George ordered a rare drink, an Old Fashioned, and finished it. He did not touch the second one that was placed in front of him, but he did a fine job on the food, manicotti for an

appetizer, a salad, lamb chops, asparagus, a potato skin and chocolate Häagen-Dazs ice cream. We talked of other sports, and when George recalled his hurdling days, he became more animated than he had been all day. His enthusiasm was not forced. He recalled running against Harrison Dillard, and against another Olympian, Walt Ashbaugh of Cornell, and against a Harvard hurdler named Pat McCormick, who became more famous as a writer and as a comedian. Names floated into our conversation, Meredith Gourdine and Andy Stanfield and George Rhoden, names that had faded into track and field history, and Steinbrenner relished the memories.

Then we talked of another athlete, of Fran Tarkenton, and Steinbrenner, knowing Tarkenton's antagonism toward him, stiffened. He tried to explain the background of Tarkenton's bitterness, and his facts became confused, and then he said, simply, "I don't care what he thinks of me. He's a great guy, terrific guy, Fran. I think the world of him. It was just a misunderstanding. We could straighten it out in a minute."

One more athlete's name came up, John McEnroe's, and again Steinbrenner glowed. He loved McEnroe's style, his combativeness, his patriotic fervor. He saw no fault in McEnroe's manners. He said he could identify with John. Ironically, a few days later, *TV Guide* announced its annual Nice Guy Award, a facetious title for the person the magazine considered the most boorish personality in sports. McEnroe came in third in the ratings. George Brett of the Kansas City Royals came in second. Steinbrenner came in first for the second straight year.

When we drove to the airport, Steinbrenner mused about his loss of privacy. He was tired of being a public figure, he said. He was tired of being abused. He was pulling back. He was going to maintain a low profile.

Not for the first time, I didn't believe him.

Bibliography

Certain publications were invaluable in preparing this biography of George Steinbrenner. First, the New York Yankees' own *Media Guides,* from 1973 through 1981, which, though they contain no biographical data about George Steinbrenner, trace the pattern of his baseball life. Second, *The Yankees,* published by Random House, divided into four eras, each era reported and analyzed by a different writer, the Steinbrenner era, appropriately called "The Money Players," wonderfully presented by Murray Chass, who has covered the Yankees on a daily basis for *The New York Times.* Third, *Inside the Yankees: The Championship Year,* from Ballantine Books, a minutely detailed study of the 1977 season, by Ed Linn, an old friend and a talented writer. Times Books' *Mr. October,* by Maury Allen, another talented friend, and Delacorte's *Number 1,* by Billy Martin and Peter Golenbock, offer insights into Steinbrenner's two most famous employees. Among magazine articles, the champion is Tony Kornheiser's "That

Damned Yankee," from *The New York Times* magazine, but Pete Axthelm's "George's Rage to Win," from *Newsweek,* and Marie Brenner's "Boss Steinbrenner," from *New York* magazine, certainly stand out. For details of Steinbrenner's life before New York, *Cleveland* magazine's "George M. Steinbrenner III" is essential. I am grateful to *Sports Illustrated* and the *New York Times,* for access to their archives, and to Mike Lupica of the *Daily News,* for a full set of his columns on Steinbrenner. I very much appreciate the daily reporting that was done by, among others, Henry Hecht for the New York *Post,* Phil Pepe for the *Daily News* and Jane Gross for the *Times,* and I appreciate the special reporting that Brent Larkin of the Cleveland *Plain Dealer* did for me. I could not possibly name every journalist and every publication whose articles on George Steinbrenner I have read, but many of them are mentioned, and quoted, in the text, and I am grateful to all of them. It may be slightly out of place within even an informal bibliography, but I do want to thank Phyllis Grann, my editor and publisher, and Sterling Lord, my literary agent and friend, for their encouragement and their patience, and Jimmy Breslin, for his impatience. While I was in the final weeks of writing this book, Breslin called me every day for only one reason: To make me feel guilty if I wasn't working.

STEINBRENNER!